NATIONAL GEOGRAPHIC KiDS

INFOPEDIA 2021

An octopus swims below the water's surface in Maui, Hawaii, U.S.A.

NATIONAL GEOGRAPHIC KiDS

INFOPEDIA
2021

NATIONAL GEOGRAPHIC

WASHINGTON, D.C.

NATIONAL GEOGRAPHIC KiDS

Welcome to National Geographic Kids' fantastic new *Infopedia 2021!*

Are you looking for adventure, fun, puzzles and games? Then this is the book for you! *Infopedia 2021* is packed with all the super stories and fascinating facts that you'll find each month in *National Geographic Kids* magazine — from astonishing animals and spectacular space to brave explorers and exciting escapades!

Learn all about our wonderful world in this year's Amazing Animals, Wonders of Nature, Geography Rocks and Space and Earth chapters. Meet incredible explorer Albert Lin and discover how he's using technology to find ancient Maya ruins. Check out different beliefs and customs in our Culture Connection section, and discover how YOU can help the environment in this year's Going Green pages. Don't miss the brilliant quizzes, puzzles, jokes and comics in our bumper Fun and Games section, and then amaze your friends and family with each chapter's bonkers Bet You Didn't Know facts!

Bursting with fantastic photographs, inspiring interviews and awesome maps, National Geographic Kids' *Infopedia 2021* is the perfect read for children who want to know about everything and more. So what are you waiting for?

Get ready to explore!

Tim Herbert
Editor, *National Geographic Kids* magazine

If you enjoy *Infopedia 2021*, look for *National Geographic Kids* magazine — it's jam-packed with adventure and fun every month!

Subscribe to *Nat Geo Kids* now by visiting natgeokids.com — enter code NGKIP205 at checkout to receive £5 off the subscription price!

Contents

GOING GREEN

HISTORY HAPPENS 220

GEOGRAPHY ROCKS 252

NATIONAL GEOGRAPHIC KIDS
ALMANAC CHALLENGE 2021

THE RESULTS ARE IN!

**Which idea won our 2020
Visionary Almanac Challenge?**
See page 25.

**Want to become part of the 2021 Almanac
Challenge?** Go to page 24 to find out more.

Colourful kites soar above the beach during the annual International Berck-sur-Mer Kite Festival in northern France.

Newly Discovered
Animals

From an **ORANGUTAN** to **COLOURFUL FISH**, here are some species recently discovered in the wild.

Wakatobi and Wangi-Wangi White-Eyes

You can't miss the pop-out peepers of the two birds recently discovered in Sulawesi, Indonesia. Aptly named white-eyes, both of these birds are marked with a white ring around each eye. The main difference between the two? The Wakatobi white-eye (left) has a yellow belly, while the Wangi-Wangi white-eye's belly is white. Found in separate areas off the coast of Sulawesi, the birds are named for their island homes.

Vibranium Fish

Wakanda forever! A marine biologist named a never-seen-before fish the Vibranium wrasse after one of his favourite films, *Black Panther*. This tiny purple fish, found off the coast of Zanzibar, lives near reefs and eats plankton.

Rain Frog

A total of 11 species of rain frogs have been identified by researchers in Ecuador. This group of new hoppers is believed to be one of the biggest discoveries of amphibians in recent years. The frogs, which vary in colour from bright yellow to dark brown, live in an area of less than 2,500 square kilometres (965 sq mi) in the rainforest.

Tapanuli Orangutan

What's the rarest great ape on the planet? Scientists say it's the Tapanuli orangutan, a new species recently identified on the island of Sumatra in western Indonesia. The Tapanuli orangutan lives exclusively in a high-elevation forest called Batang Toru, while other species are found in different parts of Sumatra and on Borneo across the Java Sea. While the discovery is exciting, it is also a reminder of just how fragile certain species are. Experts say there are just 800 of these orangutans on Earth, underlining the importance of conservation work being done to save all orangutans.

ASTEROID
SELF-DESTRUCTS

Some asteroids crash into Earth. Some barrel into other planets. And sometimes, they self-destruct. That's what is likely to be happening to one asteroid known as 6478 Gault, a space rock that's some 4 kilometres (2.5 mi) in diameter and travels in a circular orbit in an asteroid belt between Mars and Jupiter. Images from the Hubble Space Telescope showed the giant asteroid splitting apart, leaving behind two bright, dusty tails, one of which measures a whopping 805,000 kilometres (500,000 mi) long and 4,800 kilometres (3,000 mi) wide. 6478 Gault, which was first spotted by astronomers in 1988, is one of a million space rocks shooting through space. But the sight of an asteroid becoming unglued is rare: Astronomers estimate that this type of event happens just once a year.

Town Aims for
Zero Waste

The village of Kamikatsu, Japan, may be tiny, but it's making a big impact on the future of our planet. There, the 1,500 residents aim to recycle everything they use, from chopsticks to printer cartridges. In fact, 80 percent of the town's waste is recycled or composted — which is four times the rate of the country of Japan as a whole. The people of Kamikatsu sort their rubbish into some 40 different recycling bins set aside for items like aluminium cans, steel cans, paper cartons and paper flyers.

Locals also get creative with their rubbish, like repurposing old kimonos into teddy bears. While an 80 percent recycling rate is impressive, the citizens of Kamikatsu don't want to stop there: They're hoping to produce absolutely zero waste in the near future.

WILDLIFE
CROSSINGS

Overpass in Banff, Alberta, Canada

A toad in the U.K. crosses a road through an underground wildlife tunnel.

Eco-friendly bridges and tunnels help animals get from one side to the other — safely.

How did the bear cross the road?

In Banff, Canada, it walks across an overpass! Or, more specifically, a grassy bridge spanning the width of the Trans-Canada Highway. A part of a wildlife initiative meant to protect animals like bears, wolves, coyotes and moose from getting hit by cars, Banff boasts numerous wildlife crossing structures. And they don't just keep the animals safe: The overpasses protect people, too, since they can greatly reduce the amount of animal–car collisions on the roads.

Similar overpasses have been built in different parts of the world, including western Europe and other areas in Canada. And plans are under way to construct what may be the world's largest wildlife crossing over a Southern California, U.S.A., highway for animals like mountain lions, deer, lizards and snakes. The bridge, which will stretch some 61 metres (200 ft) above 10 lanes of highway, is expected to be completed in 2023.

In some places, animals head underground to get to where they want to go. Road tunnels for wildlife in areas like Banff serve as safe ways for critters to cross busy roads. And, like the overpasses, these tunnels can curb collisions between cars and wildlife.

On one stretch of highway in the Santa Cruz Mountains in California, for example, a tunnel is being built for the many mountain lions and deer that tend to dash across the four lanes — a dangerous and often fatal mission.

'ICE TSUNAMI'

Usually, a strong storm over Lake Erie in eastern Canada and western New York State, U.S.A., means there may be flooding along the shoreline. But when temperatures dip well below the freezing mark, something else can happen: an 'ice tsunami'! This wacky phenomenon happens when strong winds push blocks of ice floating in the lake towards the water's edge. The ice surges over the lake's shoreline, creating frozen, moving walls as high as three-storey buildings. An ice tsunami is a cool sight, but just like an actual tsunami, it can be damaging to anything in its path.

Robots Comfort Kids

Sure, ducks are cute. Even better when they're soft and cuddly. But what about a duck that dances, nuzzles and quacks when you tickle it? Meet My Special Aflac Duck, a robot disguised as a stuffed duck. With five special touch sensors in its cheeks, on its back and under its wings, the duck interacts with whomever is holding it. Aside from being capable of cuddling and dancing, this duck is equipped with a microphone and speaker so it can communicate with cute quacks or even groans if its owner is feeling frustrated. And this robot doesn't just make duck sounds: It will even play soothing music, like rainforest sounds, at the touch of a button. Designed to comfort and cheer up kids with cancer, the bot is available at U.S. hospitals and medical centres for anyone over three years old who is undergoing treatment. The hope is that this darling duck will calm down—and perhaps even *quack* up—any kid going through a scary situation.

DOGS AT THE MOVIES

A group of adorable dogs hit the theatre for a very good cause.

This theatre is for the dogs! A group of dogs recently took in a showing of *Billy Elliot* at a cinema in Ontario, Canada. But they weren't just checking out the film for fun: They were actually in training! All of the dogs are in the process of becoming service dogs for those with special needs, and sitting through a movie was simply practice for their future gig. A service dog attends most everyday activities with its human and needs to ignore distractions — like food and other people — so it can stay focused on its job. So, by taking the dogs to the movies, their handlers hope it will teach them to stay relaxed for a couple of hours in an environment with loud noises, flashing lights, tight spaces and potential crowds. So how did the dogs do? The handlers were quite impressed by their four-legged friends, giving them an A+ for their behaviour. Sounds like these dogs deserve a treat or two!

HOT FILMS in 2021*

- *Trolls World Tour*
- *The Boss Baby 2*
- *Rugrats*
- *Sing 2*
- *Tom and Jerry*
- *Mary Poppins 3*
- *Moana 2*
- *Zootopia 2*
- *The Little Mermaid*

*Release dates and titles are subject to change.

HIGH-TECH HELP

When carers at the Jurong Bird Park in Singapore noticed a suspicious gash on a resident hornbill's casque — the helmet-like part atop the bill — they suspected something was seriously wrong. After all, two of their hornbills had recently been diagnosed with cancer, and this bird, named Jary, was showing similar signs.

A scan confirmed the diagnosis, and Jary underwent surgery to remove the cancerous growths — and most of his casque. But it wasn't all bleak for this bird: A team of veterinary experts quickly sprang into action, using a 3D printer to create a prosthetic casque. Made to fit Jary just right, the customised casque was carefully screwed into place and sealed with a special resin so it stayed put. After some time in quarantine to recover, Jary — whose name means 'warrior with a helmet' in ancient Norse — returned to his home in the bird park, healthy and cancer free.

ECO-SHOES

One brand of shoes is taking a step in the right direction when it comes to protecting the planet. Rothy's shoes are made of discarded plastic water bottles and other recycled materials. To create the shoes, the bottles are crushed, melted into pellets and pulled into soft fibres that are knitted together to form a stretchy material. Recycled foam fills each shoe's inside. And the packaging? Even the shoe boxes are made from recycled materials. Rothy's has repurposed tens of millions of water bottles — helping stomp out the problem of too much waste on Earth.

15

Cool Events 2021

WORLD GIRAFFE DAY

Stick your neck out for giraffes and raise awareness for these enchanting animals.

21 June

SPECIAL OLYMPICS WORLD WINTER GAMES

Sweden will host this week-long event for athletes with intellectual disabilities — it's one of the largest and most inspiring sports events on the planet.

5–13 February

UEFA WOMEN'S EURO CHAMPIONSHIP

The top teams in women's football go toe to toe in this major matchup.

11 July – 1 August

WORLD LAUGHTER DAY

What's so funny? Find something to LOL about today!

5 May

RUGBY LEAGUE WORLD CUP

Men's, women's and wheelchair rugby league teams from around the world head to England to battle it out at this epic event.

23 October – 27 November

HAEUNDAE SAND FESTIVAL

This beachside fest in Busan, South Korea, featuring castle-building, sand baths and a volleyball competition, celebrates all things sand.

Late May/Early June

WORLD PASTA DAY

Did someone say spaghetti?

Pile it on your plate and eat up today!

25 October

PAN O RAMA ST. JOHN'S FESTIVAL

The tropical sounds of steel pan drums drift through the Caribbean island of St. John as local bands compete for glory in this friendly competition.

June

INTERNATIONAL MOUNTAIN DAY

There are hundreds of thousands of mountains on our planet. Find one and take a hike today!

11 December

Rooftop POOL

Designers of this sky-high swimming spot aim for new heights.

Visitors who take a dip in the Infinity London will be able to swim *and* sightsee at the same time! This splashy see-through pool — set to be the world's first infinity pool with 360-degree views — has been designed to be built some 200 metres (656 ft) atop a 55-storey luxury hotel in the British capital. The pool will be accessed by a rotating spiral staircase rising from the pool floor — a concept based on the door of a submarine. And that's not the only futuristic feature: The water will be heated using waste energy from the building's air-conditioning system. Now that's one *cool* pool.

Rendering of Infinity London's planned rooftop pool

A Chance of LADYBIRDS

Residents of San Diego, California, U.S.A., were *bugging* out when a massive swarm of ladybirds recently flew high over the coastal city. Measuring about 16 kilometres (10 mi) wide, the swarm spanned somewhere between 1,500 and 2,700 metres (5,000 and 9,000 ft) in the sky. Also known as a 'bloom', the group was so big that it registered on the National Weather Service's radar. While experts aren't sure what type of ladybirds formed this phenomenon, they think it was likely to have been a mega migration. Each summer, big groups of certain ladybird species fly from the higher elevations of California to the valleys to lay eggs.

NO UMBRELLA NEEDED. WEATHER FORECASTERS DETERMINED THE LARGE GREEN 'CLOUD' ON THE RADAR MAP ABOVE WAS ACTUALLY A SWARM OF LADYBIRDS.

Cave divers explore a tree-lined spring that forms part of the Devil's Spring System in Florida, U.S.A.

DARE TO EXPLORE

From listening to animals to reading the stars, three Nat Geo explorers share secrets about communicating with the world.

> "Don't be afraid to take things apart. Play with them, see how they work and experiment on your own."

TOPHER WHITE PREPARES TO MOUNT A LISTENING DEVICE TO A TREE THAT WILL HELP NAB ILLEGAL LOGGERS ON THE GROUND.

THE ENGINEER

Topher White attaches recycled mobile phones to trees in remote rainforests around the world, hoping to pick up the sounds of illegal loggers. He describes trying to work while being swarmed by bees.

"Even though the forests can be home to illegal loggers, sometimes what's going on in the treetops is scarier than what's on the ground. One time I was installing a phone and bees kept landing on me. Eventually I was completely covered with them! But I had to finish the job, even if it meant getting a *lot* of bee stings.

"The phones I place each have an app that turns the phone into a listening device. They capture all the sounds of the rainforest. Listening to this noise can help us pick out the sounds of things like chain saws and logging trucks. If we can pinpoint the sounds of illegal logging, we can instantly send alerts to local authorities and tribes, who are then able to stop illegal loggers on the spot. In a way, the trees are telling us when they need help."

WANT TO BE AN ENGINEER?

STUDY	Mathematics, physics
WATCH	The documentary series *The Trials of Life*
READ	*The Wild Trees* by Richard Preston

WHITE ATTACHES A DEVICE TO A TREE IN INDONESIA, A COUNTRY IN SOUTHEAST ASIA.

FROM LEFT: ASTRONOMERS HALEY FICA, MUNAZZA ALAM AND SARA CAMNASIO STAND IN FRONT OF A 6.4-METRE (21-FT)-WIDE TELESCOPE IN CHILE.

THE ASTRONOMER

Munazza Alam searches the sky for a planet that humans could live on one day. She discusses her hunt for what she calls the 'Earth Twin'.

"I spend a lot of my nights at observatories atop mountain ranges, using high-resolution telescopes that are sometimes the size of a school bus. I'm observing faraway planets outside our solar system called exoplanets. By analysing these exoplanets, I hope to discover if any of them have atmospheres similar to Earth that people could one day survive in. You could say I'm searching for Earth's twin. An 'Earth Twin' would be a rocky planet with temperatures that would support liquid water. We haven't found one yet, but I do think we're getting closer. The more we study the stars and their planets, the more we can understand what they're like. As an astronomer, it's my job to keep examining the sky in the hopes that it'll reveal new things about our galaxy and beyond."

> "If you have a curiosity, don't let that flame go out. Never let go of that enthusiasm, because it will inspire you forever."

WANT TO BE AN ASTRONOMER?

STUDY	Physics, astronomy
WATCH	*Zathura: A Space Adventure*
READ	*The Magic School Bus: Lost in the Solar System* by Joanna Cole

THE CONSERVATIONIST

Hotlin Ompusunggu works to protect the forests of Indonesia in Southeast Asia. She talks about saving orangutans and educating illegal loggers.

"I'll occasionally see orangutans frolicking in the trees above me. We've placed cameras in the forests to monitor their movements, and sometimes it looks like they might be posing for a picture — sort of like an orangutan selfie! Their population in Indonesia is decreasing, mostly because of logging, so when I see one of these photos I'm very happy. It means orangutans are still there, and it's like they're saying, 'Thank you for protecting our home'.

> "People may not always agree with you, but don't let that stop you from sharing your ideas."

"The forests of Indonesia provide natural resources like fruit, meat and wood. Often loggers will try to gain these resources illegally, which is dangerous for animals and people. By educating loggers on the impact of their actions, we can begin to create new forest guardians."

WANT TO BE A CONSERVATIONIST?

STUDY	Biology, ecology
WATCH	*Dr. Seuss' The Lorax*
READ	*My Life With the Chimpanzees* by Jane Goodall

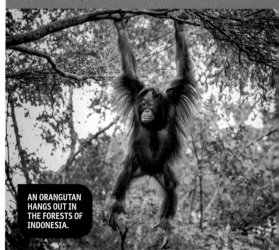

AN ORANGUTAN HANGS OUT IN THE FORESTS OF INDONESIA.

Jamal Galves
Manatee Man

N ational Geographic Explorer Jamal Galves is working so hard to save Antillean manatees in his native Belize, he's known as the 'manatee man'. Listed as a vulnerable species — or likely to become endangered unless its population numbers improve — all manatees are threatened by habitat loss and collisions with boats. "They could eventually go extinct," explains Galves. "My mission is to stop that from happening."

Growing up in Gales Point Manatee, a tiny village in the Central American country, Galves knew from the time he was 11 that he wanted to dedicate his life to the unique animals. Today, he spends his days either in the field observing manatees in their natural habitat or travelling the world advocating for their protection and better environmental laws.

"Manatees fall victim to boats, habitat destruction, pollution, climate change and poaching," Galves says. "I want to bring awareness and share the issues manatees are facing locally and internationally."

Galves is the person to call whenever an Antillean manatee is in need of help. With the Clearwater Marine Aquarium Research Institute, he's rescued those massive mammals that have become tangled in fishing gear or injured by a boat. He has also saved newborn calves abandoned on the beach, taking them to a rescue facility to be nursed back to health.

"The favourite parts about my job? Hugging manatees when I rescue them, giving them names that fit their personality, bottle-feeding babies and releasing them to the wild when they're ready," Galves says.

Manatees are already beloved animals in Belize. But Galves hopes that his work will help make them targets of conservation efforts around the world. "We need to save this species," he shares. "Because they can't save themselves."

GALVES HOLDS A BABY MANATEE THAT WAS RESCUED AFTER BEING SEPARATED FROM ITS MOTHER.

A TRACKING RADIO AND ANTENNA HELP GALVES OBSERVE AND RECORD THE BEHAVIOUR OF TAGGED MANATEES.

6 marvellous facts about manatees

1 Manatees spend almost half their day eating.

2 Belize has the highest known density of Antillean manatees in the world.

3 Manatees can hold their breath for up to 20 minutes.

4 Manatees live in water that is 16°C (60°F) or warmer.

5 Big eaters, manatees consume about 10 percent of their body weight in plants daily.

6 Elephants are closely related to manatees.

ANTILLEAN MANATEE

Be a Kids vs. Plastic Leader

NATIONAL GEOGRAPHIC KiDS
ALMANAC CHALLENGE 2021

Nearly 8.1 million tonnes (9 million tons) of plastic enter the ocean each year. That's the equivalent of unloading a dump truck of plastic into the ocean *every minute.* Help keep habitats healthy for humans and animals by participating in this year's Kids vs. Plastic Almanac Challenge.

Plastic water bottles, straws and bags might be part of your everyday life. They're called 'single-use plastics' because you use them once, then throw them away. But that plastic doesn't disappear when you're done with it: Most of it ends up in the ocean, where it can entangle animals or make them sick.

National Geographic explorers are working hard to raise awareness and solve this plastics problem. Check out what one explorer is doing to reduce single-use plastic in her own family and around the world.

Meet National Geographic Explorer and Plastic Waste Activist Jenna Jambeck

An award-winning explorer and environmental engineer, Jenna Jambeck is working hard to reduce the amount of plastic piling up in the oceans and on land. Here, Jambeck shares how she got her start in this field of science — and how you can get involved, too.

What inspired you to care about the amount of plastics in the environment?
I grew up in a town of less than 3,000 people in Minnesota, U.S.A., where there was no trash collection. We had to take our trash to the landfill ourselves, so I saw what everyone threw away and became fascinated with it.

Plus, I've always loved the ocean. When I first heard about our waste ending up in the ocean, I knew we were doing something wrong on land. Then I became dedicated to protecting the seas.

What are you working on now?
As a co-leader for the Sea to Source plastic expeditions for National Geographic, we are trying to better understand how waste moves from land into our waterways, especially rivers that can lead into the ocean. Having grown up on a river, this is especially important to me. I'm also looking at how natural disasters contribute to the plastic pollution problem.

Why is this issue so important?
The statistics are pretty scary. The amount of plastic produced around the world over the past 60 years is equivalent to the weight of 80 blue whales. A lot of that becomes waste, but only 9 percent of that waste is recycled. The rest ends up in landfill or in our environment. It litters our ocean and our shores, and animals ingest and get entangled in the plastic.

So how *can* kids help to reduce the amount of plastic they use at home?
To start, pay attention to the plastic items you use. Are they all useful? Can you imagine a different way to get the same or similar food or drink without the packaging? Can you reuse it?

Any other ways kids can get involved?
There are many ways to make a collective difference. Start clubs and groups with friends to communicate your message about plastics. Do research to empower yourself about the topic, then communicate it to others.

You can also tap into the Marine Debris Tracker (marinedebris.engr.uga.edu), which is a great tool for collecting data on what's leaking out into the environment. You can create a map of what you find in your neighbourhood — it doesn't have to be anywhere near water or the ocean — and find out what the top trash items are in your area. It's an easy way to make a big difference.

THIS YEAR'S CHALLENGE

The good news is that kids can make a difference when it comes to plastic! Join the Kids vs. Plastic Almanac Challenge at natgeokids.com/almanac.

Get inspired! Check out our top 10 tips online to reduce your plastic waste.

Take action! Tell us how many of the tips you were able to do in one month by filling out a form and taking our online poll.

Inspire and involve others! Show us the creative ways you've been able to reduce plastic waste in your home, classroom or community by sending us your stories and photos (along with your form), and your entry may appear in next year's almanac!

Take the pledge! Commit to using less plastic and earn your certificate.

Be a Kids vs. Plastic leader and remember: Awareness inspires action, which leads to change!

Get details and official rules at natgeokids.com/almanac.

LAST YEAR'S CHALLENGE

For the Almanac's 10th anniversary, we asked kids to think 10 years into the future to envision a change that would make the world better. Submissions covered a range of important issues — from finding a cure for cancer to saving endangered species — and showed how smart, creative and caring today's kids are!

The grand prize winner of the Almanac 2020 Visionary Challenge is Kai S., from Hawaii, U.S.A., who has a revolutionary idea to rid the ocean of plastic waste and save marine life. First, ban single-use plastic. Then, create a plastic-eating enzyme (a molecule that speeds up chemical reactions) to break down any plastic left in the ocean. The enzyme would be safely deployed via a self-propelled machine that looks like a whale! The machine would find, gulp up and 'digest' the plastic.

Check out the grand prize entry and more visionary ideas at natgeokids.com/almanac.

MANY VISIONARY IDEAS FOCUSED ON KEEPING THE OCEAN HEALTHY AND FREE OF PLASTIC.

Meet Your Shark Bestie

Some sharks grow more than 30,000 teeth in their lifetime.

YOU WON'T BELIEVE THESE PREDATOR PERSONALITIES.

While diving off the Bahama Islands, National Geographic photographer Brian Skerry noticed an oceanic whitetip shark swimming towards him. Soon the 2.7-metre (9-ft)-long female was gently bumping her snout against Skerry's camera.

The shark's mouth was closed, so Skerry knew she wasn't trying to bite him. Instead, she just examined his photographic equipment like a curious child. Skerry says this type of behaviour shows that sharks have all sorts of personalities. And even individuals belonging to a species that's thought to be aggressive can have a major sweet side.

PERSONALITY POWER

Hiking in the Bahamas through a mangrove forest—a group of shrubs or trees that grow in coastal waters—Skerry arrived at a wild nursery for lemon shark pups in about 30 centimetres (1 ft) of water. He put on his snorkel gear and scrambled onto his stomach to snap pics of the fish, watching as three shark pups swished closer to investigate. "Certain sharks are quicker to explore new things in their environment," Skerry says—meaning some sharks are also super social, while others within the same species prefer their me time.

Different sharks within the same species thrive in different situations. Social lemon sharks may do better when food is plentiful because they'll share with each other. But when food is scarce, the loner lemon sharks might thrive, since they don't divide their meals.

SUPERSIZED SHARK

On another diving trip, Skerry caught sight of a 4.3-metre (14-ft)-long tiger shark in the Atlantic Ocean. Skerry admits to being nervous at first, but the shark just glided over him and actually allowed Skerry to touch her. The tiger shark, known as Emma, visited the dive site almost every day during Skerry's stay. "She was just a gentle giant," says Skerry.

Skerry hopes that by showing the different personalities of sharks, people will view them

SKERRY TOOK THIS PHOTO OF A LEMON SHARK PUP FROM THE WATERY FLOOR OF A MANGROVE FOREST.

More than 450 species of sharks exist, but at least 26 of them are endangered and at least 48 are vulnerable.

THIS PHOTO, TAKEN BY BRIAN SKERRY, SHOWS A DIVER INTERACTING WITH A TIGER SHARK OFF THE BAHAMA ISLANDS.

Check out this book!

SKERRY READIES HIS CAMERA TO TAKE PHOTOS OF A SCHOOL OF CARIBBEAN REEF SHARKS.

less as scary animals and more as individuals that deserve our care and protection—even if they do have a lot of teeth!

GUARDIANS OF THE SEA

Want to help keep coral reefs in good condition? Call in the sharks! Certain sharks eat animals that prey on herbivorous (or plant-eating) fish. Since herbivorous fish eat harmful algae that grow on the reefs, a break in that chain would be bad news for coral. Thank goodness for hungry sharks.

A REMORA FISH CATCHES A RIDE ON A TIGER SHARK OFF THE BAHAMA ISLANDS.

27

awes8me
EXTREME SPORTS

CLIFF JUMPERS!

2 ON A ROLL

Who says you can't walk on water? Water zorbing brings extra thrills to a day at the lake, ocean or pool. Climb inside this giant inflatable orb and run or walk across the water's surface. You're sure to have a ball!

1 TAKE THE PLUNGE

Cannonball! A brave diver leaps off the La Quebrada Cliffs in Acapulco, Mexico. The height of the jump? About 46 metres (150 ft) — four times taller than most diving boards.

4 GO WITH THE FLOW

This sport is on fire. In ash boarding, you strap a wooden board onto your feet before shooting down the slope of an active volcano, reaching speeds of up to 80 kilometres an hour (50 mph).

3 CURVE APPEAL

Cars and motorcycles drive sideways along a wall in this dizzying display in India. Thanks to centripetal force, vehicles stay stuck to the wall as they loop around the curved course.

5 WHEELS UP

Rock-and-roll! A free rider sails over a steep rock wall in Moab, Utah, U.S.A. In free riding, cyclists use obstacles in nature — like rock formations and twisty trails — to do daring tricks and stunts.

6 BALANCING ACT

No fear here: A daredevil tiptoes along a wire as she crosses between two cliffs in the Italian Alps. A stumble at this height would be like falling from the top of the Empire State Building.

7 THROWN FOR A LOOP

Stunt cyclist Danny MacAskill seems to defy gravity by riding around a 4.9-metre (16-ft)-tall loop. Here, he's shown in a time-lapsed photo making a full circle before riding away on his bike.

8 BIG AIR

A snowboarder is flying high during the slopestyle event at the 2018 Winter Olympics in PyeongChang, South Korea. Slopestyle competitors race down a mountain dotted with obstacles like ramps, which allow them to catch major air.

DUH! Don't try these tricks on your own.

SOLO TREKS
ACROSS ANTARCTICA

It's tough enough for a team of explorers to trek across Antarctica. But imagine doing it completely on your own, towing a 136-kilogram (300-lb)-plus sled across the ice for nearly two months straight.

RIGHT: SELFIE OF COLIN O'BRADY TAKEN DURING HIS EXPEDITION. BELOW: O'BRADY ARRIVES AT THE SOUTH POLE ON DAY 40 OF HIS SOLO CROSSING.

That's just what a pair of adventurers did in separate solo trips across the coldest continent. In December 2018, both Colin O'Brady and Louis Rudd completed their respective journeys just two days apart.

What began as a race between the two men turned into a journey of survival, as both faced low visibility, biting winds and bitterly cold temperatures that could drop below minus 46°C (-50°F) during their more than 1,450-kilometre (900-mi) trek. Both men travelled with skis while dragging sleds packed with supplies. Rudd's sled weighed 150 kilograms (330 lb), while O'Brady's was 170 kilograms (375 lb). Both had scary stumbles while skiing over the icy surface. Still, neither used any sort of outside support, like supply drops or wind-harnessing kites that could have helped them pull their heavy loads. They slept in tents, made water out of snow and rationed the carefully measured food they packed to make sure they had enough fuel to last the entire way.

While O'Brady eventually completed his journey first, both men emerged as winners: Collectively, their efforts raised thousands of dollars for charity.

LEFT: LOUIS RUDD ON THE FINAL DAY OF HIS SOLO CROSSING. BELOW: RUDD ON SKIS AT THE SOUTH POLE ON DAY 40 OF HIS EXPEDITION.

HOW TO
SURVIVE A
KILLER BEE ATTACK!

1 Buzz Off
Killer bees — or Africanised honey-bees — attack only when their hive is being threatened. If you see several bees buzzing near you, a hive is probably close by. Heed their 'back off' attitude and slowly walk away.

2 Don't Join the Swat Team
Your first instinct might be to start swatting and slapping the bees. But that just makes the buzzers angry. Loud noises have the same effect, so don't start screaming, either. Just get away.

3 Don't Play Hide-and-Seek
Hives are often near water, but don't even think about outlasting the bees underwater. They'll hover and attack when you come up for air, even if you try to swim for it.

4 Make Like Speedy Gonzalez
Killer bees will chase you, but they'll give up when you're far enough away from the hive (usually about 183 metres [200 yards]). Take off running and don't stop until the buzzing does.

5 Create a Cover-Up
Killer bees often go for the face and throat, which are the most dangerous places to be stung. While you're on the run, protect your face and neck with your hands, or pull your shirt over your head.

HOW TO SURVIVE A
BEE STING!

1. De-Sting Yourself
First, get inside or to a cool place. Then, remove the stinger by scraping a fingernail over the area, like you would to get a splinter out. Do not squeeze the stinger or use tweezers unless you absolutely can't get it out any other way because squeezing it may release more venom.

2. Put It on Ice
Wash the area with soap and water and apply a cool compress to reduce swelling. Continue icing the spot for 20 minutes every hour. Place a washcloth or towel between the ice and your skin.

3. Treat It Right
With a parent's permission, take an antihistamine and gently rub a hydrocortisone cream on the sting site.

4. Hands Off
Make sure you don't scratch the sting. You'll just increase the pain and swelling.

5. Recognise Danger
If you experience severe burning and itching, swelling of the throat and/or mouth, difficulty breathing, weakness or nausea, or if you already know you are allergic to bees, get to a doctor immediately.

31

PHOTO TIPS:
Getting Started

TAKING A PHOTO IS AS EASY AS PUSHING A BUTTON, but taking a good photo requires patience and a general understanding of how photography works. Whether you're using a low-end smartphone or a high-end digital camera, check out National Geographic photographer Annie Griffiths' top tips and tricks for taking better pictures. With these expert pointers, you'll discover how to get the shot you want.

TIP 1
Get Closer When You Photograph People

Remember, it's the face of a person that makes us love people pictures, not their shoes! So move in close and show that beautiful face!

TIP 2
Take Time to Think About Your Composition

Composition is the way you place objects or people inside the frame. This is where you can be most creative. Remember, what is left OUT of the frame is as important as what is left in, so look carefully to see if anything in the shot will distract from your subject. If so, find a way to recompose, or rearrange, the photo so the distraction is left out.

TIP 3
Get Moving!

If you have taken lots of shots from one spot, try looking at the subject from another angle: above, behind, close up, far away. Professional photographers are moving all the time, always trying for a better shot.

TIP 4
Don't Photograph People in the Sun

Bright sun is usually the worst light for photographing people. The sun causes deep shadows and harsh light. Besides, everyone in the picture is usually squinting! It's much better to move your subjects to a shady spot where the light is softer.

TIP 5
Quality Not Quantity

It's far better to take fewer, more thoughtfully composed pictures, than it is to shoot like a maniac. It's not about how many photos you take. It's about how cool those photos are!

GUIDE TO
PHOTO
GRAPHY

Check out this book!

33

QUIZ WHIZ

Discover just how much you know about exploration with this quiz!

Write your answers on a piece of paper. Then check them below.

1 Which country has the highest known density of Antillean manatees in the world?
a. Bermuda
b. Belize
c. Bahrain
d. Bolivia

2 **True or false?** Of the 450-plus species of sharks, 26 of them are endangered.

3 In ash boarding, people strap on a wooden board and shoot down what?
a. a ski slope
b. a sand dune
c. an active volcano
d. a waterfall

4 Two explorers recently made history when they both completed a trek across _____.

5 In photography, _____ is the way you place objects or people inside the frame.
a. composition
b. measurement
c. correction
d. magnification

Not **STUMPED** yet? Check out the NATIONAL GEOGRAPHIC KIDS QUIZ WHIZ collection for more crazy **EXPLORATION** questions!

ANSWERS: 1. b; 2. True; 3. c; 4. Antarctica; 5. a

34

HOMEWORK HELP

How to Write a Perfect Essay

Need to write an essay? Does the assignment feel as big as climbing Mount Everest? Fear not. You're up to the challenge! The following step-by-step tips will help you with this monumental task.

1 **BRAINSTORM.** Sometimes the subject matter of your essay is chosen for you, sometimes it's not. Either way, you have to decide what you want to say. Start by brainstorming some ideas, writing down any thoughts you have about the subject. Then read over everything you've come up with and consider which idea you think is the strongest. Ask yourself what you want to write about the most. Keep in mind the goal of your essay. Can you achieve the goal of the assignment with this topic? If so, you're good to go.

2 **WRITE A TOPIC SENTENCE.** This is the main idea of your essay, a statement of your thoughts on the subject. Again, consider the goal of your essay. Think of the topic sentence as an introduction that tells your reader what the rest of your essay will be about.

3 **OUTLINE YOUR IDEAS.** Once you have a good topic sentence, you then need to support that main idea with more detailed information, facts, thoughts and examples. These supporting points answer one question about your topic sentence — 'Why?' This is where research and perhaps more brainstorming come in. Then organise these points in the way you think makes the most sense, probably in order of importance. Now you have an outline for your essay.

4 **ON YOUR MARKS, GET SET, WRITE!** Follow your outline, using each of your supporting points as the topic sentence of its own paragraph. Use descriptive words to get your ideas across to the reader. Go into detail, using specific information to tell your story or make your point. Stay on track, making sure that everything you include is somehow related to the main idea of your essay. Use transitions to make your writing flow.

5 **WRAP IT UP.** Finish your essay with a conclusion that summarises your entire essay and restates your main idea.

6 **PROOFREAD AND REVISE.** Check for errors in spelling, capitalisation, punctuation and grammar. Look for ways to make your writing clear, understandable and interesting. Use descriptive verbs, adjectives or adverbs when possible. It also helps to have someone else read your work to point out things you might have missed. Then make the necessary corrections and changes in a second draft. Repeat this revision process once more to make your final draft as good as you can.

35

AMAZING
ANIMALS

A Bengal tiger, a species that is primarily found in India, leaps through the air.

Bet You Didn't Know!

10 tail-wagging facts about

1 **A dog** can make about **100** different facial expressions.

2 **Dogs** have three times more **taste buds** than **cats.**

3 It can take up to **two months** before a newborn puppy **can wag its tail.**

4 **Most dogs have brown eyes.**

5 **The Norwegian Lundehund** has at least **six toes on each foot.**

6 **Bloodhounds** can follow **a scent** that is **four days old.**

dogs

7 Some dogs have **webbed feet.**

8 The shortest full-grown dog stands 9.65 centimetres (3.8 in) tall — as tall as a coffee mug!

9 A greyhound can reach speeds of about 72 kilometres an hour (45 mph).

10 Some 2,000 active-duty dogs serve in the U.S. military.

5 COOL CATS

True stories of amazing felines

A black cat crossed your path? It might be your lucky day! Cat lovers know that any kitty can bring good things like comfort and companionship. That's why humans have lived with feline friends for thousands of years, and why cats are still popular pets today.

1 CAT DETECTIVE

THE CAT Snowball
THE SPOT Prince Edward Island, Canada
WHY HE'S COOL Snowball helped solve a crime—a serious one. When police found white cat hairs clinging to a jacket with blood on it, they took a hard look at Snowball and DNA from cells in his hair. Since every individual's DNA is unique, scientists were able to show the hairs were Snowball's. That way, police could connect the jacket and the crime to Snowball's owner, who turned out to be the culprit. It was the first time cat DNA was used to convict a criminal. Looks like Snowball really shed some light on this crime.

2 FURRY FIRE ALARM

THE CAT Luna
THE SPOT Chester, South Carolina, U.S.A.
WHY SHE'S COOL Around 4 a.m., Emily Chappell-Root felt her cat Luna clawing, pawing and nipping at her feet. Thinking the cat wanted to show off a rabbit she had brought into their home, Chappell-Root went into the hallway. But instead of a rabbit, she saw flames coming from the kitchen. Thanks to Luna, she had time to get all six of her children, plus the other pets, out of the house. "Black cats have a reputation of being unlucky," Chappell-Root says. "But adopting Luna has been one of the luckiest things that happened to our family."

3 SURFER CAT

THE CAT Nānākuli
THE SPOT Honolulu, Hawaii, U.S.A.
WHY HE'S COOL Nānākuli the one-eyed cat knows exactly how to ride the waves: He lies down on his owner's surfboard with his paws hanging ten. His owners think that taking baths as a kitten helped the cat, nicknamed Kuli, get used to the water. Eventually they gave Kuli a tiny life jacket and let him float on a surfboard while gently splashing seawater on his paws. Now Kuli wears a lead as he surfs with his owners behind him on the board — as long as the water isn't too rough. *Cat*-abunga, dude!

KULI GETS READY TO CATCH SOME WAVES WITH OWNER ALEXANDRA GOMEZ-YOUNG.

WHAT A TEACHER'S PET! TOMBI 'HELPS' WITH CLASSWORK.

4 TOP OF THE CLASS

THE CAT Tombi
THE SPOT Izmir, Turkey
WHY HE'S COOL One morning when the school bell rang, 33 students and one stray cat filed into Özlem Pinar Ivaşçu's Year 4 classroom. "The kids started playing with him immediately," Ivaşçu says. The kitty didn't want to leave — and the students didn't want him to go. So the cat, named Tombi, was given vaccinations and a medical checkup to make sure he would be safe to have in the school. Now officially the class cat, Tombi sleeps through classes on a bookshelf and then plays with the kids during breaks. This kitty is a real class act!

CAT IN CHARGE 5

THE CAT Larry
THE SPOT London, U.K.
WHY HE'S COOL Larry has his own doorman. And an official title. And a job to do. This rescue kitty is the Chief Mouser to the Cabinet Office, meaning he keeps the home of the prime minister of the United Kingdom totally mouse free. Once, Larry almost lost his position after a former prime minister spotted a rodent in his office — and Larry didn't lift a paw. The cat's still employed though. Guess Larry is too cute to be voted out of office.

LARRY GUARDS 10 DOWNING STREET, HOME TO THE UNITED KINGDOM'S PRIME MINISTER.

Extraordinary
ANIMALS

Baby Sloths Rock Out

San Josecito de Heredia, Costa Rica
Huey is in school — and since he's a two-toed sloth at the Toucan Rescue Ranch, that means his classroom includes two rocking chairs connected by ropes and vines.

Rangers near Braulio Carrillo National Park found one-month-old Huey alone in the forest, too young to survive on his own. They brought him to the rescue centre, where staff prepare orphaned sloths to live in the wild. That's where the rocking chairs come in — they teach the sloths how to climb in real trees. "The chairs, vines and ropes aren't stable, so they sway like branches in the wind," says Pedro Montero, a biologist at the centre.

Once he aces the rocking chairs, Huey will climb on a jungle gym made of wood and tree branches. After mastering that, he'll hang out in a larger enclosure that will get him ready for life in the wild. When Huey is about two years old, staff will put a tracking collar on him. Then his keepers will leave the enclosure door open, letting Huey 'graduate' to the forest when he's ready — no cap and gown required!

You're totally rocking this.

Just call me Superpig!

Pig Saves Owner

Las Vegas, Nevada, U.S.A.
Jordan Jones was playing outside when a growling dog suddenly lunged towards him. Terrified, the boy could barely react. But just in time, Jordan's potbellied pig Dasiey jumped in front of the dog, fending off the angry animal.

Jordan's mum, Kim Jones, heard Dasiey's squeals and ran outside. "Jordan was just frozen, not moving," she says. "Dasiey was backed into a corner but still standing up to the dog." At one point Dasiey's head was locked in the dog's jaws. But she refused to give up.

Jordan's dad finally untangled Dasiey and the dog. Jordan was fine, as was Dasiey after a few stitches. "If Dasiey hadn't been there, the dog would've attacked Jordan," Jones says. "Dasiey will always be our hero."

Dog Hangs Ten

Sit? Stay? Please. I can do better than that.

Pacifica, California, U.S.A.
This dog knows how to catch—how to catch waves, that is! Abbie Girl the Australian kelpie took the top prize at the World Dog Surfing Championships two years in a row, by surfing the largest and longest waves. "She nailed it in every category," competition judge Charly Kayle says.

Owner Michael Uy started taking Abbie to the beach after adopting her more than a decade ago. Once the dog got used to the water, she eventually hopped on a surfboard. "Working kelpies herd sheep by running across their backs," Uy says, noting her breed's natural instinct might help Abbie balance. The dog also rides a custom board that's lighter, thinner and soft on top so she can dig in her claws. And nobody minds the wet dog smell!

Seal Pup Mystery

Carnforth, England, U.K.
The last thing anyone expected to see in the middle of a country road was a seal pup. But there was Ghost, 3.2 kilometres (2 mi) away from the nearest river and about 13 kilometres (8 mi) from his ocean habitat. How did the motherless youngster get so far from home?

"You never see seals this far inland," wildlife rescuer Nick Green says. "I figured whoever reported the seal had made a mistake." Seals often hunt where rivers meet the sea, so one possibility is that Ghost swam too far upriver and got lost. But the fact that he left the river and made the difficult journey over land stunned rescuers. "They feel safest in the water," Green says. "This was extremely unusual, and we'll never know the reason."

Luckily, Ghost was healthy and unharmed, so he was released back into the Irish Sea less than two weeks later. "He swam right off," Green says. The mystery remains unsolved, but at least the story has a happy ending.

Next time I'll ask for directions.

Best friends fur-ever!

INCREDIBLE ANIMAL FRIENDS

DOG CALMS CHEETAH

COLUMBUS, OHIO, U.S.A.

For the first few weeks of his life, Emmett the cheetah cub had pneumonia and required around-the-clock care. Kind humans at the Wilds conservation centre in Cumberland, Ohio, oversaw his recovery. But once Emmett was better, he moved to the Columbus Zoo and Aquarium.

Cheetahs are naturally cautious animals. But Emmett had a rough start. So the zookeepers thought it was important that he find a friend. Like people, some animals can get lonely. Having a friend—an animal to interact with, and even cuddle with—is important for development. That's where Cullen came in: This bundle of fur was destined to become Emmett's adorable puppy pal.

The pair love playing together, and they are helping the Columbus Zoo raise awareness about cheetahs to help protect this vulnerable species.

EMMETT

CULLEN

CAT CARER

Striped friends for the win.

KITTEN

EMU ▶

TE HORO, NEW ZEALAND

Sometimes cats have an unfriendly reputation. Not Kitten the cat. A longtime resident at Free as a Hawk Refuge, Kitten is known for being exceptionally nurturing towards other animals.

Kitten's owner thinks that because the cat was so well cared for when she was young, she might believe that all kinds of animals at the sanctuary need taking care of—including ducks, lambs, opossums and others.

The feline has even been caring for a baby emu that hatched at the refuge. The striped pair spend most of their time snuggled together on a comfortable couch, with Kitten grooming the sleeping emu's long, feathered neck.

FAWN BEFRIENDS RABBIT

BUFFALO, NEW YORK, U.S.A.

When Leondra Scherer, a wildlife rescuer and rehabilitator, got a call in late fall that a fawn needed help, she thought it was a mistake. Baby deer are typically born between May and August in upstate New York, and it would be rare for one to be born so late in the year. But sure enough, Scherer found an orphaned one-day-old fawn in desperate need of care.

Scherer named the fawn Pumpkin and brought her home to tend to her. Scherer would've loved for Pumpkin to have an animal companion she could interact with, but all of the other fawns at the farm were much older than Pumpkin and ready to be released back into the wild.

That's when Scherer adopted Chunk, a laid-back rabbit. "I wasn't sure if it would work," Scherer says. But when she introduced the two, Chunk immediately hopped over to the fawn for snuggles and a nap. "If you see a picture of Pumpkin and you can't see Chunk ... he's there, he's just burrowed beneath her!" Scherer says.

PUMPKIN

CHUNK

You make me so hoppy!

LLAMA COMFORTS SHEEP

May the Force be with you!

YODA

CLAIRE

LOS ANGELES, CALIFORNIA, U.S.A.

Felicity the sheep was severely mistreated until she was rescued from her former living situation. At her new home, the Barbados blackbelly sheep never quite bonded with the other sheep and spent her time alone. Until she befriended a goat named Claire, that is.

Claire was rescued around the same time as Felicity; the duo were known as pals around their new home, the Farm Sanctuary. But after a while, Claire began to spend more of her time with the other goats. In Claire's absence, a gentle llama named Yoda stepped up to look after the shy sheep.

Felicity and Yoda enjoy going for walks on the hillside, grazing in the fields and napping together. Felicity can even tuck her little body beneath Yoda's larger one when she's feeling shy or scared, which some experts say comforts the anxious sheep.

As Felicity gets used to her new home, she's also become less nervous around her human caregivers. She now takes treats from them, something she wouldn't have done previously. Maybe the sweet, soothing llama has more in common with a certain Jedi master than just a name!

WHAT IS Taxonomy?

Since there are billions and billions of living things, called organisms, on the planet, people need a way of classifying them. Scientists created a system called taxonomy, which helps to classify all living things into ordered groups. By putting organisms into categories, we are better able to understand how they are the same and how they are different. There are eight levels of taxonomic classification, beginning with the broadest group, called a domain, followed by kingdom, down to the most specific group, called a species.

Biologists divide life based on evolutionary history, and they place organisms into three domains depending on their genetic structure: Archaea, Bacteria and Eukarya. (See page 165 for 'The Three Domains of Life'.)

Where do animals come in?

Animals are a part of the Eukarya domain, which means they are organisms made of cells with nuclei. More than one million species of animals have been named, including humans. Like all living things, animals can be divided into smaller groups, called phyla. Most scientists believe there are more than 30 phyla into which animals can be grouped based on certain scientific criteria, such as body type or whether or not the animal has a backbone. It can be pretty complicated, so there is another, less complicated system that groups animals into two categories: vertebrates and invertebrates.

HEDGEHOG

SAMPLE CLASSIFICATION
PHILIPPINE TARSIER

Domain:	Eukarya
Kingdom:	Animalia
Phylum:	Chordata
Class:	Mammalia
Order:	Primates
Family:	Tarsiidae
Genus:	*Carlito*
Species:	*syrichta*

TIP:
Here's a sentence to help you remember the classification order:
Did **K**ing **P**hillip **C**ome **O**ver **F**or **G**ood **S**oup?

BY THE NUMBERS

There are 13,730 vulnerable or endangered animal species in the world. The list includes:

- **1,220 mammals**, such as the snow leopard, the polar bear and the fishing cat.
- **1,492 birds**, including the Steller's sea eagle and the black-banded plover.
- **2,494 fish**, such as the Mekong giant catfish.
- **1,367 reptiles**, including the Round Island day gecko.
- **1,597 insects**, such as the Macedonian grayling.
- **2,157 amphibians**, such as the emperor newt.
- **And more**, including 183 arachnids, 733 crustaceans, 239 sea anemones and corals, 187 bivalves and 2,039 snails and slugs.

ROUND ISLAND DAY GECKO

Vertebrates
Animals WITH Backbones

Fish are cold-blooded and live in water. They breathe with gills, lay eggs and usually have scales.

Amphibians are cold-blooded. Their young live in water and breathe with gills. Adults live on land and breathe with lungs.

Reptiles are cold-blooded and breathe with lungs. They live both on land and in water.

Birds are warm-blooded and have feathers and wings. They lay eggs, breathe with lungs and are usually able to fly. Some birds live on land, some in water and some on both.

Mammals are warm-blooded and feed on their mothers' milk. They also have skin that is usually covered with hair. Mammals live both on land and in water.

BIRD: MANDARIN DUCK

AMPHIBIAN: POISON DART FROG

Invertebrates
Animals WITHOUT Backbones

Sponges are a very basic form of animal life. They live in water and do not move on their own.

Echinoderms have external skeletons and live in seawater.

Molluscs have soft bodies and can live either in or out of shells, on land or in water.

Arthropods are the largest group of animals. They have external skeletons, called exoskeletons, and segmented bodies with appendages. Arthropods live in water and on land.

Worms are soft-bodied animals with no true legs. Worms live in soil.

Cnidaria live in water and have mouths surrounded by tentacles.

MOLLUSC: MAGNIFICENT CHROMODORID NUDIBRANCH

SPONGE: SEA SPONGE

MOLLUSC: GARDEN SNAIL

Cold-Blooded
versus
Warm-Blooded

Cold-blooded animals, also called ectotherms, get their heat from outside their bodies.

Warm-blooded animals, also called endotherms, keep their body temperature level regardless of the temperature of their environment.

BIZARRE Insects

Check out some of the strangest bugs on Earth!

The brightly coloured head of the puss moth caterpillar warns predators to stay away. This species, one of the most toxic caterpillars in North America, can spray acid from its head when it is attacked.

puss moth caterpillar

walking leaf

This flat, green insect is a master of disguise: It's common to mistake this bug for an actual leaf, thanks to its large, feathery wings. This clever camouflage provides protection from potential predators.

giraffe-necked weevil

No surprise, this bug gets its name from its extra-long neck. The males have longer necks than the females, which they use to fight other males for mating rights.

thorn bugs

One tiny thorn treehopper may not be a match for a bigger predator, but when grouped together on a branch, these spiky bugs create a prickly pack no bird wants a bite of!

spiny katydid

This katydid is covered in sharper-than-knive spikes. If a predator attacks, this species springs into action, defending itself by jabbir the enemy with its spiny legs and arms.

48

cockchafer beetle

The wild, feathery antennae on the male cockchafer may be cool to look at, but they're also helpful tools. They enable the beetle to sniff for food and feel out its surrounding environment.

acorn weevil

The acorn weevil's hollow nose is longer than its body, and perfect for drilling through the shells of acorns. A female will feast on the nut by sucking up its rich, fatty liquid, and then lay her eggs in the acorn.

pink grasshopper

Though most grasshoppers are green or brown, some — like this pink nymph — are much brighter. Pink grasshoppers are rare, most likely because they are easy for predators to spot.

man-faced stinkbug

There are more than 4,500 species of stinkbugs worldwide, including this brilliant yellow species, whose shield-shaped body displays a unique pattern resembling a tribal mask. Like all stink-bugs, this species secretes a foul-smelling liquid from scent glands between its legs when it feels threatened.

rhinoceros beetle

Gram for gram, this insect, which gets its name from the hornlike structure on the male's head, is considered one of the world's strongest creatures. It is capable of carrying up to 850 times its own body weight.

WELCOME to FOX Island

How clever scientists saved these cute critters

Native Americans likely brought island foxes to the southern Channel Islands.

A MATING PAIR OF ISLAND FOXES SHOWS AFFECTION. THE SPECIES USUALLY MATES FOR LIFE.

An island fox kit emerges from its underground den and sniffs the brush on Santa Cruz Island, some 32 kilometres (20 mi) off the southern coast of California, U.S.A. His brother follows, and the two foxes tumble over each other as they play fight. Decades ago, about 4,000 island foxes roamed Santa Cruz Island and two others in the Channel Islands National Park. But now, these two kits are part of the island fox's shrinking population—only about 200 of the species remain throughout the islands.

Out of Balance

About the size of house cats, foxes were once the top predators on these islands, eating everything from insects to mice to birds to fruit. But that started changing about 80 years ago. Before, the foxes shared their island home with bald eagles, which ate mostly fish and chased away other birds of prey. In the 1940s and 1950s, though, pesticide waste began seeping into the ocean off the California coast. It poisoned sea creatures, which over time poisoned fish-eating bald eagles, too. By 1960 all the bald eagles were gone from the islands.

BALD EAGLE

The foxes, which are excellent climbers, can grab fruit from the tips of tree branches.

Eagle Swap

Of course, the scientists still had to get the predators away from the islands. They set up bait around the island to trap the birds — but some were too smart to fall for the trick and avoided the traps. Scientists finally nabbed the last golden eagles by trapping them on the ground with a net that was shot from a helicopter. In all, the team trapped, transported and released 32 golden eagles back to the California mainland.

Now they just had to keep the golden eagles from coming back. The plan? Raising bald eagle chicks on the islands. Scientists even fed the eagles through a door so they wouldn't bond with humans.

Today, about 60 bald eagles fly over the Channel Islands. They are helping to maintain a safe habitat for the foxes so the mammals can continue to thrive.

Fox Island

With the golden eagle population dwindling, the wild foxes could safely breed again. Combined with pups from the captive foxes, scientists eventually increased the fox population to a healthy 250. Once the golden eagles were completely gone, scientists released the captive foxes back into their habitat.

A SCIENTIST CHECKS OUT A YOUNG BALD EAGLE, ONE OF THE FIRST HATCHED ON THE NORTHERN ISLANDS IN 50 YEARS.

Without the territorial bald eagles guarding the islands, golden eagles settled on three northern Channel Islands: San Miguel, Santa Rosa and Santa Cruz. Unlike bald eagles, these birds hunt mammals that live on land. Island foxes became the perfect prey. Within a decade, golden eagles nearly wiped out the foxes.

The Comeback

The foxes were in danger of disappearing from the islands forever unless someone did something — fast. Working together, scientists from the National Park Service, the Nature Conservancy and other agencies developed an amazing plan to save the island fox.

First, scientists had to keep the critters safe from eagles. So they created special traps to help them move the foxes to safety. Biologists baited the traps with cat food and simply waited for the foxes to walk in.

Scientists kept breeding pairs in 6-by-12-metre (20-by-40-ft) pens on their home islands. Inside, the foxes climbed on tree branches, rested in hammocks and hid in wooden den boxes. Then ... success! The foxes began having kits the following year. These animals were starting their comeback.

AN ISLAND FOX KIT STAYS CLOSE TO ITS DEN. KIT DENS ARE OFTEN IN ROCKS, WOOD PILES, BRUSH OR BURROWS.

The population on the three islands today is the same if not greater than it was before the golden eagles came to the islands. The curious, playful critters often greet human visitors when they arrive — and can get mischievous.

"They'll try to pull the zipper down on my tent and run off with my shoes and socks," says Chuck Graham, a wildlife photographer and kayak guide. "They're a part of the Channel Islands. They deserve to be here."

PREPARE TO BE
AMAZED BY THIS
ACROBAT
OF THE FOREST ...

THE INCREDIBLE RED PANDA

A red panda totters along the branch of an evergreen tree, placing one paw in front of the other like a gymnast on a balance beam. But then ... whoops! The panda loses its footing. A fall from this height — about 30 metres (100 ft) — could be deadly. But the panda quickly grips the branch with all four paws and some seriously sharp claws, steadies itself and keeps moving.

Red pandas spend about 90 percent of their time in the trees, says Mariel Lally, a red panda keeper at the Smithsonian's National Zoo in Washington, D.C., U.S.A. In fact, red pandas have adapted so well to life in the trees that they're famous for their incredible acrobatic skills. Check out three ways that red pandas land a perfect score with their amazing aerial act.

Where red pandas live

BUILT-IN BALANCE

A tightrope walker is all about balance. But red pandas can't exactly extend their arms like an acrobat. Instead they hold their tails straight behind them. "If they start to swing in one direction, they can move their tails the opposite way," Lally says. "It's sort of like a tightrope walker's pole."

UNDER FUR COVER

What's the best way to avoid a hungry snow leopard? Never let it see you in the first place! The small red panda's fiery coat sticks out at the zoo, but in the fir trees of the Himalayan mountains, the fur hides the panda in the reddish moss and white lichen (a plantlike organism) that often hang on the trees. Red pandas are so hard to spot that even scientists have trouble locating these creatures.

FAKE THUMB

A trapeze artist needs her thumbs to wrap her whole hand around the trapeze as she swings. Otherwise she might fly off! Same idea with red pandas. They have a special thumb-like wrist bone that gives them an extra grip when climbing down trees headfirst.

RED PANDA ON THE RUN

Smithsonian's National Zoo, Washington, D.C.

Ashley Wagner was out with her family when she spotted an animal crossing the street. At first Wagner's mum thought they'd seen a raccoon, but as soon as the creature turned its face towards them, Wagner knew it was a red panda. "He seemed very confident," she says.

Rusty the runaway red panda had arrived at the zoo just a few weeks before. As he scampered under a fence, Wagner snapped photos, shared them on social media and called the zoo. Soon a team came to the rescue, eventually nabbing him from a tree.

Today, Rusty has retired from his life on the run and settled down. The father of three red panda cubs, he lives at the Smithsonian Conservation Biology Institute.

SAVING THE RED PANDA

With their kitten-like faces, fluffy fur and waddling walk, red pandas are adorable. But these endangered animals are also ideal targets for the illegal pet trade.

Luckily, people are trying to help them. There's the Red Panda Network, which hires local people to keep watch over the red pandas in Nepal, replant bamboo and help paying tourists observe them without disturbing the creatures. Other organisations track poachers by using DNA samples from red pandas rescued from the black market to learn where the animals are being taken from.

You can help by asking your parents and older siblings not to 'like' photos and videos of red pandas on social media unless you know that the group or person posting them is trustworthy (like a wildlife photographer or a conservation group).

HOW TO SPEAK GORILLA

A YOUNG MOUNTAIN GORILLA IN THE DEMOCRATIC REPUBLIC OF THE CONGO REACHES FOR A CAMERA.

Discover five surprising ways these apes communicate

Keepers entering the gorilla enclosure at the Columbus Zoo and Aquarium in Ohio, U.S.A., often hear a noise that sounds like a babbling human. But it's just Mac, a western lowland gorilla. The ape greets his caregivers by making long, low grumbling sounds, gorilla-speak for "Hi, there!" When keepers exit the area in the evening, he makes a similar sound as if to say "Good night."

Mac isn't just making noise. Gorillas like him have things to say. And if you pick up a little gorilla language, you just might understand them.

"Apes are excellent communicators," Columbus Zoo curator Audra Meinelt says. And sound isn't the only way gorillas 'talk'. They use movements and even body odour to get their point across. It's no wonder experts think gorillas are among the most advanced animal communicators after humans. Check out these five amazing stories.

1

"What's in it for me?"

Nia, a western lowland gorilla, was excited when she discovered a new 'toy' — a plastic cup — had been added to her habitat at the Columbus Zoo. When zookeepers came to replace the cup with another toy, Nia wouldn't give it up. So Nia's keepers offered her a treat as a reward. Nia gave up the cup — and realised that things she finds in her habitat can be valuable. The next time Nia found a cup in her space, the gorilla broke it into several pieces and only gave the keepers one piece at a time ... in exchange for a treat after every piece!

Other gorillas at the zoo caught on to Nia's trick. "They'll hold out an item they think we might want, but not all the way," zookeeper Heather Carpenter says. "If we try to get it, they'll pull it back like, 'Not so fast!' Their actions are telling us that they'll give us what we want — but only when we offer something *they* want."

A WESTERN LOWLAND GORILLA GOOFS OFF IN ITS ZOO ENCLOSURE.

2 "Help!"

Anthropologist Kelly Stewart wanted to see how the wild mountain gorillas she was observing would react to her new gorilla T-shirt. But when she opened her jacket to reveal the shirt to a young female, Simba, the gorilla screamed — a sound that means "I'm scared!" in young gorillas. And *that* told the older troop members that Simba needed help. The group's leader, Uncle Bert, barrelled toward Stewart with a deep roar. Stewart quickly covered her shirt and stepped away from Simba, who stopped screaming. Uncle Bert backed off once Simba was quiet — the little gorilla was OK now that the unfamiliar 'gorilla' was gone. "I never wore that T-shirt again!" Stewart says.

3 "Follow me."

Kighoma the eastern lowland gorilla is the leader of his troop in the Democratic Republic of the Congo, a country in Africa. It's easy to spot the gorilla in charge, according to Sonya Kahlenberg of the Gorilla Rehabilitation and Conservation Education Center. Adult male leaders are identified by the silver fur on their backs. (They're called, well, silverbacks.) And they're often belching!

"It sounds like *na-oom*, kind of like a throat clearing. It means, 'I'm over here,'" Kahlenberg says. "And whenever Kighoma is ready to move, he'll make that grumbling sound and the other gorillas know to follow him."

A SILVERBACK MOUNTAIN GORILLA IN RWANDA LEADS HIS TROOP.

A GORILLA GETS A WHIFF OF SOMETHING GROSS.

4 "I'm not happy."

When zookeepers at the Dallas Zoo in Texas, U.S.A., smell a gym-sock-like odour, they know it's time to do an extra check on the gorillas. The smell comes from the male apes' armpits, and it may mean that a squirrel has entered their exhibit, or that the males aren't getting along. Either way, the stink signifies that something's not quite right.

5 "You've got this!"

Fasha the wild mountain gorilla had got her foot caught in a poacher's trap in the forests of Rwanda, Africa. She escaped, but couldn't keep up with her troop. But Icyororo the gorilla wasn't leaving her friend behind. Arms linked, they made their way through the forest. Every few minutes Icyororo turned and patted Fasha as if to say, "We're almost there."

When the pals crossed a river together, Icyororo gave Fasha a hug, demonstrating a gorilla's amazing ability to encourage their loved ones.

You can do this!

Surprise Party!

Red-eyed tree frogs astonish others with their weird behaviour.

Looking for a snack, a 76-centimetre (30-in)-long viper slithers down a tree in a steamy rainforest in Central America. Suddenly it sees a tasty-looking, 7.6-centimetre (3-in)-long red-eyed tree frog resting on a nearby leaf. The reptile lunges forward and snatches up the tiny croaker in its fanged mouth. But the snake's in for a not-so-pleasant surprise—the frog tastes terrible! The snake immediately spits out the amphibian. Landing unharmed on the forest floor, the frog blinks its big red eyes, then hops off to safety.

Red-eyed tree frogs have some features and behaviours that surprise other animals in their rainforest home, as well as the experts who study them. Discover how these jaw-dropping jumpers turn their habitat into one big surprise party.

The red-eyed tree frog oozes stinky, slightly toxic slime through its skin when a predator is near. It also doesn't taste very good!

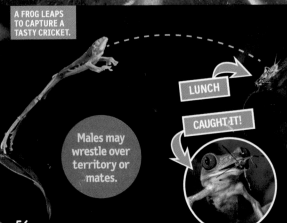

A FROG LEAPS TO CAPTURE A TASTY CRICKET.

LUNCH

CAUGHT IT!

Males may wrestle over territory or mates.

Ambush and Eat

A red-eyed tree frog might jump through the air to get closer to an insect it wants to eat. This animal also uses the element of surprise. Known as an ambush predator, the amphibian sometimes hides among the leaves in its rainforest home. The frog waits patiently until a tasty-looking moth or cricket comes within striking distance. Then it fires out its long, sticky tongue to capture the insect and pull the meal into its mouth. Now *that's* fast food.

Eye Spy

These nocturnal animals may spend the day lazing on plants, but they can still spy on their habitat. Thanks to a see-through third eyelid

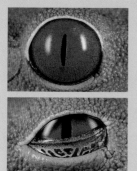

that closes over their eyeballs when resting, the amphibian can stay on the lookout for trouble while it reenergises. If a hunter does approach, the frog can leap away, startling its pursuer. The eyelid's stripes also may help hide the frog's bright red eyes from would-be predators.

Stick to It

Slick surfaces aren't a problem for this frog. It can easily clamber across wet leaves. Instead of hopping, the animal takes careful steps like a professional rock climber. It also has rounded toe pads that stick to surfaces like suction cups, and its feet produce gluey mucus to help it grip slippery surfaces. It can even cling to the undersides of leaves to hide from predators Spider-Man-style. That's a sticky surprise.

UNDERSIDE OF FOOT

A RED-EYED TREE FROG IN THE COUNTRY OF COSTA RICA SCALES A PLANT SHOOT.

One of the frog's calls sounds like a baby rattle.

Shake It Off

When researchers visited the country of Panama to study these frogs, they saw something that gave them a shock: a male frog shaking the shoot of a plant with his hind legs, similar to a person strumming a guitar string! They realised that males do this when other males come too close to their turf. The shaking creates vibrations, which intruders interpret as a signal to back off.

Why not just croak loudly to ward off intruders? "They don't want to reveal their location to the entire pond, including enemies such as frog-eating bats," biologist Michael Caldwell says. That'd shake things up *way* too much.

NORTH AMERICA
ATLANTIC OCEAN
PACIFIC OCEAN
SOUTH AMERICA

Gulf of Mexico

Caribbean Sea

BELIZE
HONDURAS
MEXICO
GUATEMALA
NICARAGUA
EL SALVADOR
PACIFIC OCEAN
COSTA RICA
PANAMA
COLOMBIA

Where red-eyed tree frogs live

MIXED-UP
MARSUPIALS?

FIND OUT WHY QUOKKAS ACT LIKE GIRAFFES, KOALAS AND BATS.

When explorers in the late 1600s first spotted this fuzzy, friendly-looking animal in Australia, they figured they'd stumbled on a house-cat-sized rat. Not even close. Quokkas might be related to kangaroos and wallabies, but they're way weirder. This marsupial has traits more often associated with other animals — and that makes it one wacky critter.

THEY REACH FOR LEAVES LIKE KOALAS

Ground-dwelling quokkas sometimes climb 1.5 metres (5 ft) up a tree trunk to reach a tasty-looking leaf or berry. That might not *sound* impressive, but it's something its closest relatives — kangaroos and wallabies — can't do. Tree-loving koalas have strong, large paws made for gripping branches all day. But the quokka can hold on only for a few minutes. Just enough time to swipe a snack!

THEY HOP LIKE RABBITS

If you spot a brown fuzz ball bouncing through the brush, it's not a rabbit — it's a leaping quokka! Although they usually crawl on all fours, quokkas also use their strong back legs to jump. These animals also create passageways in the bushes and grass as they move through the brush, similar to the underground tunnels bunnies create. Furry, cute *and* hoppy? Yes, please!

THEY CATCH Z'S LIKE BATS

OK, quokkas don't sleep while hanging from a cave or tree, but they do sometimes nap with their heads upside down. Quokkas often sleep in a sitting position with their head resting on their feet. "It's very cute," says Cassyanna Gray, a conservation officer on Australia's Rottnest Island, one place quokkas live. Also, like most bats, quokkas are mostly nocturnal, snoozing when the hot sun is out.

THEY CHEW LIKE GIRAFFES

Quokkas eat their food in a way that is similar to giraffes. Both animals use their large, flat molars to grind tough treats like leaves to release moisture and nutrients. The difference? Giraffes later regurgitate the food (meaning they basically throw it back up into their mouths — yuck!) and chew it some more. When a quokka swallows food, the meal enters its first stomach (yep, quokkas have two tummies!), where the food is broken down more before entering the second stomach.

SAY 'LEAVES'!

Quokkas have smiley faces and are sometimes friendly around people, so tourists to Australia's Rottnest Island often get too close. The extra attention could put quokkas in danger — or it might help the species survive.

Authorities on Rottnest Island protect the critters with rules against touching or feeding the quokkas. Human food can make them sick, plus giving them snacks (and even water) can make the quokkas too dependent on people. But by following the rules and keeping a safe distance, island tourists help give authorities more power to support the quokka's habitat. For instance, conservationists can use the money generated from tourism to protect the island and monitor the quokka population.

So if you want to protect the quokkas *and* get an epic picture, just use a selfie stick!

Rottnest Island, one of the places quokkas live, got its name after explorers thought quokkas were rats. (Get it? *Rat* nest? *Rott*nest?)

SCALY
SUPERHEROES
Discover the hidden powers of the pangolin.

Clark Kent and Peter Parker—the alter egos of Superman and Spider-Man—don't really stand out. And neither do pangolins in the tropical forests or grasslands of Africa and Asia where they live. But like your favourite movie heroes, this animal has a few hidden superpowers. Check them out here.

ASIA

AFRICA

INDIAN OCEAN

ATLANTIC OCEAN

AUSTRALIA

Where pangolins live

SPIDER-MAN STICKINESS!

SPIDER-MAN

Spider-Man shoots out sticky strands of webbing from his wrists to swing from one sky-scraper to another. When a pangolin is hungry, it shoots out its sticky tongue, which extends up to 41 centimetres (16 in) past its mouth. Coated in gluey saliva, the licker scoops up ants and termites, the pangolin's favourite snacks. In all, the mammal can eat some 70 million insects a year. Makes sense that this superhero-like creature would have a super appetite.

WOLVERINE CLAWS!

WOLVERINE

During fights with villains, Wolverine defends himself with long, sharp claws that pop out of his knuckles. Pangolins have claws on each of their front feet used to rip up ant and termite nests as they search for dinner. Claws also help them clutch on to branches or dig burrows for sleeping. Whether you're a superhero or a pangolin, claws really come in handy.

Eight species of pangolins exist in total.

The animal emits a stinky odour when threatened.

IRON MAN ARMOUR!

CLOSE-UP OF SCALES

IRON MAN

Iron Man sports a high-tech suit of armour that shields the superhero from weapons hurled by enemies. Pangolins wear armour, too. Their 'suits' consist of rows of overlapping scales that resemble a pine cone. Made out of keratin—the same substance as in your fingernails—the pangolin's armour is so tough that predators such as lions can't bite through it. It's too bad that this armour doesn't come with built-in jets!

ANT-MAN MOVES!

ANT-MAN

When he senses trouble, Ant-Man shrinks to the size of, well, an ant. Pangolins, which can be almost two metres (6 ft) long from head to tail tip, have their own way of shrinking. If the mammal notices a nearby predator, it'll curl into a small ball less than half its normal size and shield its stomach and face. Unable to find a vulnerable part of the pangolin to strike, many enemies give up. Tiny can be tough.

TONGUE TIME

Up to 71 centimetres (28 in) in length, a pangolin's tongue can be almost as long as its body (minus the tail)! How does it fit inside the mammal? The tongue runs from its mouth down its sternum (or breast-bone). The back end curves around organs in the lower abdomen, arching towards the backbone. At rest, the tongue's front end is coiled inside the pangolin's mouth. The animal flicks it out to grab grub.

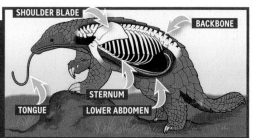

SHOULDER BLADE

BACKBONE

STERNUM

TONGUE

LOWER ABDOMEN

THE SECRET LIVES OF

Orcas don't often dive very deep — their food is usually near the surface, so they are as well.

You'd need more than 650 cans of tuna to keep an orca full!

Orcas

'FRIENDING' OTHER DOLPHINS. 'LIKING' FUN ACTIVITIES. 'CHATTING'. ORCAS MIGHT HAVE THE BEST SOCIAL NETWORK EVER.

A bottlenose dolphin flips its tail as it swims with its dolphin friends. A baby chimpanzee watches closely as its mum shows it how to crack a nut. A male wolf howls to gather the pack for a hunt.

Playing, teaching and working together are known as 'social skills'. Humans, of course, are social animals. So are bottlenose dolphins, chimps and wolves. And according to scientists, it's time to move one animal higher up the list: orcas!

Orcas are dolphins, so scientists already knew about some of their social behaviours. "We knew orcas travel in pods," says biologist Janice Waite of the National Oceanic and Atmospheric Administration (NOAA), in the United States. But new research shows that the school-bus-sized swimmers have more complex social behaviours than previously understood.

Could orcas be among the most social animals of all? Here are five stories to help you decide.

Orcas 'adopt' orphans.

Springer watched curiously as a boat approached her. The young orca had been orphaned as a calf, so no one had taught her that boat propellers could injure her. Wanting to take a closer look, Springer swam closer until ... *whoosh!* An older female orca called Nodales forcefully shoved her away from danger.

"Nodales took Springer under her wing, even though they weren't related," says Paul Spong, co-director of OrcaLab, a research station in Canada. "It didn't take long for the young orca to understand she should keep away from boats." Today, Springer is a mother herself — and she stays out of water traffic.

Orcas 'babysit' other orcas.

One day a female named Sharky moved close to a group of newborn orcas and their mothers. Sharky swam near a calf, then led it away to play with her — giving the mums a break. Waite observed Sharky behave like that with other calves as well. "She's not the only young female we've seen 'babysit' other orcas," Waite says. "We think they do it as practice for when they have calves of their own."

ORCAS APPROACH A WEDDELL SEAL, HOPING TO MAKE IT THEIR MEAL.

Orcas are team players.

A Weddell seal lies on a sheet of floating ice in Antarctica. Suddenly five orcas begin nudging the ice. Then, a large female orca begins to make whistling and clicking noises. It's like a signal: The other orcas line up, swim toward the ice and create a wave that knocks the seal into the water. Oddly, the orcas let the seal escape.

Some experts believe that the female orca was teaching hunting and teamwork to her calves. And as with any new skill, practice makes perfect!

Orcas put family first.

Researchers rarely spotted Plumper and Kaikash apart. But when older bro Plumper got sick, the researchers worried that he wouldn't be able to keep up with his younger sibling. But the brothers were inseparable. Kaikash would swim a short distance, then wait for Plumper to catch up. "This went on for hours," Spong says. "Kaikash didn't seem to mind. Like human brothers, these two had each other's backs."

Researchers now know that orca families spend most of their days together. Although adults — especially males — sometimes split from the group to hunt, they stay close enough to hear family members. Says Waite: "They're probably as close with their families as we are with ours."

Orcas play together.

Orcas are known for breaching — or leaping out of the water — to show their playful side. "They get most excited when they meet up in groups," says biologist Candice Emmons of NOAA. She's seen orcas from different pods brush against each other to say hello. She's also watched orcas smacking their tails against the water (called lobbing) to show excitement. But Emmons's favourite thing to observe is 'pec slapping'.

"That's when they touch each other with their pectoral fins, which are like their arms," Emmons says. Sort of like orca high fives!

An orca's diet consists of whales, sea lions, penguins, seals, walruses and a variety of fish and squid. *Chomp!*

I'm tougher than I look!

SEA OTTERS:
Super Cute, Super Tough

ULTIMATE FUR COAT

A sea otter wears a luxurious fur coat made up of about 800 million hairs. A shield from the sea, the coat is covered in natural oils that keep the skin and underfur dry. Because its fur is the only thing protecting a sea otter from the heat-stealing ocean water, the marine mammal spends nearly half of its day cleaning, combing and fluffing its coat.

Only a female and her pups will hunt in groups or share food.

FEEDING FRENZY

To stay warm, an otter also relies on a super-revved metabolism. It must eat three times more calories than a child needs in order to survive. A daily menu might be 7 abalone, 37 cancer crabs, 50 sea urchins or 157 kelp crabs — that's about equal in calories to 42 scoops of chocolate ice cream! Otters also have to work for their food: To eat 150 kelp crabs, the otter needs to make at least 150 dives!

S ea otters may look like cute, gentle balls of fur, but they're actually rugged, resilient predators that battle prey, the environment and other otters every day. Here's why they deserve a reputation as the tough guys of the ocean.

SEA SURVIVOR

A sea otter is about the same size as an 11-year-old child — but a whole lot tougher. A human would be lucky to last 20 minutes in an otter's home just beyond the breaking waves before hypothermia — a drop in body temperature — set in and their body shut down. Unlike whales and walruses, otters don't have blubber (a thick layer of fat) to keep them warm. So how do they survive?

Sea otters are related to skunks, weasels, badgers and river otters.

SUPER STRENGTH

Sea otters are like superheroes when it comes to strength. A hard clam or mussel shell is no match for an otter's extremely powerful jaws and strong teeth. A person would have to use a special sharp tool to pry a firmly anchored abalone from its rock. An otter has only its paws and an occasional rock. The otter also uses its strong paws to snatch and overpower large crabs while avoiding their dangerous claws.

Super swimmers, super eaters, super divers — sea otters definitely deserve their reputation as supertough marine mammals.

Incredible Powers of the OCTO US!

Octopuses may not look like wizards you know from films, but they've got many of the same tricks. They can change shape, disappear in a puff of smoke, use potions and poisons and are very good at keeping out of sight.

POTIONS AND POISONS

Blue-ringed octopuses make one of the deadliest poisons in the world. They have enough poison in their saliva to kill a human, though these molluscs mostly use their venom to paralyse prey or to defend themselves from enemies.

TRICK ARMS

When faced with danger, some octopuses will break off an arm and scoot away. The arm keeps wriggling for hours, sometimes crawling all over an attacker and distracting it. The octopus grows a new arm out of the stump.

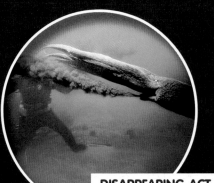

DISAPPEARING ACT

To confuse attackers, an octopus will squirt a concentrated ink out of its backside that forms a smokelike cloud. This allows enough time for the octopus to escape.

THE OCTOPUS IS THE TALLER LUMP ON THE RIGHT. THAT'S BRAIN CORAL ON THE LEFT.

MAGICAL MOVES

Octopuses can squeeze through tiny holes as if they were moving from room to room through keyholes. Some can even swim through the sand, sticking an eye up like a periscope to see if the coast is clear.

OCEAN SUPERSTARS

The fascinating lives of 6 sea turtle species

Think all sea turtles are the same? Think again! Each of these species stands out in its own way.

1 GREEN SEA TURTLE: THE CLEAN FREAK

In Hawaii, U.S.A., green sea turtles choose a 'cleaning station'—a location where groups of cleaner fish groom the turtles by eating ocean gunk, like algae and parasites, off their skin and shells. In Australia, the turtles rub against a favourite sponge or rock to scrub themselves. Clever!

2 KEMP'S RIDLEY: THE LITTLE ONE

They may be the smallest sea turtles (babies shown here), but they're not so tiny: Adults weigh as much as many 10-year-old children, and their shell is about the size of a car tyre. They're speedy, too: It takes them less than an hour to dig a nest, then lay and bury their eggs.

3 OLIVE RIDLEY: THE ULTRA-MUM

Every year, hundreds of thousands of female olive ridley sea turtles take over beaches to lay their eggs and then bury them before disappearing back into the sea. Call it safety in numbers: With thousands of turtles swarming the shoreline, they're sure to overwhelm any predator.

4 LEATHERBACK: THE MEGA-TURTLE

These giants among reptiles have shells about as big as a door and weigh as much as eight fully grown adults! Their size doesn't slow them down, though. A leatherback can swim as fast as a bottlenose dolphin.

5 HAWKSBILL: THE HEARTY EATER

What's the hawksbill's favourite snack? Sponges! These turtles gobble about 544 kilograms (1,200 lb) of sponges a year. The turtles can safely eat this sea life, which is toxic to other animals. That means there are plenty of sponges to snack on!

6 LOGGERHEAD: THE TOUGH GUY

The loggerhead sea turtle's powerful jaws can easily crack open the shells of lobsters, conchs and snails to get at the meat inside. Some loggerheads swim a third of the way around the world to find food.

67

An Amur leopard can leap up to three metres (10 ft) in the air.

THE WORLD'S RAREST LEOPARD

THESE BIG CATS GET A NEW CHANCE AT SURVIVAL.

SOFT, DENSE FUR KEEPS AMUR LEOPARDS WARM IN THE BITTER COLD.

S talking down the snowy hillside, the Amur leopard watches its prey through the trees. In the clearing below, a sika deer munches on tree bark. The leopard crouches, then suddenly springs forward, tackling the deer from three metres (10 ft) away. With a deadly combination of speed, strength and stealth, the Amur leopard seems like it has everything it needs for survival. But after decades of habitat loss and poaching, these endangered cats almost went extinct. Thanks in part to a newly established national park, Amur leopards are coming back from the brink.

Disappearing Act

Amur leopards live along the Russian–Chinese border, where they've adapted to their chilly climate with bushier fur and longer legs to trudge through the deep snow. But as hearty as they are, the leopards couldn't fight off the humans moving into their habitat or the poachers who killed them to sell their coats. At one point, there were only about 30 left in the world. They were going extinct.

Saving the Leopards

To protect these cats, scientists had to convince the government that this was something worth doing. The first step was to show where the leopards spent their time — and what land needed protection most. Using camera traps and devices that automatically take photos and videos of passing animals, experts were

AMUR LEOPARDS OFTEN DRAG THEIR PREY UP INTO A TREE BEFORE EATING.

Armed with this information, scientists approached the Russian government about coming up with a plan to protect the big cats. After proving how few leopards were left in the wild and what was needed to save them, scientists persuaded officials to take action to save the world's most endangered big cat from extinction.

able to get more information about the Amur leopards in the area. And, because a leopard's spots — called rosettes — are as unique as human fingerprints, scientists could identify individual leopards to figure out where each leopard spent most of its time.

New Territory

The camera trap footage also revealed that their home ranges were up to twice the distance of leopards in other parts of the world — and that they travelled very far to find food. That meant larger pieces of land needed to be protected for both the leopard and its prey. Better-protected prey meant more food for the leopards and their cubs.

AMUR LEOPARDS GIVE BIRTH TO ONE TO FOUR CUBS AT A TIME.

Amur leopards are named after the Amur River, a body of water that runs along the border of Russia and China.

The result: Land of the Leopard National Park. The 261,994-hectare (647,400-acre) refuge — about two and a half times bigger than where the leopards had been living — added newly protected areas to pre-existing reserves. New laws on hunting animals such as sika deer meant the big cats wouldn't run out of food. Millions of dollars were spent on anti-poaching patrols and other efforts, including a 'Leopard Tunnel' built on a stretch of busy highway so that Amur leopards and Amur tigers didn't have to dodge speeding cars.

Bouncing Back

After Land of the Leopard National Park was created in 2012, the Amur leopard population grew to 84 by 2015. Since then, more new cubs have been spotted. Throughout the forest, young leopards are now crouching nearby as their mum teaches them how to hunt. They're learning from her how to survive. And one day, some of those cubs will have babies of their own to teach.

AN AMUR LEOPARD'S LARGE PAWS WORK LIKE SNOWSHOES, LETTING THE CAT WALK ON SNOW WITHOUT SINKING.

RISE OF THE TIGER

An adult male tiger can weigh the same as eight 10-year-old kids.

Tigers live in both cold and hot climates.

Scientists find good news with the help of secret snaps.

Recently, scientists have worked to get a current global estimate of how many wild tigers exist. As part of the effort, experts in countries throughout the tiger's range, including Russia, Bangladesh, Bhutan, India and Nepal, trekked to forests and grasslands where the cats live to set up camera traps—motion-sensing or remote-controlled cameras that snap wildlife pics. They hoped the photos would give clues about the number of tigers in each nation.

Cats on Camera

To track down tigers, researchers focused on water holes and areas with boar and other tiger prey. There, they fixed multiple camera traps to trees to catch the cats from different angles. The cameras' treelike disguise made them less likely to be destroyed by curious animals. After setting up the traps, the researchers journeyed home.

Take a Number

The cameras snapped pictures of any animal that walked in front of them, using night vision to get good photos in the dark, when tigers are most active. The researchers returned to collect the devices a few months later and uploaded their pictures to computers, which analysed each tiger's coat pattern and recognised when a certain tiger appeared more than once. The computers then counted how many individuals appeared overall in the photos.

Using this data and other information, teams were able to estimate how many tigers live in the countries studied. The final tally surprised them all.

Tiger Time

Researchers estimated that about 3,890 wild tigers exist on the planet. That's up from as few as 3,200, the estimated population in 2010. Experts say this bump may be partly due to conservation efforts made by several of the countries where tigers live, such as laws to protect the cats' habitats.

Still, experts emphasise that the rise in numbers doesn't mean that tigers are out of danger. In fact, it's possible that better technology may have allowed researchers to photograph more tigers than before, making it seem as if the population is increasing. Still, analysing these 'selfies' is certainly a step in the right direction for the future of wild tigers.

A TIGER CUB INVESTIGATES A CAMERA THAT'S MOUNTED ON WHEELS AND CONTROLLED REMOTELY BY A RESEARCHER.

MARGAYS: OUT ON A LIMB

Meet the margays! These small wild cats, about the size of a house cat, are native to rainforests of Central and South America. Because of their secretive lifestyle — they spend a lot of their lives in trees, even hunting among the branches — catching a glimpse of these acrobatic cats in their natural habitat is no easy task.

BUILT TO CLIMB

With a body uniquely adapted to life in the treetops, a margay moves through the canopy like a feline gymnast. Unlike most wild cats, it can go down a tree headfirst. The margay's ankles can rotate all the way around to face backwards, which allows the cat to quickly change direction while climbing.

A margay's feet are wide and soft, with flexible toes that allow it to grab branches. Its 43-centimetre (17-in)-long tail provides balance as it moves around in the treetops.

TRACKING MARGAYS

Because margays can stay hidden in the trees, experts use radio collars to track these cats and shed some light on their daily activities. As a result, the margay's characteristics and habits aren't a complete secret. Experts have observed that these solitary animals are active mostly at night (their huge eyes help them see in the dark), hunting for birds, snakes, rodents and even small monkeys. It takes skilful climbing to accomplish that hunting feat.

SAVING MARGAY HABITAT

Though the overall margay population isn't in immediate danger, the cats are vulnerable. Margays need tropical forests to survive. Habitat destruction, especially clearing forests for farms, is their biggest threat. Today, scientists are working hard to save the habitat of these acrobats of the rainforest.

Climbing skills make margays the acrobats of the rainforest.

CLIMBING HEADFIRST DOWN A TREE IS A RARE ABILITY MARGAYS HAVE MASTERED.

Prehistoric TIMELINE

HUMANS HAVE WALKED on Earth for some 200,000 years, a mere blip in the planet's 4.5-billion-year history. A lot has happened during that time. Earth formed and oxygen levels rose in the millions of years of the Precambrian time. The productive Paleozoic era gave rise to hard-shelled organisms, vertebrates, amphibians and reptiles.

Dinosaurs ruled Earth in the mighty Mesozoic. And 65 million years after dinosaurs became extinct, modern humans emerged in the Cenozoic era. From the first tiny molluscs to the dinosaur giants of the Jurassic and beyond, Earth has seen a lot of transformation.

THE PRECAMBRIAN TIME

4.5 billion to 542 million years ago

- Earth (and other planets) formed from gas and dust left over from a giant cloud that collapsed to form the sun. The giant cloud's collapse was triggered when nearby stars exploded.
- Low levels of oxygen made Earth a suffocating place.
- Early life-forms appeared.

THE PALEOZOIC ERA

542 million to 252 million years ago

- The first insects and other animals appeared on land.
- 450 million years ago (mya), the ancestors of sharks began to swim in the oceans.
- 430 mya, plants began to take root on land.
- More than 360 mya, amphibians emerged from the water.
- Slowly, the major landmasses began to come together, creating Pangaea, a single supercontinent.
- By 300 mya, reptiles had begun to dominate the land.

What Killed the Dinosaurs?

It's a mystery that's boggled the minds of scientists for centuries: What happened to the dinosaurs? While various theories have bounced around, a recent study confirms that the most likely culprit is an asteroid or comet that created a giant crater. Researchers say that the impact set off a series of natural disasters like tsunamis, earthquakes and temperature swings that plagued the dinosaurs' ecosystem and disrupted their food chain. This, paired with intense volcanic eruptions that caused drastic climate changes, is thought to be why half of the world's species — including the dinosaurs — died in a mass extinction.

DINO TIMES

THE MESOZOIC ERA

251 million to 65 million years ago

The Mesozoic era, or the age of the reptiles, consisted of three consecutive time periods (shown below). This is when the first dinosaurs began to appear. They would reign supreme for more than 150 million years.

TRIASSIC PERIOD

251 million to 201 million years ago

- Appearance of the first mammals. They were rodent-sized.
- The first dinosaur appeared.
- Ferns were the dominant plants on land.
- The giant supercontinent of Pangaea began breaking up towards the end of the Triassic.

JURASSIC PERIOD

201 million to 145 million years ago

- Giant dinosaurs dominated the land.
- Pangaea continued its breakup, and oceans formed in the spaces between the drifting landmasses, allowing sea life, including sharks and marine crocodiles, to thrive.
- Conifer trees spread across the land.

CRETACEOUS PERIOD

145 million to 66 million years ago

- The modern continents developed.
- The largest dinosaurs developed.
- Flowering plants spread across the landscape.
- Mammals flourished, and giant pterosaurs ruled the skies over small birds.
- Temperatures grew more extreme. Dinosaurs lived in deserts, swamps and forests from the Antarctic to the Arctic.

THE CENOZOIC ERA — TERTIARY PERIOD

65 million to 2.6 million years ago

- Following the dinosaur extinction, mammals rose as the dominant species.
- Birds continued to flourish.
- Volcanic activity was widespread.
- Temperatures began to cool, eventually ending in an ice age.
- The period ended with land bridges forming, which allowed plants and animals to spread to new areas.

DINO Classification

Classifying dinosaurs and all other living things can be a complicated matter, so scientists have devised a system to help with the process. Dinosaurs are put into groups based on a very large range of characteristics.

Scientists put dinosaurs into two major groups: the bird-hipped ornithischians and the lizard-hipped saurischians.

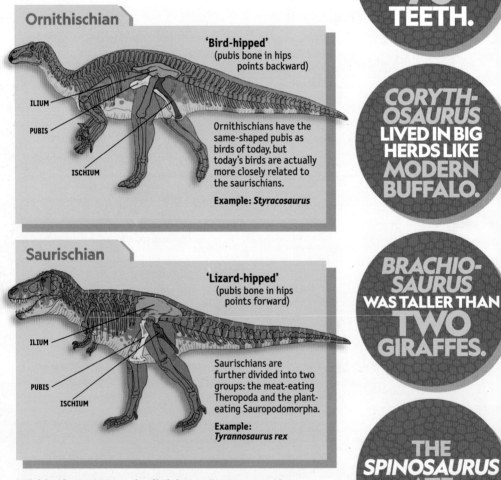

Ornithischian

'Bird-hipped'
(pubis bone in hips points backward)

ILIUM

PUBIS

ISCHIUM

Ornithischians have the same-shaped pubis as birds of today, but today's birds are actually more closely related to the saurischians.

Example: *Styracosaurus*

Saurischian

'Lizard-hipped'
(pubis bone in hips points forward)

ILIUM

PUBIS

ISCHIUM

Saurischians are further divided into two groups: the meat-eating Theropoda and the plant-eating Sauropodomorpha.

Example:
Tyrannosaurus rex

Within these two main divisions, dinosaurs are then separated into orders and then families, such as Stegosauria. Like other members of the Stegosauria, *Stegosaurus* had spines and plates along the back, neck and tail.

THE FIERCE
ALLOSAURUS
HAD NEARLY
70
TEETH.

CORYTH-
OSAURUS
LIVED IN BIG
HERDS LIKE
MODERN
BUFFALO.

BRACHIO-
SAURUS
WAS TALLER THAN
TWO
GIRAFFES.

THE
SPINOSAURUS
ATE
SHARKS.

③ NEWLY DISCOVERED DINOS

Humans have been searching for — and discovering — dinosaur remains for hundreds of years. In that time, at least 1,000 species of dinos have been found all over the world, and thousands more may still be out there waiting to be unearthed. Recent discoveries include *Suskityrannus hazelae*. Found in the western United States, the jaguar-sized cousin of *T. rex* was discovered by a 16-year-old on a high school dig trip.

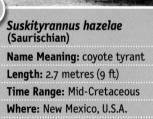

1

Suskityrannus hazelae
(Saurischian)

Name Meaning: coyote tyrant

Length: 2.7 metres (9 ft)

Time Range: Mid-Cretaceous

Where: New Mexico, U.S.A.

2

Mnyamawamtuka moyowamkia
(Saurischian)

Name Meaning: animal of the Mtuka (with) a heart-shaped tail

Length: 7.6 metres (25 ft)

Time Range: Mid-Cretaceous

Where: Tanzania

3

Bajadasaurus pronuspinax
(Saurischian)

Name Meaning: bent over forward spine

Length: 9.1 metres (30 ft)

Time Range: Early Cretaceous

Where: Argentina

Dynamite
DINO AWARDS

Spiky body armour. Razor-sharp teeth. Unimaginable strength. No doubt, all dinos are cool. But whether they were the biggest, the fiercest or the biggest-brained of the bunch, some stand out more than others. Here are seven of the most amazing dinos ever discovered.

Supersize Appetite

Big Brain

Scientists think that *Tyrannosaurus rex* could gulp down 227 kilograms (500 lb) of meat at a time — that's like eating 2,000 burgers in one bite!

Troodon, a meat-eater the size of a man, had a brain as big as an avocado stone — relatively large for a dinosaur of its small stature. Because of its big brain, scientists think *Troodon* may have been the smartest dino and as intelligent as modern birds.

Cool Camo

The birdlike *Sinornithosaurus* had feathers similar to those of modern birds. It may have also had reddish brown, yellow and black colouring that kept this turkey-sized raptor camouflaged as it hunted in the forest.

Heavy-weight

The heaviest of all dinosaurs, *Argentinosaurus* is believed to have weighed 99,790 kilograms (220,000 lb) — more than 15 elephants.

Built for Speed

Ornithomimids, a group of dinosaurs that resembled ostriches, would have given the world's fastest man a run for his money. Some of these long-limbed, toothless meat-eaters are thought to have clocked speeds of 80 kilometres an hour (50 mph).

Pint-Size Predator

Microraptor zhaoianus, the smallest meat-eating dinosaur, measured just 40 centimetres (16 in) tall. With long toe tips for grasping branches, it's thought to be closely related to today's birds.

Super Spines

Known as the 'spine lizard', *Spinosaurus* had huge spines sticking out of its back, some taller than a 10-year-old! Weighing up to 20 tonnes (22 tons), it may have been the biggest meat-eating dinosaur.

77

DINO DEFENCES

Scientists don't know for sure whether plant-eating dinos used their amazing attributes to battle their carnivorous cousins, but these herbivores were armed with some pretty wicked ways they could have used to defend themselves.

ARMOUR: *GASTONIA*
(GAS-TONE-EE-AH)

Prickly *Gastonia* was covered in heavy, defensive armour. To protect it from the strong jaws of meat-eaters it had four horns on its head, thick layers of bone shielding its brain, rows of spikes sticking out from its back and a tail with triangular blades running along each side.

SPIKES: *KENTROSAURUS*
(KEN-TROH-SORE-US)

Stand back! This cousin of *Stegosaurus* had paired spikes along its tail, which it could swing at attackers with great speed. One paleontologist estimated that *Kentrosaurus* could have swung its treacherous tail fast enough to shatter bones!

CLUB TAIL:
ANKYLOSAURUS

(AN-KYE-LOH-SORE-US)

Steer clear! *Ankylosaurus* possessed a heavy, knobby tail that it could have used to whack attackers. It may not have totally protected the tanklike late Cretaceous dino from a determined *T. rex*, but a serious swing could have generated enough force to do some real damage to its rival reptile.

WHIP TAIL:
DIPLODOCUS

(DIH-PLOD-UH-KUS)

Some scientists think this late Jurassic giant's tail — about half the length of its 27-metre (90-ft) body — could have been used like a whip and swished at high speeds, creating a loud noise that would send potential predators running.

HORNS:
TRICERATOPS

(TRI-SER-UH-TOPS)

There's no evidence *Triceratops* ever used its horns to combat late Cretaceous snack-craving carnivores. But scientists do believe the famous three-horned creature used its frills and horns in battle with other members of its species.

21 CUTEST ANIMALS OF 2021

From roly-poly pandas to scuttling crabs, there's no shortage of cute creatures on Earth. Here's Nat Geo Kids' roundup of cuddly critters that are sure to make you say *awww.*

1 HEADS OR TAILS

Ring-tailed lemurs are named for their unique striped appendages, which are as long as their bodies and help them balance as they climb and leap among the tree branches. They live exclusively on the African island of Madagascar.

2 TASTY TREAT

Eat up! A Galápagos land iguana gets ready to feast on a flower. These spiky lizards live on the Galápagos Islands, off the coast of Ecuador in South America. There, they spend their days lounging in the sun and searching for their next meal, like bright blooms, chunks of cacti and insects.

3 HAVING A BALL

When the Tierpark Berlin in Germany launched a contest to name their new female polar bear cub, more than 5,000 suggestions came streaming in. The eventual winner? Hertha, a name honouring Berlin's professional soccer team. And by chasing balls around her enclosure, the fluffy cub sure lives up to her sporty name!

5 CUB LOVE

For about the first two years of their lives, tiger cubs stay close to their mum. From birth, she feeds them and protects them, and eventually teaches them how to hunt. By the time the cubs turn two, they're ready to tackle the real world on their own—all thanks to mum.

4 DECKED OUT

That's one colourful camel! This accessorised ungulate is dressed up for the Desert Festival in Jaisalmer, India. Camels are the stars of the show at the three-day festival, which celebrates local culture. The humped mammals participate in polo matches, foot races and parades.

6

LOOKING UP

A member of the antelope family native to Africa, gerenuks have wackily long necks. Why so stretchy? All that height helps them reach the tall plants they snack on.

7

GLOW ON

Creepy crawler — or beautiful jewel? When basking in the glow of ultraviolet (UV) light, this scorpion dazzles with a blue-green sheen. Actually brownish in colour, scorpions tend to blend into the deserts and other hot, dry places they call home.

8

UP A TREE

Giant pandas — they're like adventurous kids! These roly-poly animals love to climb trees, too. They learn to climb at just a few months old, their extra-sharp claws helping them to grip the bark. And once they reach the top? A panda may lounge in the branches before heading back down.

9 JUST DUCKY

Mandy the mandarin duck made quite a splash! Visitors flocked to Central Park in New York City, U.S.A., to catch a glimpse of the attractive visitor. Because mandarin ducks are native to Asia, experts think this duck was once a pet who was abandoned—or simply flew the coop.

10 FOR THE DOG

Luigi Maestro is one pampered pooch! The dog scoots around his hometown of New York City in a variety of luxury vehicles, including a pint-size Porsche and a mini Ferrari. The cost of this car collection? About £1,200. Bow *wow*!

11

ON THE LOOKOUT

Native to parts of Africa, meerkats are constantly on alert for predators such as jackals and falcons. Clever critters, meerkats share the group's work — including guard duty and babysitting. Everything gets taken care of by working as a team. *Hakuna matata!* No worries!

BY A WHISKER

What long whiskers you have! A harbour seal sports extra-long face fringe, which helps this swimmer see and hear. The super-sensitive whiskers are packed with nerves and act as underwater antennae. Studies show a seal could still successfully find fish even if it were blindfolded and wearing headphones.

12

13

EARS TO YOU

This young goat—also known as a kid—is all ears! And better to hear you with: Goats are super sensitive to a range of sound and can even move their ears to locate the source of various noises.

BOLD BILL

This isn't your typical toucan! With a beak featuring a blend of green, red, yellow and orange, the keel-billed toucan—also known as the rainbow-billed toucan—has one of the most colourful beaks in the bird world. It's native to Latin America and is the national bird of Belize.

14

15

STICK TO IT

A red-eyed tree frog's striking eyes aren't the only thing that makes this creature stand out: Sticky toe pads let it climb up just about any surface. Paired with this tiny amphibian's awesome jumping skills, it's no wonder they're often called monkey frogs!

IN BLOOM

Everything's just *dandy*-lion for this guinea pig! Known for being cuddly, smart and sweet, guinea pigs make popular pets. Actually part of the rodent family, one possible reason for their name is the piglike squeaking noises they make.

16

FUR REAL

Thanks to its bright white coat, an arctic fox blends into its icy surroundings. Its thick, fuzzy fur also acts like a warm sleeping bag, keeping the fox cosy as temperatures dip well below freezing in its chilly habitat.

17

18

FISH FRIENDS

Nemo, is that you? Like the fish from the famous film, these bright orange clownfish live in sea anemones in warm, tropical waters. The fish clean and protect the anemone while receiving food and shelter in return.

19

STAR KITTY

Lil BUB was one cool cat! This Instagram-famous feline had more than two million followers. Fans fell for Lil BUB's sweet features, the result of an extreme case of dwarfism. Sadly, BUB passed away in 2019, but she'll be remembered for more than just cute pics. She was also an author, the star of a hit documentary and a supporter of special-needs pets.

TRICK OR TREAT

The Halloween crab is named for its *boo*-tiful colouring, from its black body to its blood-orange legs to its purple claws. Also known as the moon crab, it's often spotted scuttling along sand dunes or in the rainforests of the Pacific coast, from Mexico to Panama.

20

CROWN JEWELS

Forget glittering jewels: This caiman has a crown of butterflies! So what's with the funky headpiece? Experts say the insects feed on the salty reptile tears when minerals like sodium are otherwise hard to find.

21

QUIZ WHIZ

Explore just how much you know about animals with this quiz!

Write your answers on a piece of paper. Then check them below.

1 What type of armour did the dinosaur *Gastonia* sport?
a. horns on its head
b. a super-thick skull
c. rows of spikes on its back
d. all of the above

2 Which country is the quokka native to?
a. Argentina
b. Armenia
c. Australia
d. Angola

3 True or false? An Amur leopard's large paws help it walk on snow without sinking.

4 When faced with danger, some octopuses will _____.
a. dig a hole and hide in the sand
b. break off an arm and scoot away
c. shoot red-hot liquid from their eyes
d. scream and swim away

5 What does an orca's diet mostly consist of?
a. smaller mammals and fish
b. sea grass
c. jellyfish
d. plankton

Not **STUMPED** yet? Check out the *NATIONAL GEOGRAPHIC KIDS QUIZ WHIZ* collection for more crazy **ANIMAL** questions!

ANSWERS: 1. d; 2. c; 3. True; 4. b; 5. a

HOMEWORK HELP

Wildly Good Animal Reports

Seahorse

Your teacher wants a written report on the seahorse. Not to worry. Use these organisational tools so you can stay afloat while writing a report.

STEPS TO SUCCESS: Your report will follow the format of a descriptive or expository essay (see page 35 for 'How to Write a Perfect Essay') and should consist of a main idea, followed by supporting details and a conclusion. Use this basic structure for each paragraph, as well as the whole report, and you'll be on the right track.

1. Introduction
State your **main idea.**
   Seahorses are fascinating fishes with many unique characteristics.

2. Body
Provide **supporting points** for your main idea.
   Seahorses are very small fishes.
   Seahorses are named for their head shape.
   Seahorses display behaviour that is rare among almost all other animals on Earth.

Then **expand** on those points with further description, explanation or discussion.
   Seahorses are very small fishes.
   Seahorses are about the size of an M&M at birth, and most adult seahorses would fit in a teacup.
   Seahorses are named for their head shape.
   With long, tubelike snouts, seahorses are named for their resemblance to horses.
   A group of seahorses is called a herd.
   Seahorses display behaviour that is rare among almost all other animals on Earth.
   Unlike most other fish, seahorses stay with one mate their entire lives. They are also among the only species in which dads, not mums, give birth to the babies.

3. Conclusion
Wrap it up with a **summary** of your whole paper.
   Because of their unique shape and unusual behaviour, seahorses are among the most fascinating and easily distinguishable animals in the sea.

KEY INFORMATION

Here are some things you should consider including in your writing:
   What does your animal look like?
   What other species is it related to?
   How does it move?
   Where does it live?
   What does it eat?
   What are its predators?
   How long does it live?
   Is it endangered?
   Why do you find it interesting?

SEPARATE FACT FROM FICTION: Your animal may have been featured in a movie or in myths and legends. Compare and contrast how the animal has been portrayed with how it behaves in reality. For example, penguins can't dance the way they do in *Happy Feet*.

PROOFREAD AND REVISE: As you would do with any essay, when you're finished, check for misspellings, grammatical mistakes and punctuation errors. It often helps to have someone else proofread your work, too, as he or she may catch things you have missed. Also, look for ways to make your sentences and paragraphs even better. Add more descriptive language, choosing just the right verbs, adverbs and adjectives to make your writing come alive.

BE CREATIVE: Use visual aids to make your report come to life. Include an animal photo file with interesting images found in magazines or printed from websites. Or draw your own! You can also build a miniature animal habitat diorama. Use creativity to help communicate your passion for the subject.

THE FINAL RESULT: Put it all together in one final, polished draft. Make it neat and clean, and remember to cite your references.

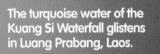

The turquoise water of the Kuang Si Waterfall glistens in Luang Prabang, Laos.

WONDERS of NATURE

THE OC

PACIFIC OCEAN

STATS

Surface area
169,479,000 sq km (65,436,200 sq mi)

Portion of Earth's water area
47 percent

Greatest depth
**Challenger Deep
(in the Mariana Trench)
-10,994 m (-36,070 ft)**

Surface temperatures
**Summer high: 32°C (90°F)
Winter low: -2°C (28°F)**

Tides
**Highest: 9 m (30 ft) near Korean Peninsula
Lowest: 0.3 m (1 ft) near Midway Islands**

Cool creatures: **giant Pacific octopus,
bottlenose whale, clownfish, great
white shark**

Clownfish

ATLANTIC OCEAN

STATS

Surface area
91,526,300 sq km (35,338,500 sq mi)

Portion of Earth's water area
25 percent

Greatest depth
**Puerto Rico Trench
-8,605 m (-28,232 ft)**

Surface temperatures
**Summer high: 32°C (90°F)
Winter low: -2°C (28°F)**

Tides
**Highest: 16 m (52 ft)
Bay of Fundy, Canada
Lowest: 0.5 m (1.5 ft)
Gulf of Mexico and Mediterranean Sea**

Cool creatures: **blue whale, Atlantic spotted
dolphin, sea turtle, bottlenose dolphin**

Bottlenose dolphin

EANS

INDIAN OCEAN

STATS

Surface area
74,694,800 sq km (28,839,800 sq mi)

Portion of Earth's water area
21 percent

Greatest depth
**Java Trench
-7,125 m (-23,376 ft)**

Surface temperatures
**Summer high: 34°C (93°F)
Winter low: -2°C (28°F)**

Tides
**Highest: 11 m (36 ft)
Lowest: 0.6 m (2 ft)
Both along Australia's west coast**

Cool creatures: **humpback whale, Portuguese man-of-war, dugong (sea cow), leatherback turtle**

Leatherback turtle

ARCTIC OCEAN

STATS

Surface area
13,960,100 sq km (5,390,000 sq mi)

Portion of Earth's water area
4 percent

Greatest depth
**Molloy Deep
-5,669 m (-18,599 ft)**

Surface temperatures
**Summer high: 5°C (41°F)
Winter low: -2°C (28°F)**

Tides
Less than 0.3 m (1 ft) variation throughout the ocean

Cool creatures: **beluga whale, orca, harp seal, narwhal**

Narwhal

To see the major oceans and bays in relation to landmasses, look at the map on pages 256 and 257.

10 cool facts about

Cold-water coral reef near Norway

1 Coral reefs are home to **one-third** of the **world's** fish species.

There's a heart-shaped coral reef in **Australia.** **2**

3 A reef fish called a **fang blenny** feeds on the **mucus of other fish.**

4 Cryptobenthics — small, often jelly-bean-sized fish — make up **half the fish species** living on a reef.

5 **The Bermuda Islands** and the **Bahamas** are really **ancient coral reefs.**

coral reefs

6 Some deep-sea corals near Hawaii, U.S.A., are more than **4,000** years old.

7 Coral reefs are found in less than **one percent** of the ocean.

8 Fire coral can cause your **skin to burn** and break out in a **red rash** if you touch it.

9 **Cold-water coral reefs** can be found off the coasts of the U.K., Ireland and Norway.

10 Coral reefs act as a barrier against **tsunamis,** protecting coasts from the huge waves and floods.

Biomes

A BIOME, OFTEN CALLED A MAJOR LIFE ZONE, is one of the natural world's major communities where plants and animals adapt to their specific surroundings. Biomes are classified depending on the predominant vegetation, climate and geography of a region. They can be divided into six major types: forest, freshwater, marine, desert, grassland and tundra. Each biome consists of many ecosystems.

Biomes are extremely important. Balanced ecological relationships among biomes help to maintain the environment and life on Earth as we know it. For example, an increase in one species of plant, such as an invasive one, can cause a ripple effect throughout a whole biome.

FOREST

Forests occupy about one-third of Earth's land area. There are three major types of forests: tropical, temperate and boreal (taiga). Forests are home to a diversity of plants, some of which may hold medicinal qualities for humans, as well as thousands of animal species, some still undiscovered. Forests can also absorb carbon dioxide, which is a greenhouse gas, and give off oxygen.

The rabbit-sized royal antelope lives in West Africa's dense forests.

FRESHWATER

Most water on Earth is salty, but freshwater ecosystems — including lakes, ponds, wetlands, rivers and streams — usually contain water with less than one percent salt concentration. The countless animal and plant species that live in freshwater biomes vary from continent to continent, but they include algae, frogs, turtles, fish and the larvae of many insects.

The place where fresh and salt water meet is called an estuary.

MARINE

The marine biome covers almost three-quarters of Earth's surface, making it the largest habitat on our planet. Oceans make up the majority of the saltwater marine biome. Coral reefs are considered to be the most biodiverse of any of the biome habitats. The marine biome is home to more than one million plant and animal species.

Estimated to be up to 100,000 years old, sea grass growing in the Mediterranean Sea may be the oldest living thing on Earth.

DESERT

Covering about one-fifth of Earth's surface, deserts are places where precipitation is less than 25 centimetres (10 in) per year. Although most deserts are hot, there are other kinds as well. The four major kinds of deserts are hot, semiarid, coastal and cold. Far from being barren wastelands, deserts are biologically rich habitats.

Some sand dunes in the Sahara are tall enough to bury a 50-storey building.

GRASSLAND

Biomes called grasslands are characterised by having grasses instead of large shrubs or trees. Grasslands generally have precipitation for only about half to three-quarters of the year. If it were more, they would become forests. Grasslands can be divided into two types: tropical (savannahs) and temperate. Some of the world's largest land animals, such as elephants, live there.

Grasslands in North America are called prairies; in South America, they're called pampas.

TUNDRA

The coldest of all biomes, a tundra is characterised by an extremely cold climate, simple vegetation, little precipitation, poor nutrients and a short growing season. There are two types of tundra: arctic and alpine. A tundra is home to few kinds of vegetation. Surprisingly, though, there are quite a few animal species that can survive the tundra's extremes, such as wolves, caribou and even mosquitoes.

Formed 10,000 years ago, the arctic tundra is the world's youngest biome.

Weather and Climate

Weather is the condition of the atmosphere — temperature, wind, humidity and precipitation — at a given place at a given time. Climate, however, is the average weather for a particular place over a long period of time. Different places on Earth have different climates, but climate is not a random occurrence. It is a pattern that is controlled by factors such as latitude, elevation, prevailing winds, the temperature of ocean currents and location on land relative to water. Climate is generally constant, but evidence indicates that human activity is causing a change in its patterns.

WOW-WORTHY WEATHER

SEEING ORANGE: Dark orange snow sometimes falls on parts of Europe, the result of storms blowing dust from the Sahara into the atmosphere, where it mixes with the white stuff.

DEEP FREEZE: In January 2019, temperatures in Mount Carroll, Illinois, U.S.A., dipped down to minus 38.9°C (-38°F), the city's and the state's coldest recorded temperature ever.

THINK PINK: 'Watermelon snow' recently appeared in the mountains of the Pacific Northwest in the United States, the result of algae that turn snow pink.

GLOBAL CLIMATE ZONES

Climatologists, people who study climate, have created different systems for classifying climates. One that is often used is called the Köppen system, which classifies climate zones according to precipitation, temperature and vegetation. It has five major categories — tropical, dry, temperate, cold and polar — with a sixth category for locations where high elevations override other factors.

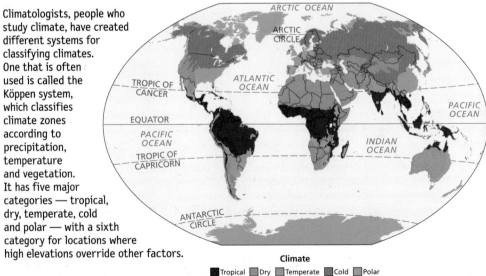

Climate
■ Tropical ■ Dry ■ Temperate ■ Cold ■ Polar

EXTREME CLIMATES

Talk about a temperature swing! The difference between the coldest place on Earth—east Antarctica—and the hottest—Death Valley, in Nevada and California, U.S.A.—is a whopping 150°C (270°F). Though they are both deserts, these two opposites are neck and neck in the race for world's most extreme climate.

HOT
DEATH VALLEY

CRAZY TEMPS	Hottest temperature ever recorded: **57°C (134°F)**
RAINFALL	Death Valley is the driest place in North America. The average yearly rainfall is about **5 centimetres (2 in)**.
ELEVATION	At **86 metres (282 ft) below sea level**, Death Valley is the lowest point in North America.
STEADY HEAT	In 2001, Death Valley experienced **160 consecutive days** of temperatures **38°C (100°F)** or hotter.

COLD
EAST ANTARCTIC PLATEAU

CRAZY TEMPS	Coldest temperature ever recorded: **minus 93°C (-135.8°F)**
RAINFALL	East Antarctica gets less than **5 centimetres (2 in)** of precipitation in a year.
ELEVATION	The record low temperature was recorded just below the plateau's **3,962-metre (13,000-ft)** ridge.
DARKNESS	During parts of winter, there is **24 hours** of darkness.

Freaky Weather

Nature can be unbelievably powerful. A major earth-quake can topple huge buildings and bring down entire mountainsides. Hurricanes, blizzards and tornadoes can paralyse major cities. But as powerful as these natural disasters are, here are five other episodes of wacky weather that will really blow you away!

1 FIRE RAINBOW

Can clouds catch fire? No, but it may look like it when you spot a circumhorizontal arc, also known as a 'fire rainbow'. This rare sight occurs when the sun travels through wispy, high-altitude cirrus clouds — and only when the sun is very high in the sky. The result? The entire cloud lights up in an amazing spectrum of colours, sometimes extending for hundreds of kilometres in the sky.

2 SNOWBALL FACTORY

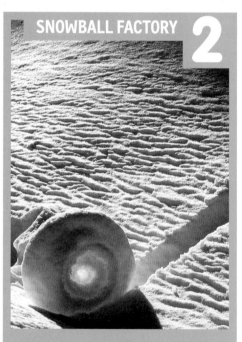

You head outside after a snowstorm and see dozens of log- or drum-shaped snowballs. These rare creations are called snow rollers, formed when wet snow falls on icy ground, so snow can't stick to it. Pushed by strong winds, the snow rolls into logs. Maybe this is nature's way of saying it's time for a snowball fight.

3 MYSTERY WAVES

Imagine you're on an ocean liner when a wall of water 10 storeys tall races towards you like an unstoppable freight train. It's a rogue wave, also called a freak wave, which can appear without warning at any time in the open sea. These waves were once considered myths, but scientists now know they are very real — and very dangerous to even the largest ships.

HOLE PUNCH CLOUDS 4

Nope, that's not a UFO — it's a rare formation in the sky called a hole punch cloud. This wild sight usually occurs when patches of high clouds freeze and fall away as ice crystals, eventually leaving a huge hole. Once unable to solve the mystery, researchers now believe that aeroplanes taking off or landing are the likely cause of these cloud holes.

5 THE MOTHER OF ALL TORNADOES

The fastest wind speed ever recorded — 512 kilometres an hour (318 mph) — occurred during a tornado near Oklahoma City, Oklahoma, U.S.A., in 1999. Scientists classify tornadoes by the damage they can do. With wind speeds of 113 kilometres an hour (70 mph), a tornado can tear branches from trees. A tornado with wind speeds of more than 483 kilometres an hour (300 mph) has the power to derail train cars, tear grass from the ground and even rip paving from the street.

WATER CYCLE

Precipitation falls

Water storage in ice and snow

Water vapour condenses in clouds

Water filters into the ground

Meltwater and surface runoff

Freshwater storage

Evaporation

Groundwater discharge

Water storage in ocean

The amount of water on Earth is more or less constant —
only the form changes. As the sun warms Earth's surface, liquid water is changed into water vapour in a process called **evaporation**. Water on the surface of plants' leaves turns into water vapour in a process called **transpiration**. As water vapour rises into the air, it cools and changes form again. This time, it becomes clouds in a process called **condensation**. Water droplets fall from the clouds as **precipitation**, which then travels as groundwater or runoff back to the lakes, rivers and oceans, where the cycle (shown above) starts all over again.

To a meteorologist — a person who studies the weather — a 'light rain' is less than 0.5 millimetre (1/48 in). A 'heavy rain' is more than 4 millimetres (1/6 in).

You drink the same water as the dinosaurs! Earth has been recycling water for more than four billion years.

Types of Clouds

If you want a clue about the weather, look up at the clouds. They'll tell a lot about the condition of the air and what weather might be on the way. Clouds are made of both air and water. On fair days, warm air currents rise up and push against the water in clouds, keeping it from falling. But as the raindrops in a cloud get bigger, it's time to set them free. The bigger raindrops become too heavy for the air currents to hold up, and they fall to the ground.

How Much Does a Cloud Weigh?

A light, fluffy cumulus cloud typically weighs about 98,000 kilograms (216,000 lb). That's about the weight of 18 elephants. A rain-soaked cumulonimbus cloud typically weighs 48 million kilograms (105.8 million lb), or about the same as 9,000 elephants.

1 STRATUS These clouds make the sky look like a bowl of thick grey porridge. They hang low in the sky, blanketing the day in dreary darkness. Stratus clouds form when cold, moist air close to the ground moves over a region.

2 CIRRUS These wispy tufts of clouds are thin and hang high up in the atmosphere where the air is extremely cold. Cirrus clouds are made of tiny ice crystals.

3 CUMULONIMBUS These are the monster clouds. Rising air currents force fluffy cumulus clouds to swell and shoot upward, as much as 21,000 metres (70,000 ft). When these clouds bump against the top of the troposphere, or the tropopause, they flatten out on top like tabletops.

4 CUMULUS These white, fluffy clouds make people sing, "Oh, what a beautiful morning!" They form low in the atmosphere and look like marshmallows. They often mix with large patches of blue sky. Formed when hot air rises, cumulus clouds usually disappear when the air cools at night.

103

HURRICANE
HAPPENINGS

A storm is coming! But is it a tropical cyclone, a hurricane or a typhoon? These weather events go by different names depending on where they form and how fast their winds get. Strong tropical cyclones are called hurricanes in the Atlantic and parts of the Pacific Ocean; in the western Pacific they are called typhoons. But any way you look at it, these storms pack a punch.

2,221 KM (1,380 mi)

diameter of the most massive tropical cyclone ever recorded, 1979's Typhoon Tip

27.8°C (82°F)

water surface temperature necessary for a tropical cyclone to form

16.6

average number of tropical storms each year in the Northeast and Central Pacific Basins

10

number of Hurricane Sandy–related pictures uploaded every second to Instagram on October 29, 2012

31

number of days Hurricane John lasted in 1994

12.1
average number of tropical storms in the Atlantic Basin each year

408 KM/H
(254 mph)

strongest gust of storm wind ever recorded

20-40 KM
(12–25 mi)

diameter of a hurricane eye

HURRICANE NAMES FOR 2021

Hurricane names come from six official international lists. The names alternate between male and female. When a storm becomes a hurricane, a name from the list is used, in alphabetical order. Each list is reused every six years. A name 'retires' if that hurricane caused a lot of damage or many deaths. Check out the names for 2021.

Ana	Henri	Odette
Bill	Ida	Peter
Claudette	Julian	Rose
Danny	Kate	Sam
Elsa	Larry	Teresa
Fred	Mindy	Victor
Grace	Nicholas	Wanda

SCALE OF HURRICANE INTENSITY

CATEGORY	ONE	TWO	THREE	FOUR	FIVE
DAMAGE	Minimal	Moderate	Extensive	Extreme	Catastrophic
WINDS	119–153 km/h (74–95 mph)	154–177 km/h (96–110 mph)	178–208 km/h (111–129 mph)	209–251 km/h (130–156 mph)	252 km/h or higher (157+ mph)
(DAMAGE refers to wind and water damage combined.)					

Avalanche!

More than 900,000 tonnes (1 million tons) of snow rumble 13 kilometres (8 mi) downhill, kicking up a cloud of snow dust visible 150 kilometres (100 mi) away.

This is not a scene from a disaster movie — this describes reality one day in April 1981. The mountain was Mount Sanford in Alaska, U.S.A., and the event was one of history's biggest avalanches. Amazingly, no one was hurt, and luckily, avalanches this big are rare.

An avalanche is a moving mass of snow that may contain ice, soil, rocks and uprooted trees. The height of a mountain, the steepness of its slope and the type of snow lying on it all help determine the likelihood of an avalanche. Avalanches begin when an unstable mass of snow breaks away from a mountainside and moves downhill. The growing river of snow picks up speed as it rushes down the mountain. Avalanches have been known to reach speeds of 249 kilometres an hour (155 mph) — about the same as the record for downhill skiing.

To protect yourself and stay safe when you play in the mountains, follow our safety tips.

Safety TIPS

SAFETY FIRST
Before heading out, check for avalanche warnings.

EQUIPMENT
When hiking, carry safety equipment, including a long probe, a small shovel and an emergency avalanche rescue beacon that signals your location.

NEVER GO IT ALONE
Don't hike in the mountain wilderness without a companion.

IF CAUGHT
If caught in the path of an avalanche, try to get to the side of it. If you can't, grab a tree as an anchor.

90 percent of AVALANCHE INCIDENTS are triggered by humans.

THE ENHANCED FUJITA SCALE

The Enhanced Fujita (EF) Scale, named after tornado expert T. Theodore Fujita, classifies tornadoes based on wind speed and the intensity of damage that they cause.

What Is a Tornado?

EF0
105–137 km/h winds (65–85 mph)
Slight damage

EF1
138–177 km/h winds (86–110 mph)
Moderate damage

EF2
178–217 km/h winds (111–135 mph)
Substantial damage

EF3
218–266 km/h winds (136–165 mph)
Severe damage

EF4
267–322 km/h winds (166–200 mph)
Massive damage

EF5
More than 322 km/h winds (200+ mph)
Catastrophic damage

TORNADOES, ALSO KNOWN AS TWISTERS, are funnels of rapidly rotating air that are created during a thunderstorm. With wind speeds of up to 483 kilometres an hour (300 mph), tornadoes have the power to pick up and destroy everything in their path.

THIS ROTATING FUNNEL OF AIR, formed in a cumulus or cumulonimbus cloud, became a tornado when it touched the ground.

TORNADOES HAVE OCCURRED IN ALL 50 U.S. STATES AND ON EVERY CONTINENT EXCEPT ANTARCTICA.

Wildfire
ANIMAL RESCUE!

I n November 2018, Jeff Hill went to check on a friend's house in the woods of Paradise, California, U.S.A. The home was part of an area that, days before, had been engulfed by the Camp Fire, the deadliest and most destructive wildfire in California history to date. As Hill got closer to the home, he stumbled upon a shocking sight: There was a horse in the garden pool!

Shivering and struggling in the water, the horse — which likely leapt into the pool to escape the flames — was weakened but alive. After Hill helped the animal out of the water, "it shook off, loved on us for a few minutes as a thank-you and walked off assuring us that she was OK," Hill posted on Facebook. Later, animal rescue workers escorted the horse to safety.

The horse was just one of thousands of animals that were in peril during the two weeks in which the Camp Fire ravaged Northern California, burning more than 62,000 hectares (about 153,300 acres) and 19,000 structures. As the fire roared toward homes, people were forced to quickly evacuate and had no choice but to leave

their pets and farm animals behind. Sadly, some animals perished in the fire, but a menagerie of displaced animals, from potbellied pigs to alpacas, were rescued by caring humans like Hill. Even injured wild animals, like bear cubs and foxes, were taken in to rescue centres, where they were treated and then released back into the woods.

Rescuing the animals was one thing, but reuniting them with their owners proved to be another challenge. While some humans were able to collect their pets right away, it took months for others to connect with their four-legged friends. Several local animal hospitals and other organisations posted albums of the animals online to help owners identify their missing pets.

The hope? That as the residents of Paradise continue to rebuild and recover from Camp Fire, they'll be able to do so with their beloved animals by their side.

Terrible Tornado

I n March 2019, a tornado touched down in the town of Beauregard, Alabama, U.S.A. But this was no ordinary tornado. First, there was its size: At nearly 1.6 kilometres (1 mi) wide, the funnel cloud was nearly four times larger than the average tornado. Then, there was its speed: With winds spinning at about 274 kilometres an hour (170 mph), it ripped homes from their foundations and trees from the ground. And finally, there was the length of its path: On the ground for a total of 113 kilometres (70 mi), it was about 20 times as long-lasting as a typical tornado.

All told, this particular twister took out thousands of homes, killing 23 people and injuring at least 100 others. Part of a system of 40 twisters to hit the southeastern United States over the course of six hours that day, the tornado in Beauregard was the most powerful and the deadliest to hit the United States in almost six years.

The destruction was beyond devastating: Homes, cars, trees and other structures were reduced to rubble. But slowly, the quiet country town with a population of some 10,000 is recovering. As donations poured in from near and far and the community came together determined to help each other, Beauregard began to rebuild — and heal.

Wicked Heat Wave

I magine a day so hot that fruit growing on trees begin to cook from the inside out. That's just what happened in parts of South Australia during a wicked heat wave in January 2019, when temperatures in some towns soared to 49°C (120°F). The hottest known weather since record-keeping began, the extreme temps caused the pits in stone fruit like peaches and nectarines to grow so hot, they burned the flesh inside the fruit. An estimated 30 percent of the stone fruit crop was destroyed as a result.

And it wasn't just fruit that took the brunt of the weather: Hundreds of flying foxes — a type of bat — died during the heat wave after succumbing to the sizzling temperatures. Thousands of fish faced the same fate due to low river levels caused by a drought. Asphalt roads melted, and dozens of brush fires broke out throughout the parched countryside.

Ultimately, the summer of 2019 set a new mark as the continent's hottest on record. And after weeks of having to keep cool by staying inside or hanging by the pools and beaches, Australians were finally given a break from the heat with rain, and lots of it: Soon after summer ends in Australia, monsoon season begins.

QUIZ WHIZ

Quiz yourself to find out if you're a natural when it comes to nature knowledge!

Write your answers
on a piece of paper.
Then check them below.

1 **True or false?** Grasslands in North America are called pampas.

2 Coral reefs are found in less than _____ percent of the ocean.
a. one
b. 50
c. 90
d. 20

3 90 percent of avalanche incidents are triggered by _____.
a. tsunamis
b. animal stampedes
c. earthquakes
d. human activity

4 **True or false?** Tornadoes have occurred on every continent except Antarctica.

5 You'd find leatherback turtles in which body of water?
a. Nile River
b. Indian Ocean
c. Chesapeake Bay
d. Arctic Ocean

Not **STUMPED** yet? Check out the *NATIONAL GEOGRAPHIC KIDS QUIZ WHIZ* collection for more crazy **NATURE** questions!

ANSWERS: 1. False. They're called prairies in North America and pampas in South America.; **2.** a; **3.** d; **4.** True; **5.** b

HOMEWORK HELP

Presentations Made Easy

Does the thought of public speaking start your stomach churning like a tornado? Would you rather get caught in an avalanche than give a speech?

Giving a presentation does not have to be a natural disaster. The basic format is very similar to that of a written essay. There are two main elements that make up a good presentation — the writing and the presentation. As you write your presentation, remember that your audience will be hearing the information as opposed to reading it. Follow the guidelines below, and there will be clear skies ahead.

Writing Your Material

Follow the steps in the 'How to Write a Perfect Essay' section on page 35, but prepare your report to be spoken rather than written.

Try to keep your sentences short and simple. Long, complex sentences are harder to follow. Limit yourself to just a few key points. You don't want to overwhelm your audience with too much information. To be most effective, hit your key points in the introduction, elaborate on them in the body and then repeat them once again in your conclusion.

A PRESENTATION HAS THREE BASIC PARTS:

- **Introduction** — This is your chance to engage your audience and really capture their interest in the subject you are presenting. Use a funny personal experience or a dramatic story, or start with an intriguing question.

- **Body** — This is the longest part of your report. Here you elaborate on the facts and ideas you want to convey. Give information that supports your main idea, and expand on it with specific examples or details. In other words, structure your presentation in the same way you would a written essay, so that your thoughts are presented in a clear and organised manner.

- **Conclusion** — This is the time to summarise the information and emphasise your most important points to the audience one last time.

Preparing Your Delivery

1 **Practice makes perfect.** Practise! Practise! Practise! Confidence, enthusiasm and energy are key to delivering an effective presentation, and they can best be achieved through rehearsal. Ask family and friends to be your practice audience and give you feedback when you're done. Were they able to follow your ideas? Did you seem knowledgeable and confident? Did you speak too slowly or too fast, too softly or too loudly? The more times you practise giving your report, the more you'll master the material. Then you won't have to rely so heavily on your notes or papers, and you will be able to give your report in a relaxed and confident manner.

2 **Present with everything you've got.** Be as creative as you can. Incorporate videos, sound clips, slide presentations, charts, diagrams and photos. Visual aids help stimulate your audience's senses and keep them intrigued and engaged. They can also help to reinforce your key points. And remember that when you're giving a presentation, you're a performer. Take charge of the spotlight and be as animated and entertaining as you can. Have fun with it.

3 **Keep your nerves under control.** Everyone gets a little nervous when speaking in front of a group. That's normal. But the more preparation you've done — meaning plenty of researching, organising and rehearsing — the more confident you'll be. Preparation is the key. And if you make a mistake or stumble over your words, just regroup and keep going. Nobody's perfect, and nobody expects you to be.

SPACE and EARTH

Instruments aboard the spacecraft Cassini, shown approaching Saturn in this artist's rendition, have helped scientists map how textures, colours and temperatures vary in Saturn's rings.

A LOOK INSIDE

The distance from Earth's surface to its centre is 6,378 kilometres (3,963 mi) at the Equator. There are four layers: a thin, rigid crust; the rocky mantle; the outer core, which is a layer of molten iron; and finally the inner core, which is believed to be solid iron.

The **CRUST** includes tectonic plates, landmasses and the ocean. Its average thickness varies from 8 to 40 kilometres (5 to 25 mi).

The **MANTLE** is about 2,900 kilometres (1,800 mi) of hot, thick, solid rock.

The **OUTER CORE** is liquid molten rock made mostly of iron and nickel.

The **INNER CORE** is a solid centre made mostly of iron and nickel.

What would happen if Earth had rings like Saturn?

It's good that Earth *doesn't* have rings. Saturn's rings are made of countless pieces of rock and ice that can be as tiny as a grain of sand or as big as a house. If Earth had similar rings, they'd be positioned in a way that would block sunlight and cast a shadow over the Northern and Southern Hemispheres during each region's winter. (That's when the hemispheres are tilted away from the sun.) Both areas would be darker and colder at these times. With less light coming in, crops and plants that depend on the sun to survive the season might die out. No thanks!

ROCK STARS

Rocks and minerals are everywhere on Earth! And it can be a challenge to tell one from the other. So what's the difference between a rock and a mineral? A rock is a naturally occurring solid object made mostly from minerals. Minerals are solid, non-living substances that occur in nature — and the basic components of most rocks. Rocks can be made of just one mineral or, like granite, of many minerals. But not all rocks are made of minerals: Coal comes from plant material, while amber is formed from ancient tree sap.

Igneous

Named for the Greek word meaning 'from fire', igneous rocks form when hot, molten liquid called magma cools. Pools of magma form deep underground and slowly work their way to Earth's surface. If they make it all the way, the liquid rock erupts and is called lava. As the layers of lava build up, they form a mountain called a volcano. Typical igneous rocks include obsidian, basalt and pumice, which is so chock-full of gas bubbles that it actually floats in water.

ANDESITE

GRANITE PORPHYRY

Metamorphic

Metamorphic rocks are the masters of change! These rocks were once igneous or sedimentary, but thanks to intense heat and pressure deep within the Earth, they have undergone a total transformation from their original form. These rocks never truly melt; instead, the heat twists and bends them until their shapes substantially change. Metamorphic rocks include slate as well as marble, which is used for buildings, monuments and sculptures.

MICA SCHIST

BANDED GNEISS

Sedimentary

When wind, water and ice constantly wear away and weather rocks, smaller pieces called sediment are left behind. These are sedimentary rocks, also known as gravel, sand, silt and clay. As water flows downhill, it carries the sedimentary grains into lakes and oceans, where they get deposited. As the loose sediment piles up, the grains eventually get compacted or cemented back together again. The result is new sedimentary rock. Sandstone, gypsum, limestone and shale are sedimentary rocks that have formed this way.

LIMESTONE

HALITE

Identifying Minerals

With so many different minerals in the world, it can be a challenge to tell one from another. Fortunately, each mineral has physical characteristics that geologists and amateur rock collectors use to tell them apart. Check out the physical characteristics below: colour, lustre, streak, cleavage, fracture and hardness.

Colour

When you look at a mineral, the first thing you see is its colour. In some minerals, this is a key factor because their colours are almost always the same. For example, azurite, below, is always blue. But in other cases, impurities can change the natural colour of a mineral. For instance, fluorite, above, can be green, red, violet and other colours as well. The change makes it a challenge to identify by colour alone.

FLUORITE

AZURITE

Lustre

'Lustre' refers to the way light reflects from the surface of a mineral. Does yours appear metallic, like gold or silver? Or is it pearly like orpiment, or brilliant like diamond? 'Earthy', 'glassy', 'silky' and 'dull' are a few other terms used to describe lustre.

ORPIMENT

DIAMOND

Streak

The 'streak' is the colour of the mineral's powder. When minerals are ground into powder, they often have a different colour than when they are in crystal form. For example, the mineral pyrite usually looks gold, but when it is rubbed against a ceramic tile called a 'streak plate', the mark it leaves is black.

PYRITE

Cleavage

'Cleavage' describes the way a mineral breaks. Since the structure of a specific mineral is always the same, it tends to break in the same pattern. Not all minerals have cleavage, but the minerals that do, like this microcline, break evenly in one or more directions. These minerals are usually described as having 'perfect cleavage'. But if the break isn't smooth and clean, cleavage can be considered 'good' or 'poor'.

MICROCLINE

GOLD

Fracture

Some minerals, such as gold, do not break with cleavage. Instead, geologists say that they 'fracture'. There are different types of fractures, and depending on the mineral, the fracture may be described as jagged, splintery, even or uneven.

Hardness

The level of ease or difficulty with which a mineral can be scratched refers to its 'hardness'. Hardness is measured using a special chart called the Mohs hardness scale. The Mohs scale goes from 1 to 10. Softer minerals, which appear on the lower end of the scale, can be scratched by the harder minerals on the upper end of the scale.

RATING	MINERAL NAME	EXAMPLES
1	TALC	BAR OF SOAP
2	GYPSUM	FINGERNAIL
3	CALCITE	COPPER PENNY
4	FLUORITE	SOFT IRON NAIL
5	APATITE	STEEL POCKETKNIFE BLADE
6	ORTHOCLASE	WINDOW GLASS
7	QUARTZ	HARDENED STEEL FILE
8	TOPAZ	TOPAZ
9	CORUNDUM	RUBY, SAPPHIRE
10	DIAMOND	DIAMOND

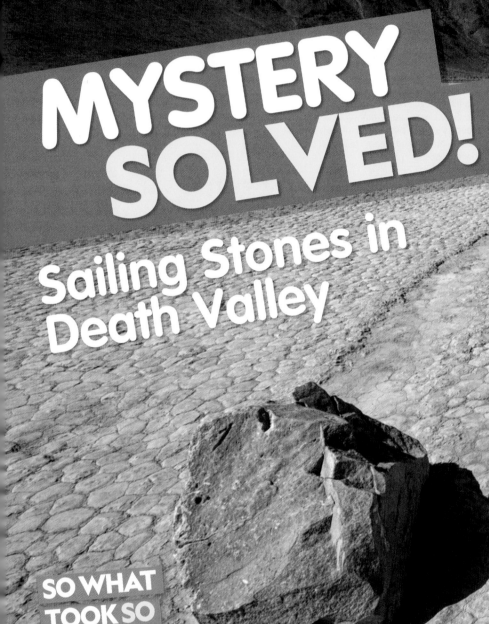

MYSTERY SOLVED!

Sailing Stones in Death Valley

SO WHAT TOOK SO LONG?

Why did it take half a century or more for scientists to figure out what was moving the stones? Several factors make observing them in action difficult to near impossible.

LOCATION: Racetrack Playa sits more than 1,100 metres (3,600 ft) above sea level and is a three-hour drive from the closest town.

ROCK TRAILS IN THE DRY LAKE BED

For decades, the remote rocks that seemed to move on their own had mostly mystified scientists and laypersons alike. The stones would sit in the same spot for years and then suddenly be found somewhere else — with long, unexplained trails behind them in the dried mud. How did these 'sailing stones' move from one place to another?

Wind, water and ice were considered the most likely explanations for the paths across Racetrack Playa — a 4.8-kilometre (3-mi)-long dry lake bed in the mountains above Death Valley, California, U.S.A., whose surface is covered with hundreds of rocks ranging from pebbles to mammoth stones weighing more than 272 kilograms (600 lb). The rock trails could be up to 244 metres (800 ft) long — zigging and zagging across the playa and sometimes showing

parallel tracks with turns in the same places. What was going on?

In 2014 scientists fitted 15 stones with motion-activated GPS units (to record their position and speed as soon as they began moving) and used time-lapse imaging and video to capture the stones' movements. What they discovered was positively earth-shattering!

After a winter storm dropped snow and rain onto the playa, the precipitation created a shallow pond about 2.5 centimetres (1 in) deep. Freezing temperatures at night caused a thin layer of ice to form on top of it, which the next day began to melt in the sun and break up into sheets. When the floating ice panels were blown by the wind, they pushed the rocks across the playa.

So, why is this remarkable? Theories to this point had assumed that the ice needed to push these huge stones would have to be very thick and that the winds needed to push the rocks would have to be hurricane-force gusts. But what the scientists observed was that the ice sheets pushing these heavy rocks were actually very thin — less than 5 millimetres (1/5 in) thick! And the wind gusts? No hurricanes here: All it took was a light breeze. The rocks moved more easily than they ordinarily would because the ground had been softened by the water — almost like the rocks were hydroplaning. After a few months, when the pond had completely dried out, the playa was marked by a new set of trails.

This riddle had finally been 'rocked' by science!

THE ROCKS ZIG AND ZAG PARALLEL TO EACH OTHER.

SPEED: Scientists estimate the sliding stones move maybe only a few minutes out of a million. When they eventually do move, the rocks move very slowly (almost too slowly even to be noticed) — one of the reasons this event wasn't easily detected before this recent use of time-lapse photography and custom-fitted rock GPS.

OCCURRENCE: The moving rocks are a rare phenomenon. Because the playa is dry the vast majority of the time, it could be a decade or longer before there is enough rain to make a pond deep enough to form the ice that pushes the rocks and, thus, create new trails — trails that form out of sight in the soft mud underneath the floating ice.

A HOT TOPIC

WHAT GOES ON
INSIDE A STEAMING, BREWING VOLCANO?

If you could look inside a volcano, you'd see something that looks like a long pipe, called a conduit. It leads from inside the magma chamber under the crust up to a vent, or opening, at the top of the mountain. Some conduits have branches that shoot off to the side, called fissures.

When pressure builds from gases inside the volcano, the gases must find an escape, and they head up toward the surface! An eruption occurs when lava, gases, ash and rocks explode out of the vent.

CRATER

VENT

CONDUIT

FISSURE

MAGMA CHAMBER

HARDENED LAVA AND ASH LAYERS

TYPES OF VOLCANOES

CINDER CONE VOLCANO
Eve's Cone, Canada

Cinder cone volcanoes look like an upside-down ice-cream cone. They spew cinder and hot ash. Some of these volcanoes smoke and erupt for years at a time.

COMPOSITE VOLCANO
Licancábur, Chile

Composite volcanoes, or stratovolcanoes, form as lava, ash and cinder from previous eruptions harden and build up over time. These volcanoes spit out pyroclastic flows, or thick explosions of hot ash that travel at hundreds of kilometres an hour.

SHIELD VOLCANO
Mauna Loa, Hawaii, U.S.A.

The gentle, broad slopes of a shield volcano look like an ancient warrior's shield. Its eruptions are often slower. Lava splatters and bubbles rather than shooting forcefully into the air.

LAVA DOME VOLCANO
Mount St. Helens, Washington, U.S.A.

Dome volcanoes have steep sides. Hardened lava often plugs the vent at the top of a dome volcano. Pressure builds beneath the surface until the top blows.

HOT SPOTS Some volcanoes form at hot spots, or holes beneath Earth's crust in the middle of a tectonic plate. As lava pushes up through the hole and forms a volcanic island, the plate keeps moving. More volcanoes form as it moves. Some hot spots are big enough to create a chain of volcanic islands, such as the Hawaiian Islands.

COLLAPSE! An erupting volcano can cause damage to itself! A caldera is a large bowl-like depression caused by the collapse of a magma chamber during an eruption. Crater Lake in Oregon, U.S.A., is a caldera that has filled with rainwater and snowfall.

10 far-out facts about

1 Luke Skywalker's **lightsaber** from *Star Wars: A New Hope* flew to the International Space Station in 2007.

2 As many as **13 people** have been in space simultaneously.

3 Astronauts say the moon smells like **wet ashes.**

4 A spacecraft **glows red hot** as it returns to Earth from space.

5 **Spiders** have travelled **into space.**

6 A Russian rocket delivered **a pizza** to the International Space Station.

space travel

7 The International Space Station circles Earth every **90 minutes.**

8 Astronauts **can grow five centimetres (2 in) taller** while in space.

A missing European spacecraft was found on the **surface of Mars** after it vanished from contact **11 years earlier.** **9**

10 Measuring about **490 metres** (1,600 ft) wide, asteroid Bennu is the **smallest object** ever orbited by a spacecraft.

International Space Station

123

A Universe of Galaxies

5 COOL FACTS TO RECORD

When astronauts first journeyed beyond Earth's orbit in 1968, they looked back to their home planet. The big-picture view of our place in space changed the astronauts' lives—and perhaps humanity. If you could leave the universe and similarly look back, what would you see? Remarkably, scientists are mapping this massive area. They see ... bubbles. Not actual soap bubbles, of course, but a structure that looks like a pan full of them. Like bubble walls, thin surfaces curve around empty spaces in an elegantly simple structure. Zoom in to see that these surfaces are groups of galaxies. Zoom in farther to find one galaxy, with an ordinary star—our sun—orbited by an ordinary planet—Earth. How extraordinary.

DIGITAL TRAVELLER!

Take a simulated flight through our universe, thanks to the data collected by the Sloan Digital Sky Survey. Search the internet for 'APOD flight through universe sdss'. Sit back and enjoy the ride!

2 DARK MATTER

The universe holds a mysterious source of gravity that cannot be properly explained. This unseen matter—the ghostly dark ring in this composite Hubble telescope photo— seems to pull on galaxy clusters, drawing galaxies towards it. But what is this strange stuff? It's not giant black holes, planets, stars or anti-matter. These would show themselves indirectly. For now, astronomers call this source of gravity 'dark matter'.

1 GALAXY CLUSTERS AND SUPERCLUSTERS

Gravity pulls things together—gas in stars, stars in galaxies. Galaxies gather, too, sometimes by the thousands, forming galaxy clusters and superclusters with tremendously superheated gas. This gas can be as hot as 100 million degrees Celsius (180 million degrees Fahrenheit), filling space between them. These clusters hide a secret. The gravity among the galaxies isn't enough to bring them together. The source of the extra gravity is a dark secret.

3 IT STARTED WHEN ...
The Big Bang

Long ago, the universe was compressed: It was hotter, smaller, denser than now, and completely uniform—almost. Extremely minor unevenness led to a powerful energy release that astronomers call the big bang. In a blip of time, the universe expanded tremendously. The first particles formed. Atoms, galaxies, forces and light ... all developed from this. Today's great filaments (see fact 4) may be organised where those first uneven patches existed.

4 FILAMENTS AND SHEETS
Bubbles of Space

What is the universe like at its grandest scale? The biggest big-picture view is jaw-dropping. Clusters and superclusters of galaxies—red and yellow areas in this illustration—along with dark matter, string together to form structures that are millions and billions of light-years long. These so-called walls, sheets or filaments surround vast voids, or 'bubbles', of nearly empty space—the blue areas. The universe has a structure, non-random and unexpected.

5 COLLISION ZONE

Saying that galaxies form clusters and superclusters is like saying two football teams simply meet. During a game, there's a lot of action and energy. Similarly, as clusters and superclusters form, there's lots going on—as evidenced by the super-high-energy x-rays that are detected (pink in this colourised image).

PLANETS

CERES

MARS

EARTH

VENUS

MERCURY

JUPITER

SUN

MERCURY

Average distance from the sun:
   57,900,000 kilometres (35,980,000 mi)
Position from the sun in orbit: 1st
Equatorial diameter: 4,878 kilometres (3,030 mi)
Length of day: 59 Earth days
Length of year: 88 Earth days
Known moons: 0
Fun fact: Mercury is home to one of the largest craters in the solar system.

VENUS

Average distance from the sun:
   108,200,000 kilometres (67,230,000 mi)
Position from the sun in orbit: 2nd
Equatorial diameter: 12,100 kilometres (7,520 mi)
Length of day: 243 Earth days
Length of year: 224.7 Earth days
Known moons: 0
Fun fact: It never rains on Venus.

EARTH

Average distance from the sun:
   149,600,000 kilometres (93,000,000 mi)
Position from the sun in orbit: 3rd
Equatorial diameter: 12,750 kilometres (7,900 mi)
Length of day: 24 hours
Length of year: 365 days
Known moons: 1
Fun fact: Earth travelled more than 8,047 kilometres (5,000 mi) in the past five minutes.

MARS

Average distance from the sun:
   227,936,000 kilometres (141,633,000 mi)
Position from the sun in orbit: 4th
Equatorial diameter: 6,794 kilometres (4,221 mi)
Length of day: 25 Earth hours
Length of year: 1.9 Earth years
Known moons: 2
Fun fact: Iron-rich soil gives Mars its reddish appearance.

This artwork shows the eight planets and five dwarf planets in our solar system. The relative sizes and positions of the planets are shown but not the relative distances between them.

SATURN

URANUS

NEPTUNE

PLUTO
HAUMEA
MAKEMAKE
ERIS

JUPITER

Average distance from the sun:
  778,412,000 kilometres (483,682,000 mi)
Position from the sun in orbit: 6th
Equatorial diameter: 142,980 kilometres (88,840 mi)
Length of day: 9.9 Earth hours
Length of year: 11.9 Earth years
Known moons: 79*
Fun fact: Jupiter is the fastest spinning planet in the solar system.

SATURN

Average distance from the sun:
  1,433,600,000 kilometres (890,800,000 mi)
Position from the sun in orbit: 7th
Equatorial diameter: 120,540 kilometres (74,900 mi)
Length of day: 10.7 Earth hours
Length of year: 29.5 Earth years
Known moons: 82*
Fun fact: Scientists believe that Saturn's rings will eventually disappear.

URANUS

Average distance from the sun:
  2,871,000,000 kilometres (1,784,000,000 mi)
Position from the sun in orbit: 8th
Equatorial diameter: 51,120 kilometres (31,760 mi)
Length of day: 17.2 Earth hours
Length of year: 84 Earth years
Known moons: 27
Fun fact: Summer on Uranus lasts 42 years.

NEPTUNE

Average distance from the sun:
  4,498,000,000 kilometres (2,795,000,000 mi)
Position from the sun in orbit: 9th
Equatorial diameter: 49,528 kilometres (30,775 mi)
Length of day: 16 Earth hours
Length of year: 164.8 Earth years
Known moons: 14
Fun fact: Large, dark spots on Neptune's surface are believed to be enormous storms.

*Includes provisional moons, which await confirmation and naming from the International Astronomical Union.

For information about dwarf planets — Ceres, Pluto, Haumea, Makemake and Eris — see page 128.

DWARF PLANETS

Haumea

Eris

Pluto

Thanks to advanced technology, astronomers have been spotting many never-before-seen celestial bodies with their telescopes. One new discovery? A population of icy objects orbiting the sun beyond Pluto. The largest, like Pluto itself, are classified as dwarf planets. Smaller than the moon but still massive enough to pull themselves into a ball, dwarf planets nevertheless lack the gravitational 'oomph' to clear their neighbourhood of other sizable objects. So, while larger, more massive planets pretty much have their orbits to themselves, dwarf planets orbit the sun in swarms that include other dwarf planets as well as smaller chunks of rock or ice.

So far, astronomers have identified five dwarf planets: Ceres, Pluto, Haumea, Makemake and Eris. There are also three newly discovered dwarf planets that will need additional study before they are named. Astronomers are observing hundreds of newly found objects in the frigid outer solar system. As time and technology advance, the family of known dwarf planets will surely continue to grow.

CERES
Position from the sun in orbit: 5th
Length of day: 9.1 Earth hours
Length of year: 4.6 Earth years
Known moons: 0

PLUTO
Position from the sun in orbit: 10th
Length of day: 6.4 Earth days
Length of year: 248 Earth years
Known moons: 5

HAUMEA
Position from the sun in orbit: 11th
Length of day: 3.9 Earth hours
Length of year: 282 Earth years
Known moons: 2

MAKEMAKE
Position from the sun in orbit: 12th
Length of day: 22.5 Earth hours
Length of year: 305 Earth years
Known moons: 1*

ERIS
Position from the sun in orbit: 13th
Length of day: 25.9 Earth hours
Length of year: 561 Earth years
Known moons: 1

*Includes provisional moons, which await confirmation and naming from the International Astronomical Union.

BLACK HOLES

A black hole really seems like a hole in space. Most black holes form when the core of a massive star collapses, falling into oblivion. A black hole has a stronger gravitational pull than anything else in the known universe. It's like a bottomless pit, swallowing anything that gets close enough to it to be pulled in. It's black because it pulls in light. Black holes come in different sizes. The smallest known black hole has a mass about three times that of the sun. The biggest one scientists have found so far has a mass about three billion times greater than the sun's. Really big black holes at the centres of galaxies probably form by swallowing enormous amounts of gas over time. In 2019, scientists released the first image of a black hole's silhouette (left). The image, previously thought impossible to record, was captured using a network of telescopes.

BLACK HOLE ➡

SPACED OUT

THE CAT Félicette

THE SPOT Space

WHY SHE'S COOL The fur really flew on 18 October 1963, when Félicette became the first cat in space. The French feline rocketed towards the stars to help researchers learn whether animals could survive the challenges of space travel. After soaring more than 160 kilometres (100 mi) above Earth, the high-flying feline safely returned home the same day. We bet she was seeing stars.

Sky Calendar
2021

Jupiter

Leonid meteor shower

Supermoon

- **3-4 JANUARY**
QUADRANTIDS METEOR SHOWER PEAK.
Featuring up to 40 meteors an hour, it is
the first meteor shower of every new year.

- **26-27 APRIL**
SUPERMOON, FULL MOON. The moon
will be full and at a close approach to
Earth, likely appearing bigger and brighter
than usual. A supermoon will be visible
April 26 in North and South America and
April 27 in other continents. Look for two
more supermoons on May 26 and June 24.

- **6-7 MAY**
ETA AQUARIDS METEOR SHOWER PEAK.
View about 30 to 60 meteors an hour.

- **17 MAY**
MERCURY AT GREATEST EASTERN
ELONGATION. Visible low in the western
sky just after sunset, Mercury will be
at its highest point above the horizon.

- **26 MAY**
TOTAL LUNAR ECLIPSE. Look for the moon
to darken and then take on a deep red
colour as it passes completely through
Earth's umbra — or dark shadow. Visible in
parts of western North America, eastern
Asia, Japan and Australia and throughout
the Pacific Ocean.

- **2 AUGUST**
SATURN AT OPPOSITION. This is your best
chance to view the ringed planet in 2021.
Saturn will appear bright in the sky and be
visible throughout the night.

- **12-13 AUGUST**
PERSEID METEOR SHOWER PEAK.
One of the best! Up to 90 meteors an
hour. Best viewing is in the direction of
the constellation Perseus.

- **22 AUGUST**
BLUE MOON, FULL MOON.
You won't see this full moon turn colours.
When there are four full moons in a season,
such as there are this summer, the third one
is called a blue moon. The second full moon
in a month is also known as a blue moon.
Both events are considered rare, happening
only once every two or three years.

- **21-22 OCTOBER**
ORIONID METEOR SHOWER PEAK.
View up to 20 meteors an hour. Look towards
the constellation Orion for the best show.

- **13-14 DECEMBER**
GEMINID METEOR SHOWER PEAK.
A spectacular show! Up to 120 multicoloured
meteors an hour.

- **2021—VARIOUS DATES**
VIEW THE INTERNATIONAL SPACE STATION.
Visit spotthestation.nasa.gov to find out
when the ISS will be flying over your
neighbourhood.

Dates may vary slightly depending on your
location. Check with a local planetarium for
the best viewing time in your area.

SUPER SUN!

THE SUN IS 99.8 PERCENT OF ALL THE MASS IN OUR SOLAR SYSTEM.

The **SUN'S** surface is about **5500°C** (10,000°F)!

There is **REAL GOLD** in the **SUN.**

Even from 150 million kilometres (93 million mi) away, the sun's rays are powerful enough to provide the energy needed for life to flourish on Earth. This 4.6-billion-year-old star is the anchor of our solar system and accounts for more than 99 percent of the mass in the solar system. What else makes the sun so special? For starters, it's larger than one million Earths and is the biggest object in our solar system. The sun also converts about 3.6 million tonnes (4 million tons) of matter to energy every second, helping to make life possible here on Earth. Now that's *sun*-sational!

Storms on the Sun!

Solar flares are 10 million times more powerful than a volcanic eruption on Earth.

With the help of specialised equipment, scientists have observed solar flares — or bursts of magnetic energy that explode from the sun's surface as a result of storms on the sun. Solar storms occur about 2,000 times every 11 years, or once every two days. Most solar storms are minor and do not impact on Earth. But the fiercer the flare, the more we may potentially feel its effects, as it could disrupt power grids or interfere with GPS navigation systems. Solar storms can also trigger stronger-than-usual auroras, light shows that can be seen on Earth.

Some solar storms travel at speeds of **4.8 MILLION KILOMETRES AN HOUR** (3 million mph).

Solar storm

131

QUIZ WHIZ

Are your space and Earth smarts out of this world? Take this quiz!

Write your answers on a piece of paper. Then check them below.

1 **True or false?** Earth's mantle is made of hot, thick, solid rock.

2 **How often do solar storms occur?**
a. once every 2 days
b. once every 200 years
c. once every 2 minutes
d. once every 2,000 years

3 **Fill in the blank.**
A rocket delivered a _____ to the International Space Station.

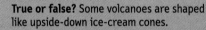

4 **What is a mineral's 'streak'?**
a. its colour when it is ground into powder
b. its weight
c. how it reflects light
d. how hard it is

5 **True or false?** Some volcanoes are shaped like upside-down ice-cream cones.

Not **STUMPED** yet? Check out the *NATIONAL GEOGRAPHIC KIDS QUIZ WHIZ* collection for more crazy **SPACE AND EARTH** questions!

ANSWERS:
1. True; 2. a; 3. pizza; 4. a; 5. True

HOMEWORK HELP

ACE YOUR
SCIENCE PROJECT

You can learn a lot about science from books, but to really experience it firsthand, you need to get into the lab and 'do' some science. Whether you're taking part in a science fair or just want to learn more on your own, there are many scientific projects you can do. So put on your goggles and lab coat, and start experimenting.

Most likely, the topic of the project will be up to you. So remember to choose something that you're interested in.

THE BASIS OF ALL SCIENTIFIC INVESTIGATION AND DISCOVERY IS THE SCIENTIFIC METHOD. CONDUCT YOUR EXPERIMENT USING THESE STEPS:

Observation/Research — Ask a question or identify a problem.

Hypothesis — Once you've asked a question, do some thinking and come up with some possible answers.

Experimentation — How can you determine if your hypothesis is correct? You test it. You perform an experiment. Make sure the experiment you design will produce an answer to your question.

Analysis — Gather your results, and use a consistent process to carefully measure the results.

Conclusion — Do the results support your hypothesis?

Report Your Findings — Communicate your results in the form of an essay that summarises your entire experiment.

Bonus!

Take your project one step further. Your school may have an annual science day, but there are also other science competitions you could take part in. Compete with other students for awards and prizes.

EXPERIMENT DESIGN
There are three types of experiments you can do.

MODEL KIT — a display, such as an 'erupting volcano' model. Simple and to the point.

DEMONSTRATION — shows the scientific principles in action, such as a tornado in a wind tunnel.

INVESTIGATION — the tip-top science project. This kind demonstrates proper scientific experimentation and uses the scientific method to reveal answers to questions.

FUN and GAMES

Young elephant seals in Antarctica

WE GAVE IT A SWIRL

Use the clues below to figure out which animals appear in these swirled pictures.

ANSWERS ON PAGE 338

1

HINT! Pink never goes out of style for this leggy creature.

2

HINT! Falsely known as a master of camouflage, this animal may actually change colour to communicate, not to blend in.

3

HINT! This teddy bear look-alike isn't really a bear.

4

HINT! This gentle giant likes to *moo*-ve in a herd.

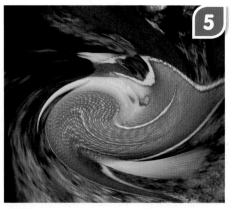

5

HINT! This animal doesn't mind spending its entire life in a school.

WHAT IN THE WORLD?

ALOHA SPIRIT

These photographs show close-up and faraway views of things you could see in Hawaii, U.S.A. On a separate sheet of paper, unscramble the letters to identify what's in each picture.

ANSWERS ON PAGE 338

EPPIEPLSNA

SNAAGDRL

TOCNCOU

AIWAAHIN SIRHT

ESA REUTLT

NVLAOOC

DAUSRFOBR

EKUULLE

GALAXY QUEST

Trace with your finger the path that Zorg the alien needs to take to get back to the mother ship. **ANSWER ON PAGE 338**

FUNNY FILL-IN

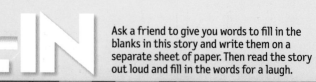

Ask a friend to give you words to fill in the blanks in this story and write them on a separate sheet of paper. Then read the story out loud and fill in the words for a laugh.

I was going to be rich! I had just invented the first electric _____ . Using
_____noun_____

a(n) _____ from _____ 's toolbox, I built it out of old _____
_____tool_____   ___relative's name___   ___noun, plural___

and rubber _____ . The first time I turned it on, the machine worked
_____noun, plural_____

_____ . I couldn't believe it! " _____ !" I quickly invited
___adverb ending in -ly___   ___exclamation___

a(n) _____ billionaire to check out my invention. I couldn't wait to sell it for
_____adjective_____

_____ million pounds and live like _____ . But when
___large number___   ___name of a celebrity___

I turned it on, something went terribly wrong. The machine started _____
                                                                   ___verb ending in -ing___

and _____ . Suddenly, it spewed _____ and shot slices of
___verb ending in -ing___   ___something slimy___

_____ in all directions. The billionaire started screaming at the top of his
_____food_____

_____ and ran out of my lab. Good thing I still get my weekly allowance.
___body part, plural___

Have you ever seen a dog that resembles its owner? Look for clues in the dog park to figure out which canine belongs to which owner. **ANSWERS ON PAGE 338**

141

WHAT IN THE WORLD?

COLOUR YOUR WORLD

These images show close-up and faraway views of rainbow-coloured objects. On a separate sheet of paper, unscramble the letters to identify what's in each picture.

ANSWERS ON PAGE 338

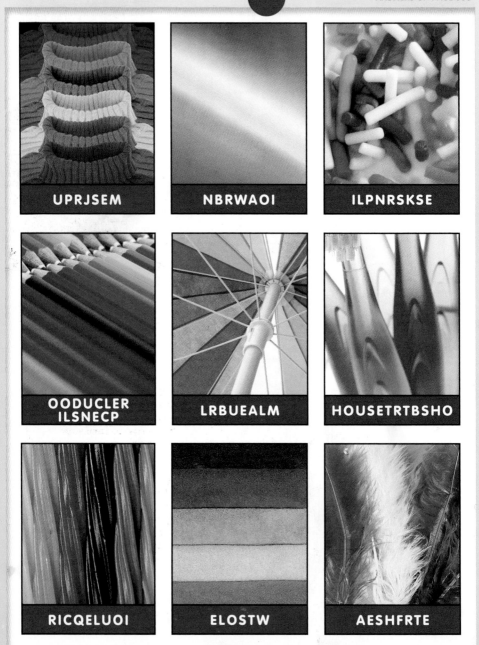

UPRJSEM

NBRWAOI

ILPNRSKSE

OODUCLER ILSNECP

LRBUEALM

HOUSETRTBSHO

RICQELUOI

ELOSTW

AESHFRTE

Just Joking

COW

KNOCK, KNOCK.

Who's there?
Olive.
Olive who?
Olive you.

Q

Why do birds fly south in the winter?

A

It's easier than walking.

EMILY: Did you know you were built upside down?
ADAM: What do you mean?
EMILY: Your nose runs and your feet smell.

You've **got** to be joking ...

Wait! I'm not nuts! I'm just nuts for you!

UNDERSEA STARS

This underwater band is jamming onstage, but it looks as if their instruments have disappeared. Or have they? Find the 10 instruments hidden in the scene. **ANSWERS ON PAGE 338**

1. piano
2. drums
3. flute
4. saxophone
5. triangle
6. violin
7. accordion
8. guitar
9. maracas
10. tambourine

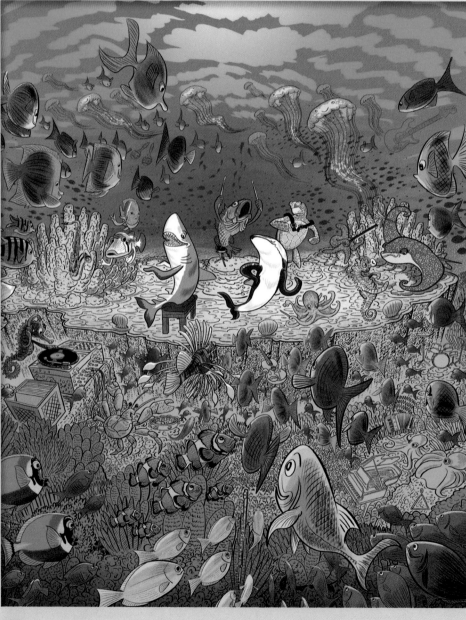

LAUGH OUT LOUD

"WHAT'S IT LIKE TO
GO FOR A WALK AND ACTUALLY
GO SOMEWHERE?"

"IT'S 'BRING YOUR IMAGINARY MONSTER
UNDER THE BED TO SCHOOL' DAY!"

"I DON'T CARE WHAT YOU SAY...
NEXT YEAR WE MIGRATE EARLIER."

"LOVE YOUR TURTLENECK!"

"IT'S GREAT YOU GOT A JOB AND ALL,
BUT YOU DIDN'T TELL ME YOU
WENT OVER TO THE DARK SIDE."

FIND THE HIDDEN ANIMALS

Animals often blend in with their environments for protection. Find each animal listed below in one of the pictures. On a separate sheet of paper, write the letter of the correct picture and the animal's name.

ANSWERS ON PAGE 338

1. pygmy seahorses
2. Brazilian long-nosed bats
3. stone grasshopper
4. grey wolf
5. lion
6. European hares

FUNNY FILL-IN

Ask a friend to give you words to fill in the blanks in this story and write them on a separate sheet of paper. Then read the story out loud and fill in the words for a laugh.

You'll never believe what happened when my family went on a(n) _____ safari in

adjective
_____ . We were having a great time snapping photos of the _____ wildlife.

country _____ adjective
We saw _____ cubs, a(n) _____ -striped _____ that could run faster

animal _____ colour _____ different animal
than _____ and a(n) _____ _____ in a tree. Then our

famous athlete _____ different animal _____ verb ending in -ing
safari vehicle suddenly _____ to a stop. The wheels had become stuck in the mud.

past-tense verb
I turned around and saw a(n) _____ the size of _____ _____

different animal _____ movie monster _____ verb ending in -ing
towards us and making a sound like a(n) _____ . It was so close I could smell its foul-

musical instrument
scented breath. I thought the animal was going to flatten us like _____ ; instead,

breakfast food, plural
it just _____ the vehicle out of the muck with its _____ and

past-tense verb _____ animal body part
_____ away. I couldn't wait to post these pictures on _____ .

past-tense verb _____ website

Play more Funny Fill-In!
natgeokids.com/ffi

147

Just Joking

JAVAN GLIDING
TREE FROG

KNOCK, KNOCK.

Who's there?
Annie.
Annie who?
Annie body home?

Q Why did the **police** stake out the baseball field?

A They heard that players were stealing bases.

Q Why couldn't the teddy bear eat his dessert?

A He was stuffed.

Q What do you get if **your parakeet** flies into the **blender?**

A Shredded tweet.

SIGNS OF THE TIMES

Seeing isn't always believing. One of these funny signs is not real. Can you figure out which one is fake?

ANSWER ON PAGE 338

1 JAIL. SCHOOL.

2 Nowhere ↓ Somewhere ↓

3 Leprechaun crossing

4 CEMETERY LANE ← DEAD END

5 SKY ↑

6 THE OTHER ST THIS ST

7 WHOA

WINDY JUMBLE

A powerful wind has whipped through this neighbourhood park. Some visitors' belongings have blown away and ended up with someone else. Figure out which items belong to the people listed on the right. On a separate piece of paper, match the correct letter with the names. We've done the first one for you.   **ANSWERS ON PAGE 338**

A Eleanor   ___ Steve   ___ Jill
___ Sam   ___ Carlos   ___ Isabel
___ Nicole   ___ Zak   ___ Daniel
                 ___ Ava

Just Joking

SEA OTTER

KNOCK, KNOCK.
Who's there?
Cash.
Cash who?
No thanks.
I prefer peanuts.

Q What do you call a **grizzly bear** with **no teeth?**

A A gummy bear.

Say this three times:

Rolling red wagons race wildly down roads.

TWO SNAKES ARE TALKING.

You've **got** to be joking ...

SNAKE 1:
"Are we venomous?"

SNAKE 2:
"Yes, why?"

SNAKE 1:
"I just bit my lip."

151

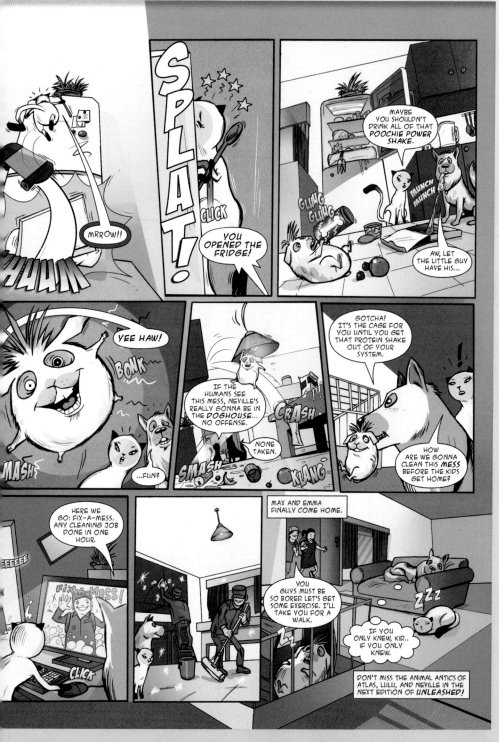

SCIENCE and TECHNOLOGY

Designed with artificial intelligence, Promobots in Perm, Russia, can recognise faces, communicate with people, answer questions and avoid obstacles as they move.

JUNGLE DISCOVERY!

National Geographic Explorer Albert Lin uses modern technology to find clues to the past.

LASER SCANS HAVE UNCOVERED 60,000 PREVIOUSLY UNKNOWN MAYA STRUCTURES.

ANCIENT MAYA RUINS HIDDEN BENEATH THE FOREST CANOPY

In northern Guatemala, thick green jungles extend for as far as the eye can see. It's hard to imagine that any humans could ever live beneath the dense jungle canopy, let alone establish an entire city. But as National Geographic Explorer Albert Lin recently discovered, this was once indeed the site of a thriving and sophisticated civilisation some 1,500 years ago.

As an explorer and engineer, Lin has carved a career out of blending cutting-edge technology with uncovering the past. In Guatemala, seeking to uncover clues from the past, he used an aerial scanning technology called LiDAR, which stands for Light Detection and Ranging. Lin and his crew fired off pulses of laser light from an aeroplane to penetrate the dense canopy, then measured how long it took for each pulse to bounce back from the ground.

A shorter return could mean that the beams bounced off of something elevated, like a temple. A longer measurement may indicate there's something much lower lurking beneath the treetops, like a deep riverbed. Then, with the help of GPS technology, Lin combined the data to create a detailed 3D map of the terrain. The result? A sprawling Maya 'megalopolis' — several large, connected cities — about the size of Italy hidden in the dense tropical forest.

And Lin didn't stop there: With his 'treasure map' in hand, Lin and his crew then trekked for hours in the jungle before locating the ancient ruins of the Maya people.

"We just followed a map created by lasers in the sky, using a helicopter to get into the jungle ... and found this,"

A NEWLY DISCOVERED MAYA PYRAMID MEASURES SEVEN STOREYS HIGH.

people — did fight in major wars with nearby civilisations. Causeways — roads built on top of bodies of water — show that they likely traded with other regions.

Lin's breakthrough casts new light on the mysterious Maya world, which reached its height between A.D. 250 and 950 before its collapse. While no one truly knows what brought about the Maya's downfall, Lin's work brings us one step closer to understanding — and appreciating — the impressively complex and sophisticated civilisation.

Says Lin: "This LiDAR data is essentially rewriting the history of the Maya."

recalls Lin of the 30-metre (100-ft)-tall ancient pyramid he discovered, which was previously mistaken by archaeologists to be a small mountain.

Among the other discoveries in the ancient Maya ruins? More than 60,000 structures, including pyramids, palaces, houses, farms and roadways linking distant cities and towns. This suggests that the Maya civilisation was much bigger than originally thought, with a population hovering between 10 and 15 million — a number much higher than previous estimates.

More LiDAR data uncovered extensive fortresses and defensive walls, which supports one theory that the Maya — previously thought to be mostly peaceful

THE NAKED EYE SEES ONLY JUNGLE (ABOVE), BUT LIN'S TECHNOLOGY HAS REVEALED AN ANCIENT MAYA PYRAMID (BELOW).

LiDAR TECHNOLOGY HAS SHOWN THAT SOME MAYA CITIES WERE MUCH LARGER THAN RESEARCHERS PREVIOUSLY THOUGHT.

Bet You Didn't Know!

10 high-tech facts about

1 Robotic luggage can follow travellers as they walk.

2 A team of Swiss researchers built a robot small enough to swim through human arteries.

3 The word 'robot' first appeared in a play written in 1929.

4 You can compete against a robot in table tennis.

5 The first robot debuted in 1961 and worked in a General Motors car factory.

6 Some robots can identify different cheeses.

robots

Diners at the **Robot Restaurant** in China have their whole meal **cooked and served by robots.** 7

Scientists have created **robots** that can eat and grow. 8

9 **Robots** at a farm in **California, U.S.A.,** are being used to **plant, care for and harvest lettuce crops.**

10 **'Care Bots'** are used in some retirement homes **to help elderly people** with day-to-day tasks.

159

FUTURE WORLD:

The year is 2070, and it's time to get dressed for school. You step in front of a large video mirror that projects different clothes on you. After you decide on your favourite T-shirt, a robot fetches your outfit. No time is lost trying to find matching socks! Chores? What chores? Get ready for a whole new home life.

STAY CONNECTED

Whether your future home is an urban skyscraper or an underwater pod, all buildings will one day be connected via a central communications hub. Want to check out a *T. rex* skeleton at a faraway museum? You can virtually connect to it just as though you were visiting it in person. But you're not just seeing something far away. Connect to a beach house's balcony and smell the salt water and feel the breeze. Buildings might also share information about incoming weather and emergencies to keep you safe.

CUSTOM COMFORT

Soon, your house may give you a personal welcome home. No need for keys — sensors scan your body and open the door. Walk into the living room, and the lighting adjusts to your preferred setting. Thirsty? A glass of water pops up on the table. Before bed, you enter the bathroom and say, "Shower, please." The water starts flowing at exactly the temperature you want.

ON LOCATION

Your room has a spectacular view of the sea ... because your house is suspended above it. New technologies will allow us to build our homes in unusual spots. In the future, 'floating' structures elevated by supporting poles above water or other hard-to-access spots (think mountain peaks) will be more common as cities become more crowded. And this won't be limited to dry land on Earth. That means that one day your family could even live in space!

Homes

ON THE GO

Homes of the future will always be on the move. Walls will be capable of expanding and contracting, and houses will rotate with the sun's movements to conserve energy. Buildings will also be capable of changing size depending on who's inside. Grandparents could 'move in' by attaching a modular section to the front, back or top of the house.

BRING ON THE BOTS

While you were outside playing with your friends, your house robot did the laundry, vacuumed and cleaned the bathroom. Meanwhile, a drone just delivered the shopping for the home-bot to put away. Minutes later, lunch is ready. The service is great ... but how will you earn your pocket money? Instead of taking out the bins or setting the table, you'll earn money by helping clean and maintain the robots.

FUTURE WORLD:

A buzzer goes off, marking the start of a race. Your heart is pounding — not that you can hear it over the sound of revving engines. Your car weaves through the other vehicles, making its way to the front of the pack. Peering through the windshield, you see the finish line ahead. Your car crosses first! The crowd roars.

You aren't actually in the car. But thanks to a pair of smart glasses you're wearing in the stands, you experienced exactly what the real driver did on the course.

"In the future, advanced technology will enable us to feel as if we're part of the event," says Aymeric Castaing, founder of Umanimation, a future-tech media company. Take a peek at more ways we'll be entertained by 2060 and beyond — but first, check out two terms to know.

1. Augmented reality (AR): Technology that layers computer-generated images onto things in the real world (like in Pokémon GO)

2. Virtual reality (VR): A computer-generated experience that makes you feel as if you're inside a totally different world

SUPER STADIUMS

Didn't see that catch? No worries: In the future, 3D holograms could appear in midair above the field to show replays of sports moments. For some events, you'll even get a seat in a flying pod that can put you close to the action. (The pod even flies you home afterwards!) Meanwhile, say goodbye to long lines for food or team jerseys. Through an app, flying drones will deliver anything you order right to your seat.

GAME ON

A colourful alien zooms directly toward you, attempting to knock you aside with its spaceship. You put your hands in front of you, blocking the alien with a powerful force field. A crowd cheers your dramatic victory.

To the group assembled in front of you in the park, it looks like you just took down an alien spaceship — thanks to virtual reality (VR) goggles and a suit with motion sensors. Everything you saw through your goggles was projected onto a video screen at a virtual gaming playground. There the audience can watch and cheer as you go up against the aliens. They can also wear headsets and feel as if they're in outer space, too!

Entertainment

MUSEUMS TO GO

Museums of the future will blend real life with augmented and virtual reality. For example, you can check out a sculpture at an art museum with AR glasses, getting details about the artist and style. Then, using your VR headset, you can draw your own masterpiece inspired by what you saw. Not feeling creative? "Using your in-home VR headset and a 3D printer, you can create what you saw in the museum in your bedroom," Castaing says. It's like taking the museum home with you — sort of.

THE BIG SCREEN

There won't be a bad seat in the house at cinemas in the future. Films will surround the audience with 3D screens in every direction ... including the floor and ceiling. You'll feel like you're underwater at the latest ocean adventure blockbuster. Plus, robots will deliver the snacks you've ordered from your seat's tablet directly to your rotating chair.

DROID BEATS

Ready to rock out to your favourite band? Whether it's pop-star robots or a robot orchestra conductor, future music may be in non-human hands. And audiences won't just hear music played by robots — they'll be able to see it. Augmented reality (AR) glasses will allow audiences to see which notes are coming out of the instruments in front of them. "AR glasses could even enable beginning musicians to take their lessons on the go," Castaing says. "The glasses could essentially become their teacher."

WHAT IS LIFE?

This seems like such an easy question to answer. Everybody knows that singing birds are alive and rocks are not. But when we start studying bacteria and other microscopic creatures, things get more complicated.

SO WHAT EXACTLY IS LIFE?
Most scientists agree that something is alive if it can do the following: reproduce; grow in size to become more complex in structure; take in nutrients to survive; give off waste products; and respond to external stimuli, such as increased sunlight or changes in temperature.

KINDS OF LIFE
Biologists classify living organisms by how they get their energy. Organisms such as algae, green plants and some bacteria use sunlight as an energy source. Animals (like humans), fungi and some Archaea use chemicals to provide energy. When we eat food, chemical reactions within our digestive system turn our food into fuel.

Living things inhabit land, sea and air. In fact, life also thrives deep beneath the oceans, embedded in rocks kilometres below Earth's crust, in ice and in other extreme environments. The life-forms that thrive in these challenging environments are called extremophiles. Some of these draw directly upon the chemicals surrounding them for energy. Since these are very different forms of life than what we're used to, we may not think of them as alive, but they are.

HOW IT ALL WORKS
To try and understand how a living organism works, it helps to look at one example of its simplest form — the single-celled bacterium called *Streptococcus*. There are many kinds of these tiny organisms, and some are responsible for human illnesses. What makes us sick or uncomfortable are the toxins the bacteria give off in our bodies.

A single *Streptococcus* bacterium is so small that at least 500 of them could fit on the dot above this letter *i*. These bacteria are some of the simplest forms of life we know. They have no moving parts, no lungs, no brain, no heart, no liver and no leaves or fruit. Yet this life-form reproduces. It grows in size by producing long chain structures, takes in nutrients and gives off waste products. This tiny life-form is alive, just as you are alive.

What makes something alive is a question scientists grapple with when they study viruses, such as the ones that cause the common cold and smallpox. They can grow and reproduce within host cells, such as those that make up your body. Because viruses lack cells and cannot metabolise nutrients for energy or reproduce without a host, scientists ask if they are indeed alive. And don't go looking for them without a strong microscope — viruses are a hundred times smaller than bacteria.

Scientists think life began on Earth some 4.1 to 3.9 billion years ago, but no fossils exist from that time. The earliest fossils ever found are from the primitive life that existed 3.6 billion years ago. Other life-forms, some of which are shown below, soon followed. Scientists continue to study how life evolved on Earth and whether it is possible that life exists on other planets.

MICROSCOPIC ORGANISMS

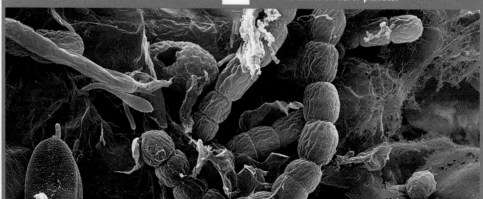

The Three Domains of Life

Biologists divide all living organisms into three domains: Bacteria, Archaea and Eukarya. Archaean and Bacterial cells do not have nuclei, but they are so different from each other that they belong to different domains. Since human cells have a nucleus, humans belong to the Eukarya domain.

1 BACTERIA

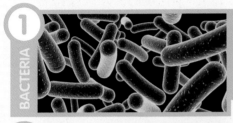

DOMAIN BACTERIA: These single-celled microorganisms are found almost everywhere in the world. Bacteria are small and do not have nuclei. They can be shaped like rods, spirals or spheres. Some of them are helpful to humans, and some are harmful.

2 ARCHAEA

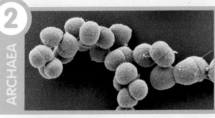

DOMAIN ARCHAEA: These single-celled microorganisms are often found in extremely hostile environments. Like Bacteria, Archaea do not have nuclei, but they have some genes in common with Eukarya. For this reason, scientists think the Archaea living today most closely resemble the earliest forms of life on Earth.

3 EUKARYA

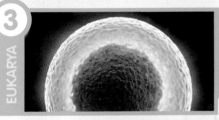

DOMAIN EUKARYA: This diverse group of life-forms is more complicated than Bacteria and Archaea, as Eukarya have one or more cells with nuclei. These are the tiny cells that make up your whole body. Eukarya are divided into four groups: fungi, protists, plants and animals.

WHAT IS A DOMAIN? Scientifically speaking, a domain is a major taxonomic division into which natural objects are classified (see page 46 for 'What Is Taxonomy?').

FYI

FUNGI

KINGDOM FUNGI (about 100,000 species): Mainly multicellular organisms, fungi cannot make their own food. Mushrooms and yeast are fungi.

PROTISTS

PROTISTS (about 250,000 species): Once considered a kingdom, this group is a 'grab bag' that includes unicellular and multicellular organisms of great variety.

PLANTS

KINGDOM PLANTAE (about 400,000 species): Plants are multicellular, and many can make their own food using photosynthesis (see page 166 for 'Photosynthesis').

ANIMALS

KINGDOM ANIMALIA (about 1,000,000 species): Most animals, which are multi-cellular, have their own organ systems. Animals do not make their own food.

HOW DOES YOUR GARDEN GROW?

The plant kingdom is about 400,000 species strong, growing all over the world: on top of mountains, in the sea, in frigid temperatures — everywhere. Without plants, life on Earth would not be able to survive. Plants provide food and oxygen for animals and humans.

Plants have three distinct characteristics:

1. Most have chlorophyll (a green pigment that makes photosynthesis work and turns sunlight into energy), while some are parasitic. Parasitic plants don't make their own food — they take it from other plants.

2. Plants cannot change their location on their own.

3. Their cell walls are made from a stiff material called cellulose.

Photosynthesis

Plants are lucky — most don't have to hunt or shop for food. Most use the sun to produce their own food. In a process called photosynthesis, a plant's chloroplast (the part of the plant where the chemical chlorophyll is located) captures the sun's energy and combines it with carbon dioxide from the air and nutrient-rich water from the ground to produce a sugar called glucose.

Plants burn the glucose for energy to help them grow. As a waste product, plants emit oxygen, which humans and other animals need to breathe. When we breathe, we exhale carbon dioxide, which the plants then use for more photosynthesis — it's all a big, finely tuned system. So the next time you pass a lonely houseplant, give it thanks for helping you live.

Plant a BUTTERFLY GARDEN

TAILED JAY

BUCKEYE

SPICEBUSH SWALLOWTAIL

BENEFITS OF BUTTERFLIES

Sure, butterflies are pretty. But they're also pollinators. Like bees, they travel to flowers seeking nectar. In the process, they spread pollen from one area to another, helping other plants grow. That's why 'nectar plants' are an important part of your butterfly garden. They help spread the growth of valuable plants to many other places.

SUPPLY LIST

- BUTTERFLY-FRIENDLY PLANTS
- HOST PLANTS TO LAY EGGS ON

RED-SPOTTED PURPLE

MONARCH

EASTERN TIGER SWALLOWTAIL

1 Choose a spot for your garden. Butterflies like lots of sun, so make sure you plant your garden in an area that gets at least six hours of direct sunlight a day.

2 Besides sun, butterflies need protection from wind and rain. Make sure trees or shrubs are part of your butterfly garden.

3 Find out what butterflies you should attract. Look in a field guide or ask a ranger at a local park which butterfly species are common in your area.

4 Certain butterflies like certain types of plants. Your local nursery can help guide you to the right ones. Many butterflies are attracted to coneflower, lilac and purple verbena. Try to pick plants that are native to the area where you are planting, and that bloom at different times of the year. That way, butterflies are always attracted to your garden.

5 Butterflies will also need some host plants, such as milkweed, to lay their eggs on. Your nursery can help you select the best ones.

6 Set up some chairs or a bench and watch your garden. Butterflies are less shy than birds and usually don't mind people being around them.

167

Your Amazing Body!

YOUR SKIN SHEDS AND REGROWS ABOUT ONCE A MONTH.

The human body is a complicated mass of systems — nine systems, to be exact. Each system has a unique and critical purpose in the body, and we wouldn't be able to survive without all of them.

The **NERVOUS** system controls the body.

The **MUSCULAR** system makes movement possible.

The **SKELETAL** system supports the body.

The **CIRCULATORY** system moves blood throughout the body.

The **RESPIRATORY** system provides the body with oxygen.

The **DIGESTIVE** system breaks down food into nutrients and gets rid of waste.

The **IMMUNE** system protects the body against disease and infection.

The **ENDOCRINE** system regulates the body's functions.

The **REPRODUCTIVE** system enables people to produce offspring.

weird but true!

YOUR **BRAIN** CAN HOLD **100 TIMES** MORE INFORMATION THAN AN AVERAGE **COMPUTER.**

A speck of **blood** contains about **5 million red blood cells.**

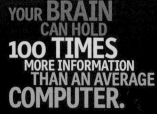

Your hands and wrists contain 26 percent of the bones in your body.

BY the NUMBERS

BRAIN POWER

Your brain is the tops—literally. It's the most complex organ in your body, an amazing supercomputer that controls everything you do. Check out some incredible info behind the numbers that nourish your noggin.

YOUR BRAIN CAN HOLD

1 MILLION

GIGABYTES OF DATA. IF YOUR BRAIN WERE LIKE A DVR, IT COULD HOLD **3 MILLION** HOURS OF TELEVISION SHOWS.

FRONTAL LOBE

PARIETAL LOBE

OCCIPITAL LOBE

TEMPORAL LOBE

CEREBELLUM

YOUR BRAIN IS ABOUT

15 CENTIMETRES (6 IN) LONG.

YOUR BRAIN WEIGHS ABOUT

1.3

KILOGRAMS (3 LB).

LIKE THE EARTH, YOUR BRAIN IS DIVIDED INTO

2

HEMISPHERES.

YOUR BRAIN CONTAINS

BILLIONS

OF NERVE CELLS.

ABOUT

2/3

OF YOUR BRAIN IS MADE UP OF SPECIALISED FATS.

THE BRAIN HAS

12

NERVE PAIRS THAT CONTROL THINGS LIKE TASTE AND HEARING.

LOOK OUT!

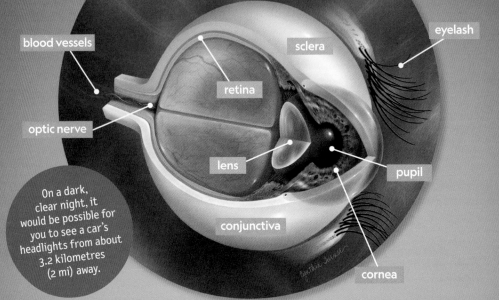

blood vessels

sclera

eyelash

retina

optic nerve

lens

pupil

conjunctiva

cornea

On a dark, clear night, it would be possible for you to see a car's headlights from about 3.2 kilometres (2 mi) away.

Your eyes are two of the most amazing organs in your body.

These small, squishy, fluid-filled balls have almost three-quarters of your body's sensory receptors. They're like two supersmart cameras, but more complex.

So how do you see the world around you? It begins when you open the protective cover of your eyelid and let in the light. Light enters your eye through the window of your cornea and passes through the aqueous humour, a watery fluid that nourishes the eye tissue. It enters the black circle in the iris (the coloured part of your eye), called the pupil. Because people need to be able to see in both bright and low light, muscles in the iris automatically make the pupil smaller when the light is strong and wider when the light is dim. Light then travels to the lens, whose muscles adjust it to be able to see objects both near and far. Then the light goes through the vitreous humour (a clear jellylike substance) to the retina. The retina, a layer of about 126 million light-sensitive cells, lines the back of your eyeball. When these cells absorb the light, they transform it into electrical signals that are sent along the optic nerve to the brain. The brain then makes sense of what you are seeing.

A TOPSY-TURVY WORLD

Turn this over in your mind: You're looking at the world topsy-turvy, and you don't even know it. Like a camera lens, your lens focuses light, creates an image and turns it upside down.

Yep, when your lens focuses light inside your eye, it flips the image so it lands on your retina upside down. But, your brain knows to flip the image automatically to match your reality. But what if your reality suddenly

CAMERA LENS

changed? A well-known experiment in the mid-20th century in which a person wore special light-inverting goggles showed that his brain actually adjusted to the new, inverted world by eventually seeing the reversed view as normal! It is thought that newborns see the world upside down for a short while, until their brains learn how to turn things right-side up.

AWESOME
OPTICAL ILLUSIONS

Ready to work your brain and show your visual alertness? Ponder these puzzling pictures to see what you see!

WHICH CIRCLE IS **BIGGER?**

Both of these circle clusters have an orange circle surrounded by purple ones. But which orange circle is bigger? The answer may surprise you: neither! The two orange circles are the same size. The one on the right may appear bigger because it's surrounded by purple circles that are smaller than it is. The one on the left seems smaller because it's surrounded by purple circles that are larger than it is.

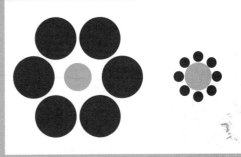

RABBIT OR DUCK?

It's a duck! Or is it a rabbit? Can you see it both ways? A recent study using this illusion suggests that the more easily people can switch back and forth between the two images, the more creative they are.

SPINNING CIRCLES

Do you see all the spinning circles? Don't look too long, or you might get dizzy! This illusion plays with your peripheral vision (vision from the sides of your eyes, not the middle). Sometimes when you look out the sides of your eyes, you see movement where really there are only patterns.

MUSCLE POWER

With its strong bones and flexible joints, your skeleton is built to be on the go.

But without muscles, it won't go anywhere! You need muscle power to make your body walk, run, skip, rub your nose or even just sit up without toppling over.

The muscles that do these jobs are called skeletal muscles. You have about 650 of them, and you can control what they do. Sometimes, it takes a lot of skeletal muscles to make even a simple move. Your tongue alone contains eight muscles!

You also have muscles that work without your having to do a thing. Most of these muscles are called smooth muscles. Sheets of smooth muscle line your blood vessels, throat, stomach, intestines, lungs and other organs. They are hard at work keeping your blood circulating and your food digesting while you're busy doing other things. And there's also that mighty muscle, your heart. It pumps thanks to cardiac muscles, which are found only in the heart.

THE HIBERNATION MYSTERY

Very sick people often lie in bed for a long time as they recover. This lack of exercise weakens muscles—a process called 'muscle atrophy'. Preventing atrophy may be possible someday thanks to researchers who study hibernating animals.

Bears, for example, spend winter sleeping but do not suffer severe atrophy. When they wake up in the spring, they're as strong as—well, bears! Scientists are

studying the muscles and blood of bears, ground squirrels and other hibernators to find out how they stay in shape while sleeping. The answers may one day help people suffering from muscle atrophy when they're sick or in the hospital for a long time.

Some of your body's strongest muscles aren't in your arms or legs. They're in your jaws! These strong muscles are called the masseters. They help you chew by closing your lower jaw. Clenching your teeth will make your masseters bulge so you can feel them.

BODY ELECTRIC

The nerve signal that tells your muscles to move is super fast! It zooms at 400 kilometres an hour (250 mph), as fast as the fastest racing car.

Your body is just humming with electricity.

Nerve cells from head to toe speak to each other through electrical signals. The electrical signals zap down each nerve cell and, when they get to the end, jump across a tiny gap called a synapse (see image below). How does the signal jump across the gap?

The nerve produces special chemicals that can flow across the gap to the next cell. There, a new electrical charge travels down the next nerve. Messages jump from neuron to neuron in a chain of electrical-chemical-electrical-chemical signals until they reach their destination.

Because nerves don't actually touch, they can change the path of their signals easily. They can make new connections and break old ones. This is how your brain learns and stores new information.

BUNDLE OF NERVES

A three-centimetre (1.2-in) section of your brain stem (called the medulla oblongata) controls some of your body's most important functions, such as breathing and heart rate. Amazingly, it also contains your body's motor and sensory nerves and is where nerves from the left and right sides of your body cross each other on their journey towards your cerebrum.

SENSORY NERVES pull in information from nerve endings in your eyes, ears, skin, hands and other parts of your body and then send this information to your brain.

MOTOR NERVES send messages from your brain to your muscles, telling them to contract, to run or to walk.

Bet You Didn't Know!

A reflex is a nerve message that doesn't go through your brain. When you touch a hot cooker, for example, a sensory neuron picks up the message ("Hot!") and passes it to a motor neuron in your spinal cord. The motor neuron then sends a message to your hand, telling it to move ("Quick!").

THE INVADERS ARE COMING!

BACTERIA

FUNGUS

VIRUS

Images are not to scale.

Every 6.5 square centimetres (1 sq in) of your skin hosts about **six million bacteria.**

PROTOZOA (CAN BE TRANSMITTED BY MOSQUITOES)

ADD IT UP

So you know that you have bacteria on your skin and in your body. But do you know how many? One hundred trillion — that's 100,000,000,000,000! Most are harmless and some are pretty friendly, keeping more dangerous bacteria at bay, protecting you from some skin infections and helping your cuts heal.

Some microorganisms (tiny living things) can make your body sick. They are too small to see with the naked eye. These creatures — bacteria, viruses, fungi and protozoa — are what you may know as germs.

Bacteria are microscopic organisms that live nearly everywhere on Earth, including on and in the human body. 'Good' bacteria help our digestive systems work properly. Harmful bacteria can cause illnesses, including ear infections and tonsillitis.

A virus, like a cold or the flu, needs to live inside another living thing (a host) to survive; then it can grow and multiply throughout the host's body.

Fungi get their food from the plants, animals or people they live on. Some fungi can get on your body and cause skin diseases such as ringworm.

Protozoa are single-celled organisms that can spread disease to humans through contaminated water and dirty living conditions. Protozoa can cause infections such as malaria, which occurs when a person is bitten by an infected mosquito.

174

GERM **SHOWDOWN**

Scientists in Wales studied three greeting styles to determine which was the cleanest. Find out which one has the upper hand.

HANDSHAKE

AN AVERAGE HANDSHAKE TRANSFERRED **MORE THAN 5 TIMES AS MUCH BACTERIA** AS A FIST BUMP. (A STRONG HANDSHAKE TRANSFERRED **10 TIMES** AS MUCH.)

HIGH FIVE

A HIGH FIVE PASSED **TWICE AS MANY** GERMS AS A FIST BUMP.

FIST BUMP

WINNER:

FIST BUMPS HAVE THE **LEAST SKIN-TO-SKIN CONTACT** OF THE GREETINGS, WHICH MAKES IT LESS LIKELY FOR MICROBES TO JUMP **FROM ONE HAND TO ANOTHER.**

WHAT DIED?

CONCEPTS
decomposition, microbiology, decay, organic materials, bacteria, insects, corpse fauna

HOW LONG IT TAKES
two to four days, possibly longer in cold weather

WHAT YOU NEED
food samples
containers
outdoor thermometer
magnifying lens
dissecting microscope
insect identification guides
optional: camera, smartphone
or video camera

If you leave food out, SOMETHING will come to live on it or lay eggs on it. In this observation, discover what arrives to make the most of your leftovers.

What comes to get food that's left out?

176

WHAT TO DO

DAY ONE:

1 WORK IN AN OPEN-AIR area, compost heap or compost bin — a place that is open to insects but not birds or other animals. Ask an adult to help you choose a location.

2 SET UP FOUR containers with a small sample of food inside each. If you want, these samples can represent the four food groups: vegetable/fruit, meat/fish, bread/grains and milk/dairy.

DAYS TWO TO FOUR:

3 KEEP A CAREFUL record of what you observe through your senses. Each day, record the temperature in the area where your samples are. Note whether you can see signs that bugs or other creatures have been attracted to your samples, including any film or mould that forms. You may want to photograph the samples every day to compare them.

4 EVERY ONE OR TWO days (decide which interval you want to study), remove the samples from the containers to examine them with a magnifying lens and microscope. Count, try to identify and sketch the bugs and other life-forms that colonise each sample. Add descriptions to your notes, including sensory observations: texture, colour and smell — but not taste!

WHAT TO EXPECT?
You may see mould, biofilm or scum, bugs, worms, flies and so on.

WHAT'S GOING ON?
Nature abhors a vacuum. If there is food, something will come to eat it.

OUR TRY

We put out duplicate food — chicken soup, blackberry jam and cat food — every other day for six days. We set out the food in the garden, in a cat box with a brick on top, but that didn't stop coyotes from pulling it apart and getting the food on the second night. After that we replaced the food and kept the cat box in the garage, where flies could still get to it. After we opened it to see what we had and examine it with the microscope, we dumped the cat box near the compost heap — and later, we had a glorious infestation of beetles.

QUESTION THIS!

- What would happen to this food if nothing were able to reach it?

- What would happen to this food if you let more time pass?

177

QUIZ WHIZ

Test your science and technology smarts by taking this quiz!

Write your answers on a piece of paper. Then check them below.

1 What did explorers recently discover in the Guatemalan rainforest?

a. an ancient city
b. a new species of bird
c. a crater the size of the Grand Canyon
d. a mysterious spaceship

2 True or false? Butterflies are pollinators, like bees.

3 Scientists have created robots that can _____.

a. identify different types of cheese
b. help humans with daily tasks
c. play table tennis
d. all of the above

4 How many species are in the kingdom Animalia?

a. 10
b. 1,000
c. 10,000
d. 1,000,000

5 True or false? Your brain weighs about 6 kilograms (13 lb).

Not **STUMPED** yet? Check out the *NATIONAL GEOGRAPHIC KIDS QUIZ WHIZ* collection for more crazy **SCIENCE AND TECHNOLOGY** questions!

ANSWERS:
1. a; 2. True; 3. d; 4. d; 5. False. It weighs about 1.3 kilograms (3 lb).

178

This Is How It's Done!

Sometimes, the most complicated problems are solved with step-by-step directions. These 'how-to' instructions are also known as a process analysis essay. While scientists and engineers use this tool to program robots and write computer code, you also use process analysis every day, from following a recipe to putting together a new toy or gadget. Here's how to write a basic process analysis essay.

Step 1: Choose Your Topic Sentence

Pick a clear and concise topic sentence that describes what you're writing about. Be sure to explain to the reader why the task is important — and how many steps there are to complete it.

Step 2: List Materials

Do you need specific ingredients or equipment to complete your process? Mention these right away so the readers will have all they need to do this activity.

Step 3: Write Your Directions

Your directions should be clear and easy to follow. Assume that you are explaining the process for the first time, and define any unfamiliar terms. List your steps in the exact order the reader will need to follow to complete the activity. Try to keep your essay limited to no more than six steps.

Step 4: Restate Your Main Idea

Your closing idea should revisit your topic sentence, drawing a conclusion relating to the importance of the subject.

EXAMPLE OF A PROCESS ANALYSIS ESSAY

Downloading an app is a simple way to enhance your tablet. Today, I'd like to show you how to search for and add an app to your tablet. First, you will need a tablet with the ability to access the internet. You'll also want to ask a parent for permission before you download anything onto your tablet. Next, select the specific app you're seeking by going to the app store on your tablet and entering the app's name into the search bar. Once you find the app you're seeking, select 'download' and wait for the app to load. When you see that the app has fully loaded, tap on the icon and you will be able to access it. Now you can enjoy your app and have more fun with your tablet.

With a population of more than five million, Abidjan, Côte d'Ivoire (Ivory Coast), in Africa, is one of the largest French-speaking cities in the world.

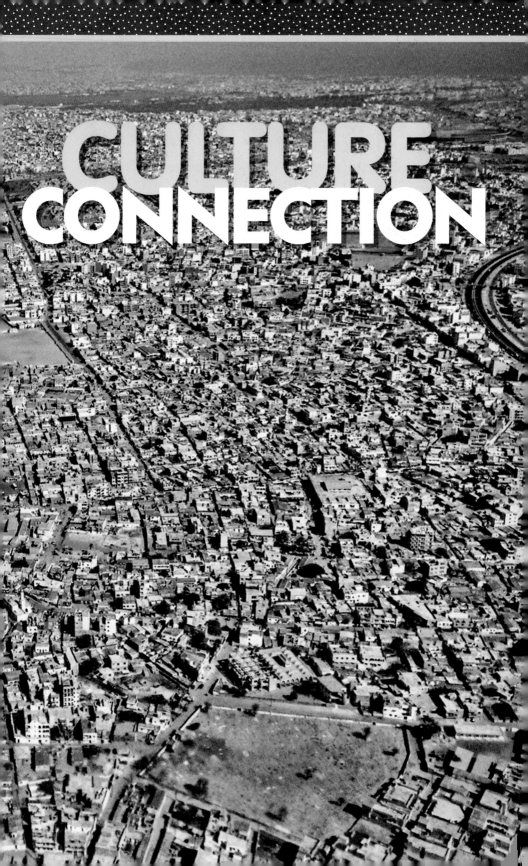

CULTURE CONNECTION

EIGHT
Works of Mind-Bending
STREET ART

**YOUR EYES DON'T DECEIVE YOU!
THESE OPEN-AIR WORKS OF ART
WILL MAKE YOU STOP IN YOUR TRACKS.**

1

RUNAWAY RAILCAR
This 3D painting depicting a soon-to-be precarious predicament was part of a 'Magic Art' special exhibition in the city of Hangzhou, China.

2

ABOUT FACE
Toronto, Canada—based visual artist Dan Bergeron created this amazing illusion as part of his 'Face of the City' series, which incorporates the surfaces of urban walls into his works of art.

3

HOLE-Y MOLEY!
Whoa — that's a bad one. Actually, it's a really great illusion by artists 3D Joe and Max displayed in Trafalgar Square, London, U.K., calling attention to the pitfalls of potholes.

4

NOAH'S ARK
This sprawling three-dimensional reimagining of the flood story was painted on Valois Square in Wilhelmshaven, Germany.

5 HANGING AROUND

Created outside the main entrance to the Corinthia Hotel in London, U.K., this incredible 3D depiction features the likeness of a crystal chandelier in the hotel's Lobby Lounge.

6 WHERE'S WALLY?

French street artist Oakoak's illusion references the children's book series that challenges readers to find the hidden main character among large groups of people in different locations.

7 LONG JUMP

Can you make it across the abyss? This amazing 3D scene is painted on the dam on Dunajec River in Niedzica, Poland.

8 DIVE IN!

Artists 3D Joe and Max created this work to commemorate the two-year anniversary of the London 2012 Olympics. It features iconic scenery as well as athletes from the games.

183

Bet You Didn't Know!

10 edible facts about food

1 Haggis, a meal of simmered sheep heart, liver and lungs, is served alongside mashed potatoes in Scotland.

2 In Poland, stuffed cabbage rolls are called **gołąbki —** which means 'little pigeons'.

3 Food trucks at the Texas, U.S.A., State Fair serve a dish of **pickles fried in red Kool-Aid.**

4 Fish-shaped marshmallows covered in **chocolate** are a favourite sweet in **New Zealand.**

5 Because of its strong smell, **durian fruit is banned** in some trains, buses and hotels in Asia.

Durian

from around the world

6 Bunny chow — curry served in hollow bread — is popular in **South Africa.**

7 In Thailand, **crickets** are farmed for **food.**

8 Traditional Mongolian cuisine includes food made from the **'five snouts'** — goats, cows, horses, yaks and camels.

9 **Natto,** a blend of **fermented soybeans** popular in Japan, is said to **smell like sweaty socks.**

10 Ant eggs are a high-end food in Mexico, where they're known as *escamoles.*

CELEBRATIONS

1 **CHINESE NEW YEAR**
12 February
Also called Lunar New Year, this holiday marks the new year according to the lunar calendar. Families celebrate with parades, feasts and fireworks. Young people may receive gifts of money in red envelopes.

2 **NYEPI**
14 March
A national day of silence, this Hindu holiday marks Lunar New Year in Bali, Indonesia, and encourages meditation and reflection. Those who follow traditional customs do not talk, use electricity, travel or eat for 24 hours.

3 **ST. PATRICK'S DAY**
17 March
This celebration sparks parties across the planet. Major monuments like the Christ the Redeemer statue in Rio de Janeiro, Brazil, and the London Eye in England are cast in green light to celebrate Irish culture and honour Ireland's patron saint.

4 **QINGMING FESTIVAL**
4 April
Also known as Grave Sweeping Day, this Chinese celebration calls on people to return to the graves of their deceased loved ones. There, they tidy up the graves, as well as light firecrackers, burn fake money and leave food as an offering to the spirits.

5 **EASTER**
4 April
A Christian holiday that honours the resurrection of Jesus Christ, Easter is celebrated by giving baskets filled with gifts, decorated eggs or sweets to children.

6 **VESAK DAY**
April or May, date varies by country
Buddhists around the world observe Buddha's birthday with rituals including chanting and prayer, candlelight processions and meditation.

7 **RAMADAN AND EID AL-FITR**
12 April* – 13 May**
A Muslim holiday, Ramadan is a month long, ending in the Eid al-Fitr celebration. Observers fast during this month — eating only after sunset. People pray for forgiveness and hope to purify themselves through observance.

8 **BERMUDA DAY**
28 May
The first day of the year that Bermudians take a dip in the ocean. It is also traditionally the first day on which Bermuda shorts are worn as business attire. To celebrate the holiday, there is a parade in Hamilton, and a road race from the west end of the island into Hamilton.

9 **ST. JOHN'S NIGHT**
23 June
In Poland, people celebrate the longest day of the year — also known as the summer solstice — with rituals that include lighting bonfires, floating flower wreaths down a stream and releasing thousands of paper lanterns into the night sky.

10 **BORYEONG MUD FESTIVAL**
July
During the Boryeong Mud Festival in South Korea, people swim, slide and wrestle in the mud, then kick back and relax to music and fireworks.

*Begins at sundown.
**Dates may vary slightly by location.

Around the World

11 ## ROSH HASHANAH
6*–8 September
A Jewish holiday marking the beginning of a new year on the Hebrew calendar. Celebrations include prayer, ritual foods and a day of rest.

12 ## DÍA DE LOS MUERTOS
31 October – 2 November
There's nothing scary about Día de los Muertos ('Day of the Dead'), a Mexican holiday that celebrates and honours the deceased. The three-day festival involves family gatherings, street fairs and visits to graveyards to leave gifts for loved ones who have passed away.

13 ## DIWALI
4 November
India's largest and most important holiday. People light their homes with clay lamps to symbolise the inner light that protects against spiritual darkness.

14 ## HANUKKAH
28 November* – 6 December
This Jewish holiday is eight days long. It commemorates the rededication of the Temple in Jerusalem. Hanukkah celebrations include the lighting of menorah candles for eight days and the exchange of gifts.

15 ## CHRISTMAS DAY
25 December
A Christian holiday marking the birth of Jesus Christ, Christmas is usually celebrated by decorating trees, exchanging presents and having festive gatherings.

2021 CALENDAR

JANUARY
S	M	T	W	T	F	S
					1	2
3	4	5	6	7	8	9
10	11	12	13	14	15	16
17	18	19	20	21	22	23
24	25	26	27	28	29	30
31						

FEBRUARY
S	M	T	W	T	F	S
	1	2	3	4	5	6
7	8	9	10	11	12	13
14	15	16	17	18	19	20
21	22	23	24	25	26	27
28						

MARCH
S	M	T	W	T	F	S
	1	2	3	4	5	6
7	8	9	10	11	12	13
14	15	16	17	18	19	20
21	22	23	24	25	26	27
28	29	30	31			

APRIL
S	M	T	W	T	F	S
				1	2	3
4	5	6	7	8	9	10
11	12	13	14	15	16	17
18	19	20	21	22	23	24
25	26	27	28	29	30	

MAY
S	M	T	W	T	F	S
						1
2	3	4	5	6	7	8
9	10	11	12	13	14	15
16	17	18	19	20	21	22
23	24	25	26	27	28	29
30	31					

JUNE
S	M	T	W	T	F	S
		1	2	3	4	5
6	7	8	9	10	11	12
13	14	15	16	17	18	19
20	21	22	23	24	25	26
27	28	29	30			

JULY
S	M	T	W	T	F	S
				1	2	3
4	5	6	7	8	9	10
11	12	13	14	15	16	17
18	19	20	21	22	23	24
25	26	27	28	29	30	31

AUGUST
S	M	T	W	T	F	S
1	2	3	4	5	6	7
8	9	10	11	12	13	14
15	16	17	18	19	20	21
22	23	24	25	26	27	28
29	30	31				

SEPTEMBER
S	M	T	W	T	F	S
			1	2	3	4
5	6	7	8	9	10	11
12	13	14	15	16	17	18
19	20	21	22	23	24	25
26	27	28	29	30		

OCTOBER
S	M	T	W	T	F	S
					1	2
3	4	5	6	7	8	9
10	11	12	13	14	15	16
17	18	19	20	21	22	23
24	25	26	27	28	29	30
31						

NOVEMBER
S	M	T	W	T	F	S
	1	2	3	4	5	6
7	8	9	10	11	12	13
14	15	16	17	18	19	20
21	22	23	24	25	26	27
28	29	30				

DECEMBER
S	M	T	W	T	F	S
			1	2	3	4
5	6	7	8	9	10	11
12	13	14	15	16	17	18
19	20	21	22	23	24	25
26	27	28	29	30	31	

HALLOWEEN PET PARADE

Forget sweets — these trick-or-treaters want belly scratches! Millions of pets will don a disguise for Halloween. Check out a few of the craziest getups.

What spell can I cast to get some oats and hay?

DISGUISED AS HARRY POTTER, RAMSEY THE HORSE MAKES MAGIC.

Stop in the name of the paw, er, law!

COREY THE DACHSHUND IS ARRESTING IN HIS WILD WEST SHERIFF GARB.

If you dress up your pet, check that the outfit is comfortable and allows the animal to breathe and walk safely.

I am one classy kitty.

ELROY THE CAT SHOWS GREAT STYLE DRESSED AS THE MAD HATTER FROM *ALICE'S ADVENTURES IN WONDERLAND.*

I'm ready to say "I do" to a chew toy and a belly rub.

TANK THE ENGLISH BULLDOG ROCKS A BRIDAL COSTUME.

What's Your Chinese Horoscope?
Locate your birth year to find out.

In Chinese astrology the zodiac runs on a 12-year cycle, based on the lunar calendar. Each year corresponds to one of 12 animals, each representing one of 12 personality types. Read on to find out which animal year you were born in and what that might say about you.

RAT
1972, '84, '96, 2008, '20
Say cheese! You're attractive, charming and creative. When you get angry, you can have really sharp teeth!

HORSE
1966, '78, '90, 2002, '14
Being happy is your 'mane' goal. And while you're clever and hardworking, your teacher may tell you off for horsing around.

OX
1973, '85, '97, 2009, '21
You're smart, patient and as strong as an ... well, you know what. Though you're a leader, you never brag.

SHEEP
1967, '79, '91, 2003, '15
Gentle as a lamb, you're also artistic, compassionate and wise. You're often shy.

TIGER
1974, '86, '98, 2010, '22
You may be a nice person, but no one should ever enter your room without asking—you might attack!

MONKEY
1968, '80, '92, 2004, '16
No 'monkey see, monkey do' for you. You're a clever problem-solver with an excellent memory.

RABBIT
1975, '87, '99, 2011
Your ambition and talent make you jump at opportunity. You also keep your ears open for gossip.

ROOSTER
1969, '81, '93, 2005, '17
You crow about your adventures, but inside you're really shy. You're thoughtful, capable, brave and talented.

DRAGON
1976, '88, 2000, '12
You're on fire! Health, energy, honesty and bravery make you a living legend.

DOG
1970, '82, '94, 2006, '18
Often the leader of the pack, you're loyal and honest. You can also keep a secret.

SNAKE
1977, '89, 2001, '13
You may not speak often, but you're very clever. You always seem to have a stash of cash.

PIG
1971, '83, '95, 2007, '19
Even though you're courageous, honest and kind, you never hog all the attention.

Try This! GINGERBREAD HOUSES

YOU WILL NEED

- VANILLA FROSTING
- CREAM OF TARTAR
- CARDBOARD
- RECTANGULAR GINGER BISCUITS
- SERRATED KNIFE (ASK FOR A PARENT'S HELP)
- ASSORTED SWEETS, PRETZELS AND BISCUITS, INCLUDING SQUARE CARAMELS (NOT SHOWN)
- SHREDDED COCONUT

WHAT TO DO

MIX THE 'GLUE': Frosting will hold each biscuit building together. Combine a tub of ready-made vanilla frosting with 1 gram cream of tartar. To apply the frosting, squeeze it out of a sealed freezer bag with a hole cut in one corner.

BUILD THE HOUSE:

BASE Cut a piece of cardboard that's big enough to hold the scene.

WALLS The front and back walls are each made of a whole biscuit turned horizontally. Ask a parent to create the two remaining sides. For each, use a serrated knife to gently saw the top of a whole biscuit into a peak (inset, above). Run a bead of frosting along the bottom edge and sides of the biscuits. 'Glue' them together in a rectangle on top of the cardboard. Prop up the walls while you work.

PEAKED ROOF Run frosting along the tops of the walls. Place two whole biscuits — turned horizontally — on top of the sides, using frosting to hold them in place. Let the frosting set overnight.

WAGON USE RECTANGULAR BISCUITS FOR THE BOTTOM AND HALF A BISCUIT FOR THE BACK. 'GLUE' THE PIECES IN PLACE. ADD PRETZEL WHEELS AND A CARAMEL UNDER THE WAGON FOR SUPPORT.

SILO CUT OFF THE TOPS OF TWO CONES, THEN FROST THE OPEN ENDS TOGETHER. STICK ON COLOURFUL LIQUORICE AND TOP WITH A FOIL MUFFIN CASE.

SNOWMAN SKEWER TWO MARSHMALLOWS ONTO A PRETZEL STICK. USE GUM-DROPS FOR THE HAT, EYES AND NOSE; PRETZELS FOR THE ARMS; AND STRING LIQUORICE FOR A SCARF.

Fun Winter Gift Idea

Snow Globes

YOU WILL NEED
- SMALL JAR WITH A LID (A BABY FOOD JAR WORKS WELL.)
- SANDPAPER
- INSTANT-BONDING GLUE (FOLLOW DIRECTIONS ON THE TUBE AND USE WITH ADULT SUPERVISION.)
- PLASTIC ANIMAL OR FIGURINE THAT FITS IN THE JAR
- NAIL POLISH REMOVER
- BABY OIL
- SMALL HANDFUL OF WHITE GLITTER

WHAT TO DO
Turn the jar's lid upside down. Use sandpaper to scuff the inside of the lid. Glue the bottom of the figurine to the centre of the lid. (Nail polish remover cleans glue off skin and surfaces.) Dry for four hours. Fill the jar with baby oil. Add glitter. To seal, put glue around the rim of the jar. Close the lid tightly and dry for four hours. Turn the jar over, and let it snow!

DOGHOUSE Follow the steps at left, but use small biscuits for all sides and the roof.

BARN Use rectangular biscuits for the barn's roof and sides. For the front and back, cut a peak in a whole biscuit (inset, above left).

DECORATIONS 'Glue' on your favourite treats to create doors, rooftops, trees and anything else you can imagine. Let everything set overnight. Cover the cardboard base with shredded coconut to finish your snowy scene.

DOG 'GLUE' TWO GUMDROPS TOGETHER TO FORM THE BODY. STICK ON PIECES OF GUMDROPS FOR THE EARS, NOSE AND TAIL.

MONEY AROUND THE WORLD!

Jordan's HALF-DINAR COIN has seven sides.

ACCORDING to some **PEOPLE,** **CANADA'S $100 BANKNOTE** gives off the scent of **MAPLE SYRUP.**

A British businessman created his own currency — named the **PUFFIN** — for an island he owned off England.

IN FEBRUARY 2015, SCUBA DIVERS OFF ISRAEL FOUND OVER 2,600 GOLD COINS DATING BACK AS FAR AS THE NINTH CENTURY.

BANCO CENTRAL DE CHILE
20 MIL PESOS
20000
VEINTE MIL PESOS

A **20,000**-PESO BANKNOTE FROM CHILE CONTAINS INK THAT CHANGES **COLOUR WHEN TILTED.**

The INCA called gold 'THE SWEAT OF THE SUN' and silver 'THE TEARS OF THE MOON'.

THE U.K. DECIMAL HALFPENNY WENT INTO CIRCULATION IN FEBRUARY **1971** AND WAS WITHDRAWN IN DECEMBER **1984.**

I knew I should've tried a fake ATM instead

IN 2002, A MAN OPENED A FAKE BANK AND TOOK IN **$650,000** BEFORE HE WAS CAUGHT.

COINS CREATED IN **1616** FOR WHAT IS NOW **BERMUDA** WERE NICKNAMED **'HOGGIES'** BECAUSE THEY PICTURED **HOGS.**

A 1913 U.S. LIBERTY HEAD NICKEL—ONE OF ONLY FIVE IN EXISTENCE— **SOLD AT** AUCTION FOR MORE THAN **$3.1 MILLION.**

THE PHRASE **'BRING HOME THE BACON'** STARTED AFTER A 12TH-CENTURY PRIEST REWARDED A MARRIED COUPLE WITH A SIDE OF BACON.

A BRITISH ARTIST MADE A DRESS OUT OF USED **BANKNOTES** FROM AROUND THE **WORLD.**

MONEY TIP! WHEN YOU GET YOUR ALLOWANCE OR A CASH GIFT, BREAK IT INTO **SMALLER NOTES.** SPEND ONLY HALF AND STASH THE REST IN YOUR **PIGGY BANK.**

193

15 Ways to Say Hello

1. ARMENIAN: **Barev**
2. DUTCH: **Goedendag**
3. FINNISH: **Hei**
4. FRENCH: **Bonjour**
5. GREEK: **Yia sou**
6. HEBREW: **Shalom**
7. HINDI: **Namaste**
8. ICELANDIC: **Halló**
9. ITALIAN: **Ciao**
10. MANDARIN: **Ni hao**
11. RUSSIAN: **Privyet**
12. SPANISH: **Hola**
13. SWAHILI: **Jambo**
14. TURKISH: **Merhaba**
15. WELSH: **Helô**

LANGUAGES IN PERIL

TODAY, there are more than 7,000 languages spoken on Earth. But by 2100, more than half of those may disappear. In fact, experts say one language dies every two weeks, due to the increasing dominance of larger languages, such as English, Spanish and Mandarin. So what can be done to keep dialects from disappearing? Efforts like National Geographic's Enduring Voices Project have been created to track and document the world's most threatened indigenous languages, such as Tofa, spoken only by people in Siberia, and Magati Ke, from Aboriginal Australia. The hope is to preserve these languages — and the cultures they belong to.

10 LEADING LANGUAGES

Approximate population of first-language speakers (in millions)

1. Chinese*	1,311
2. Spanish	460
3. English	379
4. Arabic	341
5. Hindi	319
6. Bengali	228
7. Portuguese	221
8. Russian	154
9. Japanese	128
10. Punjabi	93

Some languages have only a few hundred speakers, while Chinese has about 1.3 billion native speakers worldwide. That's nearly triple the next largest group of language speakers. Colonial expansion, trade and migration account for the spread of the other most widely spoken languages. With growing use of the internet, English is becoming the language of the technology age.

*Includes all forms of the language.

By the NuMBers

HIT THE **BOOKS**

Got a minute? If you spend a little time reading each day, by the time you reach high school you'll be a reading wizard. Check out how many times you can read *Harry Potter and the Philosopher's Stone* if you read a little —or a lot—every day.

IF YOU READ **1 HOUR** EVERY DAY

EVERY YEAR, A YEAR 7 PUPIL WILL HAVE READ: **3,285,000 words**

THAT'S THE SAME AS READING *HARRY POTTER AND THE PHILOSOPHER'S STONE:* **42 times**

FROM YEAR 1 TO THE END OF SIXTH FORM, YOU'LL HAVE READ FOR NEARLY: **198 days**

IF YOU READ **20 MINUTES** EVERY DAY

EVERY YEAR, A YEAR 7 PUPIL WILL HAVE READ: **1,095,000 words**

THAT'S THE SAME AS READING *HARRY POTTER AND THE PHILOSOPHER'S STONE:* **14 times**

FROM YEAR 1 TO THE END OF SIXTH FORM, YOU'LL HAVE READ FOR NEARLY: **66 days**

IF YOU READ **5 MINUTES** EVERY DAY

EVERY YEAR, A YEAR 7 PUPIL WILL HAVE READ: **273,750 words**

THAT'S THE SAME AS READING *HARRY POTTER AND THE PHILOSOPHER'S STONE:* **3.5 times**

FROM YEAR 1 TO THE END OF SIXTH FORM, YOU'LL HAVE READ FOR NEARLY: **14 days**

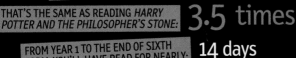

MYTHOLOGY

GREEK

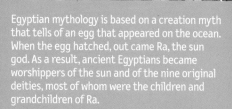

EGYPTIAN

The ancient Greeks believed that many gods and goddesses ruled the universe. According to this mythology, the Olympians lived high atop Greece's Mount Olympus. Each of these 12 main gods and goddesses had a unique personality that corresponded to particular aspects of life, such as love or death.

Egyptian mythology is based on a creation myth that tells of an egg that appeared on the ocean. When the egg hatched, out came Ra, the sun god. As a result, ancient Egyptians became worshippers of the sun and of the nine original deities, most of whom were the children and grandchildren of Ra.

THE OLYMPIANS

Aphrodite was the goddess of love and beauty.

Apollo, Zeus's son, was the god of the sun, music and healing. Artemis was his twin.

Ares, Zeus's son, was the god of war.

Artemis, Zeus's daughter and Apollo's twin, was the goddess of the hunt and of childbirth.

Athena, born from the forehead of Zeus, was the goddess of wisdom and crafts.

Demeter was the goddess of fertility and nature.

Hades, Zeus's brother, was the god of the underworld and the dead.

Hephaestus, the son of Hera, was the god of fire.

Hera, the wife and older sister of Zeus, was the goddess of women and marriage.

Hermes, Zeus's son, was the messenger of the gods.

Poseidon, the brother of Zeus, was the god of the seas and earthquakes.

Zeus was the most powerful of the gods and the top Olympian. He wielded a thunderbolt and was the god of the sky and thunder.

THE NINE DEITIES

Geb, son of Shu and Tefnut, was the god of the earth.

Isis (Ast), daughter of Geb and Nut, was the goddess of fertility and motherhood.

Nephthys (Nebet-Hut), daughter of Geb and Nut, was protector of the dead.

Nut, daughter of Shu and Tefnut, was the goddess of the sky.

Osiris (Usir), son of Geb and Nut, was the god of the afterlife.

Ra (Re), the sun god, is generally viewed as the creator. He represents life and health.

Seth (Set), son of Geb and Nut, was the god of the desert and chaos.

Shu, son of Ra, was the god of air.

Tefnut, daughter of Ra, was the goddess of rain.

All cultures around the world have unique legends and traditions that have been passed down over generations. Many myths refer to gods or supernatural heroes who are responsible for occurrences in the world. For example, Norse mythology tells of the red-bearded Thor, the god of thunder, who is responsible for creating lightning and thunderstorms. And many creation myths, especially those from some of North America's native cultures, tell of an earth-diver represented as an animal that brings a piece of sand or mud up from the deep sea. From this tiny piece of earth, the entire world takes shape.

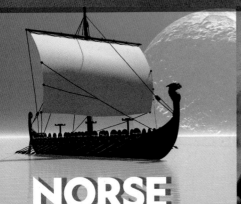

NORSE

ROMAN

Norse mythology originated in Scandinavia, in northern Europe. It was complete with gods and goddesses who lived in a heavenly place called Asgard that could be reached only by crossing a rainbow bridge.

While Norse mythology is lesser known, we use it every day. Most days of the week are named after Norse gods, including some of these major deities.

NORSE GODS

Balder was the god of light and beauty.

Freya was the goddess of love, beauty and fertility.

Frigg, for whom Friday was named, was the queen of Asgard. She was the goddess of marriage, motherhood and the home.

Heimdall was the watchman of the rainbow bridge and the guardian of the gods.

Hel, the daughter of Loki, was the goddess of death.

Loki, a shape-shifter, was a trickster who helped the gods — and caused them problems.

Skadi was the goddess of winter and of the hunt. She is often represented as 'The Snow Queen'.

Thor, for whom Thursday was named, was the god of thunder and lightning.

Tyr, for whom Tuesday was named, was the god of the sky and war.

Wodan, for whom Wednesday was named, was the god of war, wisdom, death and magic.

Much of Roman mythology was adopted from Greek mythology, but the Romans also developed a lot of original myths as well. The gods of Roman mythology lived everywhere, and each had a role to play. There were thousands of Roman gods, but here are a few of the stars of Roman myths.

ANCIENT ROMAN GODS

Ceres was the goddess of the harvest and motherly love.

Diana, daughter of Jupiter, was the goddess of hunting and the moon.

Juno, Jupiter's wife, was the goddess of women and fertility.

Jupiter, the patron of Rome and master of the gods, was the god of the sky.

Mars, the son of Jupiter and Juno, was the god of war.

Mercury, the son of Jupiter, was the messenger of the gods and the god of travellers.

Minerva was the goddess of wisdom, learning and the arts and crafts.

Neptune, the brother of Jupiter, was the god of the sea.

Venus was the goddess of love and beauty.

Vesta was the goddess of fire and the hearth. She was one of the most important of the Roman deities.

GREEK MYTHS

POSEIDON: GOD OF THE SEAS

Poseidon—along with his brother Hades and his sisters, Hestia, Demeter and Hera —was swallowed at birth by his father, Cronus. Then a sixth child, Zeus, who was never swallowed, and thus had never known humiliation, freed them. Poseidon sized things up: Zeus was a force to be reckoned with—he was the guy to follow.

For 10 long years, the six brothers and sisters fought their father and aunts and uncles—the mighty Titans. It was a nasty war, but what war isn't? Poseidon gritted his teeth and did his part. He was no coward, after all. But now and then there was a lull in the battle, perhaps because Zeus got distracted or because the Titans needed a rest. Who knew? Whatever the case, Poseidon was grateful, and in those moments he took refuge in visiting Pontus, the ancient god of all the waters, the partner to his grandmother Gaia, Mother Earth, and his grandfather Uranus, Father Heaven. He swam in Pontus's waters, and despite how badly his life had gone so far, despite all the long years of savage war, he was happy.

Best of all, Poseidon found a friend in Nereus. He loved the watery depths as much as Poseidon did. Together they plunged to the corals and sponges that lived along the seabed. They rode on the backs of turtles. They flapped their arms like the rays they followed, then let their arms hang in the water, moving at the whim of the currents.

But then it was back to war ... until the glorious moment when the hundred-handed sons of Gaia joined the battle on Zeus's side, and then the Cyclopes gave Zeus the thunderbolt and Hades the helmet that made him invisible and Poseidon the trident. It worked, that

POSEIDON, GOD OF THE SEAS, WITH HIS TRIDENT

TREASURY OF GREEK MYTHOLOGY

CHECK OUT THIS BOOK!

With his hair flying out behind him, he swam the seas in search of those who might need help. And when he wasn't patrolling, he let himself be absorbed in the watery mysteries.

That's when he discovered the finest mystery ever. She was the daughter of the sea god Phorcys and the sea goddess Ceto. That heritage made her the perfect wife in Poseidon's eyes. She was one of three sisters, called the Gorgons. The other two sisters were immortal, like the gods. But Medusa, as she was called, was mortal.

Poseidon found her mortality that much more alluring. How amazing to know someone vulnerable. He put his arms out and let the serpents of her hair swarm around them. Good! Those serpents could bite and poison —good protection. He gingerly touched the wings that jutted from her shoulder blades. Good! Those wings could carry her far from an attacker. He stroked her scales. Very good! They were harder than armour. And most assuring of all, she had a special power: Anything mortal that looked directly at her face would turn instantly to stone.

And so Poseidon felt almost safe in loving Medusa. They reveled together comfortably in his sea kingdom. At least for a while ...

trident. Poseidon struck it on the ground and the entire Earth shook. The Olympian gods won.

Zeus appointed Poseidon ruler of the seas. Poseidon knew his brother felt the seas were an inferior realm. Ha! Nothing could've pleased Poseidon more.

THE MORTAL MEDUSA EMBRACES HER HUSBAND, POSEIDON.

World Religions

Around the world, religion takes many forms. Some belief systems, such as Christianity, Islam and Judaism, are monotheistic, meaning that followers believe in just one supreme being. Others, like Hinduism, Shintoism and most native belief systems, are polytheistic, meaning that many of their followers believe in multiple gods.

All of the major religions have their origins in Asia, but they have spread around the world. Christianity, with the largest number of followers, has three divisions — Roman Catholic, Eastern Orthodox and Protestant. Islam, with about one-fifth of all believers, has two main divisions — Sunni and Shiite. Hinduism and Buddhism account for almost another one-fifth of believers. Judaism, dating back some 4,000 years, has more than 13 million followers, less than one percent of all believers.

CHRISTIANITY

Based on the teachings of Jesus Christ, a Jew born about 2,000 years ago in the area of modern-day Israel, Christianity has spread worldwide and actively seeks converts. Followers in Switzerland (above) participate in an Easter season procession with lanterns and crosses.

BUDDHISM

Founded about 2,400 years ago in northern India by the Hindu prince Gautama Buddha, Buddhism spread throughout East and Southeast Asia. Buddhist temples have statues, such as the Mihintale Buddha (above) in Sri Lanka.

HINDUISM

Dating back more than 4,000 years, Hinduism is practised mainly in India. Hindus follow sacred texts known as the Vedas and believe in reincarnation. During the festival of Navratri, which honours the goddess Durga, the Garba dance is performed (above).

Novice Monks

Members of the Wild Boars youth football team were rescued from a flooded Thai cave in July 2018. A few weeks later, 11 of the boys were ordained as novice Buddhist monks and spent nine days in a monastery. This act honoured Saman Gunan, a Thai Navy SEAL who died while rescuing them.

ISLAM

Muslims believe that the Quran, Islam's sacred book, records the words of Allah (God) as revealed to the Prophet Muhammad beginning around A.D. 610. Believers (above) circle the Kaaba in the Haram Mosque in Mecca, Saudi Arabia, the spiritual centre of the faith.

JUDAISM

The traditions, laws and beliefs of Judaism date back to Abraham (the Patriarch) and the Torah (the first five books of the Old Testament). Followers pray before the Western Wall (above), which stands below Islam's Dome of the Rock in Jerusalem.

QUIZ WHIZ

How vast is
your knowledge about
the world around you?
Quiz yourself!

Write your answers
on a piece of paper.
Then check them below.

1 Chinese astrology uses _____ to represent personality traits.

a. mythical characters
b. animals
c. numbers
d. letters

2 Natto, a delicacy popular in Japan, is said to smell like _____.

a. vinegar
b. marshmallows
c. peanut butter
d. sweaty socks

3 A rare U.S. nickel from 1913 sold at auction for more than _____.

a. $3,000,000
b. $300,000
c. $30,000
d. $3,000

4 _____ is a holiday honouring the patron saint of Ireland.

5 **True or false?** In Greek mythology, the snake-headed Medusa was immortal.

Not **STUMPED** yet? Check out the
NATIONAL GEOGRAPHIC KIDS QUIZ WHIZ collection
for more crazy **CULTURE** questions!

ANSWERS: 1. b; 2. d; 3. a; 4. St. Patrick's Day; 5. False. She was mortal.

HOMEWORK HELP

Explore a New Culture

STAMPS OF BRAZIL

CURRENCY AND COINS OF BRAZIL

FLAG OF BRAZIL

YOU'RE A STUDENT, but you're also a citizen of the world. Writing a report on a foreign nation or your own country is a great way to better understand and appreciate how different people live. Pick the country of your ancestors, one that's been in the news or one that you'd like to visit one day.

Passport to Success

A country report follows the format of an expository essay because you're 'exposing' information about the country you choose.

The following step-by-step tips will help you with this monumental task.

 1 RESEARCH. Gathering information is the most important step in writing a good country report. Look to internet sources, encyclopedias, books, magazine and newspaper articles and other sources to find important and interesting details about your subject.

2 ORGANISE YOUR NOTES. Put the information you have gathered into a rough outline. For example, sort everything you have found about the country's system of government, climate, etc.

3 WRITE IT UP. Follow the basic structure of good writing: introduction, body and conclusion. Remember that each paragraph should have a topic sentence that is then supported by facts and details. Incorporate the information from your notes, but make sure it's in your own words. And make your writing flow with good transitions and descriptive language.

4 ADD VISUALS. Include maps, diagrams, photos and other visual aids.

 5 PROOFREAD AND REVISE. Correct any mistakes, and polish your language. Do your best!

6 CITE YOUR SOURCES. Be sure to keep a record of your sources.

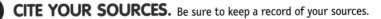

Students in Lahore, Pakistan, hit the runway to model recycled waste clothing in the Roots Ivy Recycling Fashion Fiesta to urge environmental support through education.

GOING
GREEN

Bet You Didn't Know!

10 recyclable facts

1
Nearly **half** of all fruits and vegetables grown are **wasted.**

2
It can take up to **200 years** for an aluminium can to decompose.

3
More than **95 percent** of food waste could have been **composted.**

Glass is 100 percent **recyclable** and can be used again and again. **4**

5
The average American **throws away** about **0.4 kilogram** (almost 1 lb) **of food a day.**

A mall in **Sweden** sells only recycled, reused and sustainably produced goods. **6**

about trash

7 One million plastic drinks bottles are sold every minute around the world.

8 Single-use plastic makes up about **40 percent** of all plastic produced.

9 In terms of weight, it's estimated that the ocean will contain **more plastic than fish** by 2050.

10 Mount Everest has banned single-use plastics to reduce litter left by trekkers and climbers.

Plastic bags floating in the ocean

Save the Ocean!

DUCK RESCUE

A CARING HUMAN RESCUES AN INJURED BIRD FROM A PLASTIC RING.

When white-faced whistling ducks are alarmed, they stand up straight and freeze.

A white-faced whistling duck walks backwards with its head between its feet. It shakes its beak, stops to rest and shakes again. The duck's odd movements catch the attention of Glenda Maguire, who's been watching the visiting animal from her patio in South Africa. Using her camera to zoom in for a closer look, she sees a ring of white plastic — likely from a milk bottle — wrapped around the duck's mouth and neck. She wants to help, but she knows if she tries to catch it, the wild duck will fly away and not come back to the lake.

Maguire sets out an animal trap with food pellets near the water. But the duck seems scared of the trap and later flies away. Maguire hopes that someone will save the duck before it's too late.

RIVER TO SEA

Freshwater streams, lakes and rivers are often the starting point for plastic that ends up in the ocean. "On a windy day you can see plastic bags and bottles tumbling around on the ground," says Carlie Herring, a research analyst with the National Oceanic and Atmospheric Administration in the U.S. "Those items might end up in a stream, then a river and eventually the ocean."

One group of researchers found hundreds of thousands of pieces of plastic in just one square mile of North America's Great Lakes, one of the world's largest freshwater systems. That includes microplastic — supersmall plastic pieces about the size of the full stop at the end of this sentence. According to Herring, micro-plastics have been found in drinking water and may hurt wildlife like the white-faced whistling duck, which could mistake the plastic for food.

TAKING FLIGHT

After two days, the little duck returns to the lake. But it's clearly in trouble. "It was just hanging its head, as if it had given up," Maguire says. But finally, three days later, the duck eventually walks into Maguire's cage and — *snap!* — she pulls a string to close the door. After retrieving the bird, she wraps a towel around it and carefully cuts the plastic loop off before releasing the duck back into the wild.

The exhausted duck spends two days resting and eating nearby as its flock comes and goes. Eventually the duck is ready to fly away and return to its family.

Save the Ocean!

SEAL RESCUE

FISHERMEN SCOOP UP A HARBOUR SEAL TRAPPED IN PLASTIC NETS.

Harbour seals can't rotate their hind flippers forward to walk on land—they can only scoot forward on their bellies.

Experts think just one fishing net can entangle up to 40 animals.

In the northeastern United States, about 880 seals were accidentally caught in fishing nets over a seven-year period.

A harbour seal pup floats in the water off the coast of Maine, U.S.A. The young seal has recently left its mother's care—and it's already in trouble. The little seal has a massive tangle of fishing nets wrapped around its body. Without help, the pup will not escape. Luckily a fishing boat passes by, and the people on board prepare to rescue the helpless animal.

POLAR PROBLEMS

Harbour seals live in coastal waters in the Northern Hemisphere, which includes polar habitats in the Arctic. It might seem like this region—and southern polar habitats around Antarctica—would be plastic free because few people live there. But ocean currents carry the rubbish to these regions, where it has nowhere to go.

"The ocean is the ultimate transporter on our planet," environmental engineer Jenna Jambeck says. "Once plastic that floats enters the ocean, the currents can take it all over the world, including to the Arctic." In fact, one study of the Svalbard Islands near the North Pole found polar bears and reindeer entangled in plastic.

Scientists have also discovered microplastics frozen in Arctic sea ice: One study shows 12,000 particles of microplastic in one litre—or about four cups—of sea ice. "When even the sea ice has microplastic—well, then pollution is everywhere," says Carlie Herring, a research analyst with the National Oceanic and Atmospheric Administration in the U.S. Experts worry that as the ice caps melt, they'll release these microplastics into the seas, putting more animals like the harbour seal pup in danger.

SAVED SEAL

The fishermen quickly scoop the seal out of the water and onto their boat. One of the fishermen holds the seal in place, using a knife to slowly cut the thick netting off the animal, one rope at a time. The seal is still at first but tries to wiggle away as it feels the net loosen. The fishermen keep the marine mammal calm for just a few more minutes until all the rope is off.

Finally the animal is no longer trapped in plastic. A fisherman gently lowers the pup into the water. The uninjured seal floats for a few seconds as it gets used to its surroundings. Then it gracefully swims away.

Pollution

Cleaning Up Our Act

So what's the big deal about a little dirt on the planet? Pollution can affect animals, plants and people. In fact, some studies show that more people die every year from diseases linked to air pollution than from car accidents. And right now nearly one billion of the world's people don't have access to clean drinking water.

A LITTLE POLLUTION = BIG PROBLEMS

You can probably clean your room in a couple of hours. (At least we hope you can!) But you can't shove air and water pollution under your bed or stuff them into the wardrobe. Once released into the environment, pollution — whether it's oil leaking from a boat or chemicals spewing from a factory's chimney — can have a lasting environmental impact.

KEEP IT CLEAN

It's easy to blame things like big factories for pollution problems. But some of the mess comes from everyday activities. Exhaust fumes from cars and rubbish in landfills can seriously trash Earth's health. We all need to pitch in and do some housecleaning. It may mean cycling more and riding in cars less. Or not dumping water-polluting oil or household cleaners down the drain. Look at it this way: Just as with your room, it's always better not to let Earth get messed up in the first place.

kids VS. PLASTIC

A straw stuck in a sea turtle's nostril. A seahorse swimming along with its tail curled around a cotton bud. Seabirds washing up on sandy shores, entangled in plastic bags. Sadly, we do not have to look too far to see how animals are directly impacted by the staggering amount of plastic piling up on our planet. We've created more than 6.3 billion tonnes (6.9 billion tons) of plastic waste, with only a small percentage landing in recycling bins. The rest of it lingers in landfills and winds up in our oceans. In fact, 700 species of animals are threatened because of ocean waste — and among seabirds, a whopping 90 percent eat discarded plastic, according to a study. But as scary as these stats are, we can do something about them. Experts say it all starts with reducing the amount of plastic we use, including options for reusable containers or those materials that can't fully break down in the ocean. You can also pledge to do your part to reduce the plastic problem by visiting natgeokids.com/plastic. Together, we can work to cut back on plastic and protect our planet — and everything on it.

Declining Biodiversity

Saving All Creatures, Great and Small

Earth is home to a huge mix of plants and animals — millions and possibly billions of species — and scientists have officially identified and named only about 1.9 million so far! Scientists call this healthy mix biodiversity.

THE BALANCING ACT

The bad news is that half of the planet's plant and animal species may be on the path to extinction, mainly because of human activity. People cut down trees, build roads and houses, pollute rivers, overfish and overhunt. The good news is that many people care. Scientists and volunteers race against the clock every day, working to save wildlife before time runs out. By building birdhouses, planting trees and following the rules for hunting and fishing, you can be a positive force for preserving biodiversity, too. Every time you do something to help a species survive, you help our planet to thrive.

Green sea turtle

Habitats Threatened

Living on the Edge

Even though tropical rainforests cover only about 7 percent of the planet's total land surface, they are home to half of all known species of plants and animals. Because people cut down so many trees for lumber and firewood and clear so much land for farms, hundreds of thousands of acres of rainforest disappear every year.

SHARING THE LAND

Wetlands are also important feeding and breeding grounds. People have drained many wetlands, turning them into farm fields or sites for other industries. More than half the world's wetlands have disappeared within the past century, squeezing wildlife out. Balancing the needs of humans and animals is the key to lessening habitat destruction.

Jaguar

211

kids

MAKE THIS > POM-POM DECORATIONS
TO AVOID THAT > PLASTIC BALLOONS

vs. PLASTIC

POM-POM PUFFS

Help keep Earth healthy by ditching single-use plastic items. Decorate your next party with paper pom-pom balls instead of balloons.

Why? Balloons released into the air or left outside can end up in the ocean, where they might entangle animals or be mistaken for food.

❯ MATERIALS

- 8 sheets of equal-sized tissue paper (Bigger tissue paper will make bigger pom-poms.)
- 1 craft pipe cleaner
- Scissors
- String (optional)

NOTE: Please look for recycled tissue paper when possible.

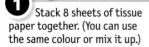

❯ STEPS

1 Stack 8 sheets of tissue paper together. (You can use the same colour or mix it up.)

2 Fold the tissue paper back and forth in 2.5-centimetre (1-in) sections like an accordion. Press each fold firmly.

3 Wrap the pipe cleaner around the centre of the folded tissue-paper stack, then twist the pipe cleaner to secure it.

4 Trim the pipe cleaner with scissors, then wrap the end of the pipe cleaner around itself so the wire doesn't poke out.

5 Cut both ends of the tissue-paper stack into rounded, pointed or frilly shapes.

6 Flip the tissue-paper stack on its side.

7 Separate each layer of tissue paper one at a time.

8 Pull the layers up and toward the centre.

9 To hang your pom-pom, tie a piece of string to the centre of the pipe cleaner.

10 WAYS YOU CAN SAVE THE OCEAN FROM PLASTIC

1 Opt for reusable containers and bottles for your food and drinks.

2 Stock up on metal or paper straws—and stop using plastic straws altogether.

3 Encourage restaurants in your community to stop offering plastic utensils. Find tips for talking to restaurants at natgeokids.com/KidsVsPlastic.

4 Convince your family to switch over to tote bags instead of plastic bags when you go food shopping.

5 Always be sure to recycle as many plastic items as you can.

6 Don't be a litterbug! Any refuse left in the environment may blow into creeks or rivers and eventually make its way into the ocean.

7 Instead of tossing plastic junk away, try to see if you can repurpose or 'upcycle' any of it to create something new.

8 Hungry? Reach for fruits like apples, bananas and oranges over snack packs, which use extra packaging.

9 Organise a local beach, lake or creek cleanup with your friends and family.

10 Reduce your plastic waste at school: Use pencils made of wood instead of plastic mechanical pencils.

A GLOBAL RACE TO ZERO WASTE

BOTH SWEDEN (MAIN PHOTO) AND SINGAPORE (INSET) ARE WORLDWIDE LEADERS IN RECYCLING AND WASTE REDUCTION.

It's an ambitious goal, but one that some countries hope to achieve in less than 10 years. The aim? Zero waste, meaning every single piece of rubbish will be reused or composted. The idea may seem impossible, but several spots are coming close.

Take Sweden, for example. Less than one percent of the country's household waste ends up in landfill. Rather, the Swedes recycle nearly everything — some 1.5 billion bottles and cans annually — and the rest winds up at waste-to-energy plants to produce electricity. The programme is so successful that Sweden actually imports rubbish from other places, such as the United Kingdom, Norway and Ireland,

DUBAI — HOME TO THE FAMOUS PALM JUMEIRAH ISLAND — IS AIMING TO GO WASTE FREE BY 2030.

to keep up the rapid pace of its incinerators.

Other places narrowing in on zero waste? The Himalayan country of Bhutan is aiming for that status by 2030, while Singapore and Dubai have announced similar timelines. In the United States, individual cities like San Francisco and New York have also declared their dedication to going zero waste. The U.S. National Park Service, as well as major corporations like Lego and Nike, are also making big moves towards creating zero waste — all in an effort to make this world a cleaner place.

So what's the secret to zero waste? It's all about enforcing the rules of reducing, reusing and recycling. In Sweden, for example, recycling stations must be no more than 300 metres (984 ft) from any residential area. And in Bhutan — which is aspiring to become the world's first nation to have an all-organic farming system — composting from food scraps is the norm. Simple practices like these, as well as educating the public on the problems that stem from too much rubbish, can lead to major changes. And, perhaps, zero waste around the world one day.

FROM FILTH **TO** FASHION

Order up! One creative company called Garbage Gone Glam made this dress out of restaurant menus. Other things they've made? A cocktail dress out of playing cards and a ball gown out of old magazines!

HOW SOME WASTE TRAVELS FROM THE RECYCLING CENTRE TO THE CATWALKS — AND EVEN TO YOUR WARDROBE

A hat made out of an old football brings new meaning to the term 'header'.

This eco-friendly bag is made from 365 recycled computer keyboard keys.

This head-piece, made from recycled corrugated cardboard, is hard to top!

LEVI STRAUSS & CO. MAKES JEANS OUT OF OLD COTTON T-SHIRTS.

This bow tie made out of an old aluminium can is both fashion-forward and eco-friendly.

WORLD ENERGY & MINERALS

Almost everything people do — from cooking to powering the International Space Station — requires energy. But energy comes in different forms. Traditional energy sources, still used by many people in the developing world, include burning dried animal dung and wood. Industrialised countries and urban centres around the world rely on coal, oil and natural gas — called fossil fuels because they formed from decayed plant and animal material accumulated from long ago. Fossil fuel deposits, either in the ground or under the ocean floor, are unevenly distributed on Earth, and only some countries can afford to buy them.

Fossil fuels are also not renewable, meaning they will run out one day. And unless we find other ways to create energy, we'll be stuck. Without energy we won't be able to drive cars, use lights or send emails to friends.

TAKING A TOLL

Environmentally speaking, burning fossil fuels isn't necessarily the best choice, either: Carbon dioxide from the burning of fossil fuels, as well as other emissions, are contributing to global warming. Concerned scientists are looking at new ways to harness renewable, alternative sources of energy, such as water, wind and sun.

HIGH VOLTAGE

It seems like we use electricity for everything — from TVs and mobile phones to air conditioners and computers. In fact, power plants generate 3.7 times more electrical power than they did just 40 years ago. How they do this can differ around the world. Is it from burning coal or from taming the energy in moving water? Here's the global breakdown.

5% OTHER, SUCH AS GEOTHERMAL, SOLAR, WIND, HEAT, ETC.

5% OIL

10.9% NUCLEAR

16.2% HYDROPOWER

40.4% COAL

22.5% NATURAL GAS

Electricity travels at the speed of light — about 299,340 kilometres a second (186,000 mi/s).

216

Climate CHANGE

POLAR BEAR ON A PIECE OF MELTING ICEBERG

Rising Temperatures, Explained

Fact: The world is getting warmer.
Earth's surface temperature has been increasing. In the past 50 years, our planet has warmed twice as fast as in the 50 years before that. This is the direct effect of climate change, which refers not only to the increase in Earth's average temperature (known as global warming), but also to the long-term effects on winds, rain and ocean currents. Global warming is the reason glaciers and polar ice sheets are melting — resulting in rising sea levels and shrinking habitats. This makes survival for some animals a big challenge. Warming also means more flooding along the coasts and drought for inland areas.

Why are temperatures climbing?
Some of the recent climate changes can be tied to natural causes — such as changes in the sun's intensity, the unusually warm ocean

SCIENTISTS ARE CONCERNED THAT GREENLAND'S ICE SHEET HAS BEGUN TO MELT IN SUMMER. BIRTHDAY CANYON, SHOWN HERE, WAS CARVED BY MELTWATER.

currents of El Niño and volcanic activity — but human activities are a major factor as well.

Everyday activities that require burning fossil fuels, such as driving petrol-powered cars, contribute to global warming. These activities produce greenhouse gases, which enter the atmosphere and trap heat. At the current rate, Earth's global average temperature is projected to rise between 1 and 6.4°C (1.8 and 11.5°F) by the year 2100, and it will get even warmer after that. And as the climate continues to warm, it will unfortunately continue to affect the environment and our society in many ways.

217

QUIZ WHIZ

What's your eco-friendly IQ? Find out with this quiz!

Write your answers on a piece of paper. Then check them below.

1 **True or false?** Sweden imports waste from other countries to recycle.

2 Researchers found hundreds of thousands of _____ in just one square mile of North America's Great Lakes.
a. pieces of plastic   c. boats
b. fish   d. snakes

3 What's considered a major threat to harbour seals?
a. pollution
b. fishing nets
c. microplastics
d. all of the above

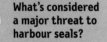

4 Some 700 species of animals are severely threatened because of _____ waste.
a. ocean
b. food
c. electronic
d. paper

5 **True or false?** In the past 50 years, Earth has warmed twice as fast as in the 50 years before that.

Not **STUMPED** yet? Check out the *NATIONAL GEOGRAPHIC KIDS QUIZ WHIZ* collection for more crazy **ENVIRONMENT** questions!

ANSWERS: 1. True; 2. a; 3. d; 4. a; 5. True

HOMEWORK HELP

Write a Letter That Gets Results

Knowing how to write a good letter is a useful skill. It will come in handy when you want to persuade someone to understand your point of view. Whether you're emailing your member of parliament or writing a letter for a school project or to your grandma, a great letter will help you get your message across. Most importantly, a well-written letter leaves a good impression.

CHECK OUT THE EXAMPLE BELOW FOR THE ELEMENTS OF A GOOD LETTER.

Your address

Date

Salutation
Always use 'Dear' followed by the person's name; use Mr, Mrs, Ms or Dr as appropriate.

Introductory paragraph
Give the reason you're writing the letter.

Body
The longest part of the letter, which provides evidence that supports your position. Be persuasive!

Closing paragraph
Sum up your argument.

Complimentary closing
Sign off with 'Sincerely' or 'Thank you'.

Your signature

Abby Jones
12 Green Street
Lincoln
LN3 4EG

22 April 2021

Dear Ms Headteacher,

I am writing to you about how much excess energy our school uses and to offer a solution.

Every day, we leave the computers on in the classroom. The TVs are plugged in all the time, and the lights are on all day. All of this adds up to a lot of wasted energy, which is not only harmful for the Earth, as it increases the amount of harmful greenhouse gas emissions into the environment, but is also costly to the school. In fact, I read that schools spend more on energy bills than on computers and textbooks combined!

I am suggesting that we start an Energy Committee to monitor the use of lighting, air-conditioning, heating and other energy systems within our school. My idea is to have a group of students dedicated to working out ways we can cut back on our energy use in the school. We can do room checks, provide reminders to students and teachers to turn off lights and computers, replace old lightbulbs with energy-efficient products and even reward the classrooms that do the most to save energy.

Above all, I think our school could help the environment tremendously by cutting back on how much energy we use. Let's see an Energy Committee at our school soon. Thank you.

Sincerely,

Abby Jones

Abby Jones

COMPLIMENTARY CLOSINGS

Sincerely, Sincerely yours, Thank you, Regards, Best wishes, Respectfully,

219

HISTORY HAPPENS

Petra, an ancient city carved into the cliffs of southern Jordan, was voted one of the New Seven Wonders of the World.

Bet You Didn't Know!

10 awesome facts about the

1 Egypt's **Lighthouse** of **Alexandria,** the world's first lighthouse, used **mirrors** to **reflect sunlight** for miles out to sea.

2 **Australian Aboriginals,** people from the world's oldest living culture, have **existed** for at least **50,000 years.**

3 The ancient **Celts** believed the **head** was the **seat of the soul.**

4 An ancient **'snack bar'** was recently **unearthed** in the **ruins** of the **city** of **Pompeii,** in Italy.

5 In **China,** the earliest **writing** dates to around **1200** B.C. and was **inscribed on the bones of animals.**

Ancient Aboriginal rock art, Australian outback

ancient world

6 Ancient Egyptians lined linen bandages with **honey** to get them to **stick to skin.**

7 A 2,400-year-old Greek **sailing vessel** was **discovered** at the **bottom of the Black Sea.**

8 People have lived in the **Citadel** — the world's oldest neighbourhood, in northern Iraq — **for at least 7,000 years.**

9 Many ancient Mesopotamians had **working toilets** in their **homes.**

10 Archaeologists found traces of **chocolate** in **pots** from the **Maya civilisation,** dating back more than **2,500 years.**

The Search for Alexander the Great's
Lost Tomb

ARCHAEOLOGIST CALLIOPE LIMNEOS-PAPAKOSTA

A PAINTING OF ALEXANDER ON HORSEBACK AT THE BATTLE WITH PORUS IN 326 B.C.

After a long day of digging,

Greek archaeologist Calliope Limneos-Papakosta was ready to go home. She had spent many years of her career scouring the grounds of Alexandria, Egypt, in the hopes of finding Alexander the Great's tomb. But upon coming up empty-handed once again, Papakosta was just about to conclude her latest dig.

Until, that is, one of her assistants called her over. A flash of white poking out of the dirt caught her eye. She began to dig. Turns out that white object was part of a remarkably intact statue of Alexander the Great — and just the sign Papakosta needed to continue her search for the ancient conqueror-turned-pharaoh's tomb.

CAPITAL GAINS

How did the ancient city of Alexandria come to be? In 332 B.C., Alexander the Great, a king from ancient Greece, defeated the Persians to take over Egypt as the new leader of the land. He went to work quickly, establishing a new capital at the mouth of the Nile River. It soon became one of the most powerful cities in the world — and an education epicentre that included one of the most famous libraries ever built.

By the time of his death, Alexander the Great had amassed the largest empire in the entire ancient world, spanning some 4,800 kilometres (3,000 mi). It's said that when he died in 323 B.C. at the age of just 32, his body was embalmed in honey and buried in a tomb in Alexandria.

SUNKEN CITY

The actual location of Alexander's final resting spot is a mystery that has baffled experts for decades. After a tsunami tore through the city in A.D. 356, many devastating earthquakes followed. This led to rising sea levels, causing the ancient part of the city to sink. As time

PAPAKOSTA AND HER TEAM HAVE UNCOVERED THE FOUNDATION WALLS OF A MONUMENTAL BUILDING IN ALEXANDRIA DATING TO THE ERA OF ALEXANDER THE GREAT.

ARTIST'S RENDERING OF ANCIENT ALEXANDRIA

passed and new portions of the city were built on top of the ancient section, Alexander's tomb went way underground.

NEW DISCOVERIES

So while experts know Alexander's tomb was buried somewhere, its location is still unclear. For several years following the discovery of that one statue, Papakosta continued her search, relying on a combination of ancient accounts, old maps and modern technology to determine where to dig. With the help of a tool called electrical resistivity tomography (ERT), which shoots electrical current into the soil to detect any objects buried below, her

team has been able to uncover more parts of the city's ancient royal quarter — including a Roman road and the remnants of a large public building that may be linked to the tomb.

THE SEARCH CONTINUES

As for the tomb itself? Its location remains unknown. But as experts like Papakosta keep searching, the hope is that this long-standing mystery will soon be solved.

225

GUARDIANS
OF THE TOMB

Back in 1974, Chinese farmers who were digging for water got a shock. Staring up from the soil was a face, eyes wide open, with features that looked almost human. But this was not a skeleton: It was one of thousands of life-sized soldiers made of baked clay called terracotta — and they had been buried for 2,200 years.

BURIED TREASURE

Row upon row of the soldiers — each face as different and as realistic as the next — were hidden in a pit about the size of two football pitches near Xi'an, which was China's capital city for nearly 2,000 years. Archaeologists eventually found four pits, some containing statues of horse-drawn chariots, cavalry (soldiers on horseback) and high-ranking officers.

BODYGUARDS

Who could have built this huge underground army? Experts assume it was China's first emperor, Qin Shihuangdi (Chin She-hwong-dee). The brilliant but brutal ruler, who created the first unified China, was known for his big ideas and even bigger ego. It's believed that because Qin Shihuangdi had killed so many people during his reign, he may have wanted a large army to protect him from his victims' ghosts once he died. He probably had the clay soldiers created to guard his tomb, which was just 1.6 kilometres (1 mi) away from where the pits were discovered.

FINAL REWARDS

As it turned out, the emperor's living enemies — not the dead ones — took revenge. In 206 B.C., a few years after Qin Shihuangdi's death, invading armies destroyed the pits, burying the warriors and cracking every figure. The pits caved in more as time went on, and the soldiers were lost to the ages.

Experts have since pieced a thousand soldiers back together. But some 6,000 figures are still buried. As work continues, who knows what secrets these soldiers have yet to tell?

STATUES OF ARCHERS, LIKE THE ONE ABOVE, WERE BURIED HOLDING REAL CROSSBOWS.

ANCIENT CRAFTSMEN MADE THOUSANDS OF LIFE-SIZED TERRACOTTA WARRIORS, EACH WITH A UNIQUE FACE.

UNDER
RECONSTRUCTION

Experts have painstakingly rebuilt and restored a thousand terracotta warriors found in underground pits near the emperor's tomb. The complex is so vast that excavations may continue for generations.

A warrior's head poking out of the dirt still has traces of red paint. Originally all of the warriors were painted bright colours.

Workers brush dirt away from the collapsed roof that sheltered the terracotta warriors.

ASIA
CHINA
PACIFIC OCEAN

TERRACOTTA WARRIORS

CHINA

HORSE-DRAWN CHARIOT

A toppled terracotta warrior lies in its 2,200-year-old underground tomb.

227

Buried Secrets

Who built this ancient Egyptian monument?

A huge stone lion looms over the passing boats on Egypt's Nile River. It serves as a giant guardian to some of the country's famous pyramids, human-made tombs that seem to stretch all the way to the sun. The ancient sand-coloured statue known as the Sphinx is nearly as tall as Buckingham Palace, with paws longer than a bus.

How many hidden chambers are inside? Scientists are still digging up clues to answer that question, but they might have an answer for one of the monument's biggest mysteries: Who built it?

SET IN STONE

In ancient Egypt, people worshipped sphinxes as mythical creatures with the power to ward off evil. Some think the Sphinx was built as a protector of the pyramids, which were once used as burial places for Egyptian kings. Nobody's sure when the Sphinx was built, but experts believe it was already ancient when Egyptian queen Cleopatra saw it around 47 B.C. Since then, many other historical figures have visited the monument. But which historical figure *built* the monument?

FACE OFF

Historians' two top suspects are Pharaoh Khufu, who ruled Egypt from 2589 to 2566 B.C., and his son, Pharaoh Khafre, who reigned from 2558 to 2532 B.C. Most experts agree that one of these rulers oversaw the construction of the statue and had his own face carved atop the giant lion. But which one was it — Khufu or Khafre?

Some think the Sphinx is the work of Khufu. They say the statue's face matches a sculpture of the king discovered in A.D. 1903.

But most experts, including Egyptologist Mark Lehner, think Khufu's son, Khafre, built the Sphinx. As father and son, the pair shared a resemblance.

HISTORIANS THINK THE SPHINX MIGHT'VE LOOKED LIKE THIS BEFORE WIND AND WATER WORE AWAY ITS COLOURS.

THE SPHINX SITS NEAR SIX PYRAMIDS, INCLUDING THE GREAT PYRAMID AT GIZA.

THE STATUE WASN'T FULLY UNCOVERED UNTIL 1936, ABOUT 70 YEARS AFTER THIS SNAP WAS TAKEN.

Egypt's Nile River is the world's longest river, flowing 7,081 kilometres (4,400 mi) through eastern Africa.

Early Egyptians named their land Kemet, or 'black land', for its rich river mud.

In Egypt, camels are called 'ships of the desert'. Like ships, they carry goods and people.

ATLANTIC OCEAN
EUROPE
ASIA
EGYPT
AFRICA
INDIAN OCEAN

Mediterranean Sea
ISRAEL
JORDAN
SPHINX ★ Cairo
SAUDI ARABIA
LIBYA
Nile River
E G Y P T
Red Sea
S U D A N

But Lehner says the most convincing evidence lies in a temple that was built in front of the statue. Lehner believes that the temple and the Sphinx are part of the same master building plan overseen by one person. Ancient workers built the temple on top of part of another structure that's been proven to be the work of Khafre. Lehner believes that this means the Sphinx and its temple must have been constructed after Khafre's first structure was built — Khufu wouldn't have been around to build on top of Khafre's lower structure. "To me, that's strong evidence that the Sphinx couldn't have been Khufu's," Lehner says.

DISAPPEARING ACT

Today the ancient Egyptians' work is crumbling. Centuries of wind and water have ground away at the Sphinx's limestone, and shifting sands have threatened to cover much of it. Archaeologists work tirelessly to repair the structure to keep it from completely disappearing.

By preserving the Sphinx, experts are also protecting clues that might still be hidden in the statue's stone. Someday, these could be the keys that unlock even more of the Sphinx's secrets.

HISTORY'S MYSTERIES

CURIOUS CLUES, COLD CASES AND UNSOLVED PUZZLES FROM THE PAST

THE MYSTERY — DOES THE YETI EXIST?

POSSIBLE YETI FOOTPRINTS

HIKERS COULD BE MISTAKING A TIBETAN BLUE BEAR FOR A YETI.

The yeti is also known as the Abominable Snowman.

THE BACKGROUND

The word 'yeti' means 'little manlike animal' in the Tibetan language. According to legend, yetis are hairy (and not so little) ogres that look like a cross between a human and a bear. People today still report seeing the mysterious creatures roaming Asia's Himalayan mountains. The fur-covered monster reportedly stands 2.4 metres (8 ft) tall, weighs some 181 kilograms (400 lb) and snacks on goats. Debate has raged for centuries about whether this creature is man, bear or myth.

THE CLUES

In 1986, a man hiking in the Himalaya photo-graphed what he thought was a yeti in the snow. Other believers have tried testing furry scalps and hair samples, hoping they belonged to an unknown animal. One man even collected what he said was a yeti finger!

WHAT THE YETI COULD BE

So far, nothing proves that the yeti exists. Test results showed that the scalp belonged to a goat, and the hair samples were from a bear. That 1986 photograph turned out to be a weird rock shape. And the 'yeti finger'? Tests revealed it was actually from a human. (That's a whole other mystery!) Some scientists believe that the Tibetan blue bear, a rare type of brown bear that walks upright, is being mistaken for a yeti.

THE MYSTERY

WHY IS THIS ANCIENT MUMMY MOANING?

Sheepskin and a strange dried-out paste covered Unknown Man E.

THE BACKGROUND

Back in 1886, the director of the Egyptian Antiquities Service was removing the wrappings of a mummy that had been discovered in Egypt's Valley of the Kings when he got a scary surprise. The mummy's mouth was open, its eyes were shut and its nostrils were flared, as though he was in pain.

WHAT COULD'VE HAPPENED

Experts guessed that Unknown Man E, as the mummy came to be known, may have been poisoned — a punishment for a crime. In 2008, a team of scientists used CT scans, DNA evidence and x-rays to figure out who the mummy was. By comparing the high-tech results with descriptions from ancient Egyptian scrolls, experts think it might be Prince Pentewere. He was suspected of plotting the murder of his father, Pharaoh Ramses III in 1155 B.C. As a member of the royal family, he might have been killed by being forced to drink poison rather than face execution. Researchers are still trying to unravel the clues on this mummy mystery.

THE SCREAMING MUMMY IS NICKNAMED UNKNOWN MAN E.

THE MYSTERY

WHY DID PEOPLE VANISH FROM THE LOST COLONY OF ROANOKE?

The lost colonists of Roanoke included entire families — 90 men, 17 women and 11 children.

A REPLICA OF A 16TH-CENTURY SHIP

THE BACKGROUND

About a hundred English colonists arrived in 1587 to Roanoke Island, a spot near modern-day Manteo, North Carolina, U.S.A. Not long after, the colony's governor, John White, travelled back to England for more supplies. When White returned in 1590, he found an empty village. What happened?

THE CLUES

Archaeologists found artefacts like broken bowls that likely belonged to the colonists on Mettaquem, a nearby Native American settlement. They also found buried cannons and coffins that might date back to when the colonists lived in the area where the Mettaquem would've been.

One theory to what happened to the colonists is that they faced some kind of threat, so they split into smaller groups and fled. The artefacts found at Mettaquem may mean some of them sought shelter there, but to this day, the disappearance of the colonists remains a mystery.

ROANOKE GOVERNOR JOHN WHITE (POINTING) FOUND THE WORD 'CROATOAN' ON A TREE. EXPERTS WONDER IF THE COLONISTS FLED TO THIS NEARBY ISLAND (NOW CALLED HATTERAS ISLAND).

231

SUPER SNEAKY CODE BREAKERS

>> **CHECK OUT SNEAKY WAYS PEOPLE HAVE SENT MESSAGES.**

You need to tell your best friend a secret. But if anyone else reads your note, you're busted. Get the sneaky scoop on ways other people have delivered secret messages. You just might find a new way to get that info to your BFF!

SPIES ARE ENCOURAGED TO MAKE UP THEIR OWN CODES. SO THIS LACE PATTERN COULD MEAN "I HAVE INFORMATION."

AND THIS LACE PATTERN COULD MEAN "FOLLOW ME."

THE METHOD: SHOELACES
THE MESSENGER: U.S. SPIES
THE STORY: Yeah, you learned how to tie your shoes years ago. But do you know how to send a message with your trainers? In the 1950s, the U.S. Central Intelligence Agency created a book of tips to teach spies ways to communicate in public in case they were being watched. One tip: Lace up your trainers. Tied one way, the laces might mean "I have information"; tied another, "Follow me." The spies could communicate while everyone else probably just thought: That guy can't tie his shoes correctly!

THE HISTORIAN HERODOTUS

THE METHOD: TATTOOED HEAD
THE MESSENGER: HISTIAEUS OF MILETUS
THE STORY: Around 513 B.C., Histiaeus was forced out as the ruler of an ancient city in what's now Turkey. So he wanted to send a message to his supporters: to revolt against the king who took away his power. According to the Greek historian Herodotus (who lived around the same time), Histiaeus summoned a slave, shaved his head and tattooed the message onto the man's scalp. After the slave's hair grew back, he travelled to Greece with instructions to shave his head again. Message received!

THE METHOD: SECRET SCARVES
THE MESSENGER: BELGIAN SPIES
THE STORY: "An old lady knitting doesn't look like a threat," says Vince Houghton, the historian and curator at the International Spy Museum in Washington, D.C. That's why during World War I (in the 1910s), Belgian resistance fighters asked women who lived near railways to keep track of the types of trains passing by, which gave the fighters information about the German invaders' movements. The women would knit a bumpy stitch for one type of train, and knit a small hole in the fabric for another. Then they'd pass the cosy scarf to a soldier so the cloth could be decoded.

Make Invisible Ink

You'll need:
- bicarbonate of soda
- water
- small cup
- paper
- paintbrush
- sponge
- grape juice

Step one Mix equal amounts of bicarbonate of soda and water in a small cup.

Step two Write your message on paper using the mixture and the paintbrush.

Step three Wait for the paper to dry, then pass the note to your friend.

Step four To reveal the message, use a sponge or brush to paint the paper with grape juice.

THE METHOD: SONGS
THE MESSENGER: SLAVES IN THE UNITED STATES
THE STORY: African-American slaves in the 1800s couldn't talk openly about their plans to escape to freedom — so they secretly sang about it. For instance, 'Swing Low, Sweet Chariot' might sound like a religious song. But for slaves, the 'sweet chariot' was code for the Underground Railroad, the network of people who helped slaves head to northern states and Canada, where slavery was illegal. The song 'Wade in the Water' warned escaped slaves to get in the water so dogs would lose their scent trail. With these methods, hundreds of people escaped slavery.

THE METHOD: ORANGE JUICE
THE MESSENGER: JOHN GERARD
THE STORY: In 1597, a priest named John Gerard was imprisoned in the Tower of London in England by Queen Elizabeth I. He asked the warden to let him send letters written in charcoal. But then he scrawled another message on top using the juice from an orange — which was only visible when the juice was dry and the page heated. With his invisible ink, he coordinated an escape out of a window and into a boat rowed by his supporters.

The slight acidity of the juice reacts with bicarbonate of soda to reveal your message.

233

MONARCHS
OF ENGLAND AND THE UNITED KINGDOM

England first became a united kingdom under the kings of Wessex, who drove out Viking invaders in the 10th century. The English kings conquered Wales in the 13th century, and the kingdoms of England and Scotland were joined together in 1603. After 1707, the country was known as the United Kingdom and now includes Northern Ireland. Many different houses have ruled the country; the current queen, Elizabeth II, is a member of the House of Windsor.

HOUSE OF WESSEX

Egbert (802–839)
Aethelwulf (839–855)
Aethelbald (855–860)
Aethelbert (860–866)
Aethelred (866–871)
Alfred the Great (871–899)
Edward the Elder (899–925)
Athelstan (925–939)
Edmund the Magnificent (939–946)
Eadred (946–955)
Eadwig (Edwy) All-Fair (955–959)
Edgar the Peaceable (959–975)
Edward the Martyr (975–978)
Aethelred the Unready (978–1013)

HOUSE OF DENMARK

Sweyn Forkbeard (1014)

HOUSE OF WESSEX
RESTORED, FIRST TIME

Aethelred the Unready (1014–1016)
Edmund Ironside (1016)

HOUSE OF DENMARK
RESTORED

Canute the Great (1016–1035)
Harold I Harefoot (1035–1040)
Harthacanute (1040–1042)

HOUSE OF WESSEX
RESTORED, SECOND TIME

Edward the Confessor (1042–1066)
Harold II (1066)

NORMANS

William I the Conqueror (1066–1087)
William II Rufus (1087–1100)
Henry I Beauclerc (1100–1135)
Stephen (1135–1154)
Matilda (1141)

PLANTAGENET
Angevin Line

Henry II Curtmantle (1154–1189)
Richard I the Lionheart (1189–1199)
John Lackland (1199–1216)
Henry III (1216–1272)
Edward I Longshanks (1272–1307)
Edward II (1307–1327)
Edward III (1327–1377)
Richard II (1377–1399)

Lancastrian Line

Henry IV Bolingbroke (1399–1413)
Henry V (1413–1422)
Henry VI (1422–1461, 1470–1471)

Yorkist Line

Edward IV (1461–1470, 1471–1483)
Edward V (1483)
Richard III Crookback (1483–1485)

HOUSE OF TUDOR

Henry VII Tudor (1485–1509)
Henry VIII (1509–1547)
Edward VI (1547–1553)
Lady Jane Grey (1553)
Mary I Tudor (1553–1558)
Elizabeth I (1558–1603)

HOUSE OF STUART

James I (1603–1625)
Charles I (1625–1649)

The 900-year-old Domesday Book — outlining the land conquered by King William I in 1066 — was printed on dried animal skins!

KING WILLIAM I THE CONQUEROR

KING JOHN LACKLAND

THE COMMONWEALTH

Oliver Cromwell* (1649–1658)
Richard Cromwell* (1658–1659)

HOUSE OF STUART
RESTORED

Charles II (1660–1685)
James II (1685–1688)

HOUSE OF ORANGE
AND STUART

William III (1689–1702)
Mary II (1689–1694)

HOUSE OF STUART

Anne (1702–1714)

HOUSE OF HANOVER

George I (1714–1727)
George II (1727–1760)
George III (1760–1820)
George IV (1820–1830)
William IV (1830–1837)
Victoria (1837–1901)

HOUSE OF SAXE-
COBURG-GOTHA

Edward VII (1901–1910)

HOUSE OF WINDSOR

George V (1910–1936)
Edward VIII (1936)
George VI (1936–1952)
Elizabeth II (1952–present)

*Held title of Lord Protector

Elizabeth I's court ate 8,200 sheep, 2,330 deer, 1,240 oxen, 1,870 pigs, 760 calves and 53 wild boar in one year.

Charles, Prince of Wales, wrote a children's book about an old man who lives in a cave.

Queen Elizabeth II is the last surviving head of state who served in uniform during World War II. (She was a driver and a mechanic.)

QUEEN ELIZABETH I

QUEEN VICTORIA

KING HENRY VIII

QUEEN ELIZABETH II

235

LEADERS OF THE WORLD

Each of the 195 independent countries in the world has its own leader or leaders. Whatever the leader is called, he or she is called upon to take charge of the direction of the country's growth — politically, economically and socially.

Some countries have more than one person who has an executive role in the government. That second person is often a prime minister or a chancellor. This varies depending on the type of government in the country.

Over the next several pages, the countries and their leaders are listed in alphabetical order according to the most commonly used version of each country's name. Disputed areas such as Northern Cyprus and Taiwan and dependencies such as Bermuda, Greenland and Puerto Rico, which belong to independent nations, are not included in this listing. The date given for leaders taking office is the date of their first term.

Note the colour key at the bottom of the pages, which assigns a colour to each country based on the continent on which it is located.

NOTE: These facts are current as of press time.

Colour
Key by
Continent

Afghanistan

President
Ashraf Ghani Ahmadzai
Took office: 29 September 2014

Albania

President
Ilir Meta
Took office: 24 July 2017

Prime Minister
Edi Rama
Took office: 10 September 2013

Algeria

Interim President
Abdelkader Bensalah
Took office: 9 April 2019

Prime Minister
Noureddine Bedoui
Took office: 11 March 2019

> To learn more about world leaders, go online:
> cia.gov/library/
> publications/
> world-leaders-1

Andorra

Co-Prince
Emmanuel Macron
Took office: 14 May 2017

Co-Prince
Archbishop Joan-Enric Vives i Sicília
Took office: 12 May 2003

Executive Council President
Xavier Espot Zamora
Took office: 16 May 2019

Angola

President João Manuel Goncalves Lourenço
Took office: 26 September 2017

Antigua and Barbuda

Governor General
Rodney Williams
Took office: 14 August 2014

Prime Minister
Gaston Browne
Took office: 13 June 2014

Argentina

President
Alberto Ángel Fernández
Took office: 10 December 2019

Armenia

President Armen Sarkissian
Took office: 9 April 2018

Prime Minister
Nikol Pashinyan
Took office: 8 May 2018

Australia

Governor General
Sir David Hurley
Took office: 1 July 2019

Prime Minister
Scott Morrison
Took office: 24 August 2018

SCOTT MORRISON began volunteering for his LOCAL GOVERNMENT when he was just NINE YEARS OLD.

Austria

**President
Alexander Van Der Bellen**
Took office: 26 January 2017

**Chancellor
Sebastian Kurz**
Took office: 7 January 2020

Azerbaijan

President Ilham Aliyev
Took office: 31 October 2003

**Prime Minister
Ali Asadov**
Took office: 8 October 2019

Bahamas

**Governor General
Cornelius A. Smith**
Took office: 28 June 2019

**Prime Minister
Hubert Minnis**
Took office: 11 May 2017

Bahrain

**King Hamad bin Isa
al-Khalifa**
Began reign: 6 March 1999

**Prime Minister
Khalifa bin Salman al-Khalifa**
Took office: 1971

Bangladesh

President Abdul Hamid
Took office: 24 April 2013

**Prime Minister
Sheikh Hasina**
Took office: 6 January 2009

Barbados

**Governor General
Sandra Mason**
Took office: 8 January 2018

**Prime Minister
Mia Mottley**
Took office: 25 May 2018

Belarus

**President
Aleksandr Lukashenko**
Took office: 20 July 1994

**Prime Minister
Sergey Rumas**
Took office: 18 August 2018

Belgium

King Philippe
Began reign: 21 July 2013

**Prime Minister
Sophie Wilmes**
Took office: 26 October 2019

Belize

**Governor General
Sir Colville Norbert Young, Sr.**
Took office: 17 November 1993

**Prime Minister
Dean Oliver Barrow**
Took office: 8 February 2008

Benin

President Patrice Talon
Took office: 6 April 2016

Bhutan

**King Jigme Khesar
Namgyel Wangchuck**
Began reign: 14 December 2006

**Prime Minister
Lotay Tshering**
Took office: 7 November 2018

THE KING OF BHUTAN is officially known as the DRAGON KING.

Bolivia

**Interim President
Jeanine Áñez Chávez**
Took office: 12 November 2019

Bosnia and Herzegovina

**Presidency members:
Milorad Dodik
Sefik Dzaferovic
Zeljko Komsic**
Took office: 20 November 2018

Chairman of the Council of Ministers Denis Zvizdic
Took office: 11 February 2015

Botswana

**President
Mokgweetse Eric Masisi**
Took office: 1 April 2018

Brazil

**President
Jair Bolsonaro**
Took office: 1 January 2019

Brunei

Sultan Hassanal Bolkiah
Began reign: 5 October 1967

HASSANAL BOLKIAH lives in a PALACE with more than 1,750 ROOMS.

Bulgaria

President Rumen Radev
Took office: 22 January 2017

**Prime Minister
Boyko Borissov**
Took office: 4 May 2017

Burkina Faso

**President Roch Marc
Christian Kabore**
Took office: 29 December 2015

**Prime Minister
Christophe Dabiré**
Took office: 24 January 2019

Burundi

President Pierre Nkurunziza
Took office: 26 August 2005

Cabo Verde

President
Jorge Carlos Fonseca
Took office: 9 September 2011

Prime Minister
Ulisses Correia e Silva
Took office: 22 April 2016

JORGE CARLOS FONSECA has written books of POETRY and ESSAYS.

Cambodia

King Norodom Sihamoni
Began reign: 29 October 2004

Prime Minister Hun Sen
Took office: 14 January 1985

Cameroon

President
Paul Biya
Took office: 6 November 1982

Prime Minister
Joseph Dion Ngute
Took office: 4 January 2019

Canada

Governor General
Julie Payette
Took office: 2 October 2017

Prime Minister
Justin Trudeau
Took office: 4 November 2015

JUSTIN TRUDEAU once STARRED in a TELEVISION MINISERIES.

Central African Republic

President
Faustin-Archange Touadera
Took office: 30 March 2016

Prime Minister
Firmin Ngrébada
Took office: 25 February 2019

Chad

President
Lt. Gen. Idriss Déby Itno
Took office: 4 December 1990

Chile

President
Sebastián Piñera Echenique
Took office: 11 March 2018

Hello From Costa Rica

Sloth

China

President
Xi Jinping
Took office: 14 March 2013

Premier
Li Keqiang
Took office: 16 March 2013

Colombia

President
Iván Duque Márquez
Took office: 7 August 2018

> **IVÁN DUQUE MÁRQUEZ was a SINGER in a rock band called PIG NOSE.**

Comoros

President
Azali Assoumani
Took office: 26 May 2016

Congo

President
Denis Sassou-Nguesso
Took office: 25 October 1997

Costa Rica

President
Carlos Alvarado Quesada
Took office: 8 May 2018

Côte d'Ivoire (Ivory Coast)

President
Alassane Dramane Ouattara
Took office: 4 December 2010

Prime Minister
Amadou Gon Coulibaly
Took office: 11 January 2017

Croatia

President
Kolinda Grabar-Kitarovic
Took office: 19 February 2015

Prime Minister
Andrej Plenkovic
Took office: 19 October 2016

Cuba

President Miguel Díaz-Canel Bermúdez
Took office: 10 October 2019

Cyprus

President
Nikos Anastasiades
Took office: 28 February 2013

> **NIKOS ANASTASIADES has a TWIN BROTHER.**

Czechia (Czech Republic)

President Milos Zeman
Took office: 8 March 2013

Prime Minister Andrej Babis
Took office: 13 December 2017

Democratic Republic of the Congo

President Felix Tshisekedi
Took office: 24 January 2019

Prime Minister
Sylvestre Ilunga Ilukamba
Took office: 20 May 2019

Denmark

Queen Margrethe II
Began reign: 14 January 1972

Prime Minister
Mette Frederiksen
Took office: 27 June 2019

Djibouti

President
Ismail Omar Guelleh
Took office: 8 May 1999

Prime Minister
Abdoulkader Kamil Mohamed
Took office: 1 April 2013

Dominica

President
Charles A. Savarin
Took office: 2 October 2013

Prime Minister
Roosevelt Skerrit
Took office: 8 January 2004

Dominican Republic

President
Danilo Medina Sánchez
Took office: 16 August 2012

Ecuador

President
Lenín Moreno Garces
Took office: 24 May 2017

> **LENÍN MORENO GARCES is the first WHEELCHAIR USER to be elected as a HEAD OF STATE IN LATIN AMERICA.**

Egypt

President
Abdelfattah Elsisi
Took office: 8 June 2014

Prime Minister
Mostafa Madbouly
Took office: 7 June 2018

El Salvador

President Nayib Armando Bukele Ortez
Took office: 1 June 2019

Equatorial Guinea

President Teodoro Obiang Nguema Mbasogo
Took office: 3 August 1979

Prime Minister Francisco Pascual Eyegue Obama Asue
Took office: 23 June 2016

Eritrea

President Isaias Afworki
Took office: 8 June 1993

Estonia

President Kersti Kaljulaid
Took office: 10 October 2016

Prime Minister Juri Ratas
Took office: 21 November 2016

Eswatini (Swaziland)

King Mswati III
Began reign: 25 April 1986

Prime Minister Ambrose Mandvulo Dlamini
Took office: 29 October 2018

Ethiopia

President Sahle-Work Zewde
Took office: 25 October 2018

Prime Minister Abiy Ahmed
Took office: 2 April 2018

SAHLE-WORK ZEWDE is ETHIOPIA'S FIRST FEMALE PRESIDENT.

Fiji

President Jioji Konousi Konrote
Took office: 12 November 2015

Prime Minister Voreqe 'Frank' Bainimarama
Took office: 22 September 2014

Finland

President Sauli Ninisto
Took office: 1 March 2012

Prime Minister Sanna Marin
Took office: 10 December 2019

France

President Emmanuel Macron
Took office: 14 May 2017

Prime Minister Edouard Philippe
Took office: 15 May 2017

Gabon

President Ali Ben Bongo Ondimba
Took office: 16 October 2009

Prime Minister Julien Nkoghe Bekale
Took office: 15 January 2019

Gambia

President Adama Barrow
Took office: 19 January 2017

ADAMA BARROW worked as a DEPARTMENT STORE SECURITY GUARD.

Georgia

President Salome Zourabichvili
Took office: 16 December 2018

Prime Minister Giorgi Gakharia
Took office: 8 September 2019

Germany

President Frank-Walter Steinmeier
Took office: 19 March 2017

Chancellor Angela Merkel
Took office: 22 November 2005

Ghana

President Nana Addo Dankwa Akufo-Addo
Took office: 7 January 2017

Greece

President Katerina Sakellaropoulou
Took office: 13 March 2020

Prime Minister Kyriakos Mitsotakis
Took office: 8 July 2019

Grenada

Governor General Cecile La Grenade
Took office: 7 May 2013

Prime Minister Keith Mitchell
Took office: 20 February 2013

Guatemala

President Alejandro Giammattei
Took office: 14 January 2020

Guinea

President Alpha Condé
Took office: 21 December 2010

Prime Minister Ibrahima Fofana
Took office: 22 May 2018

Guinea-Bissau

President José Mário Vaz
Took office: 17 June 2014

Prime Minister position vacant

Guyana

President
David Granger
Took office: 16 May 2015

Haiti

President
Jovenel Moise
Took office: 7 February 2017

Prime Minister
Fritz William Michel
Took office: 22 July 2019

Honduras

President
Juan Orlando Hernandez Alvarado
Took office: 27 January 2014

Hungary

President Janos Ader
Took office: 10 May 2012

Prime Minister
Viktor Orban
Took office: 29 May 2010

Iceland

President
Gudni Thorlacius Johannesson
Took office: 1 August 2016

Prime Minister
Katrin Jakobsdittir
Took office: 30 November 2017

India

President
Ram Nath Kovind
Took office: 25 July 2017

Prime Minister
Narendra Modi
Took office: 26 May 2014

A style icon, NARENDRA MODI inspired the 'MODI JACKET' that's popular in India.

Indonesia

President Joko Widodo
Took office: 20 October 2014

JOKO WIDODO is a former FURNITURE MAKER.

Iran

Supreme Leader
Ayatollah Ali Hoseini-Khamenei
Took office: 4 June 1989

President
Hasan Fereidun Rohani
Took office: 3 August 2013

Iraq

President
Barham Salih
Took office: 1 October 2018

Prime Minister
Adil Abd Al-Mahdi
Took office: 25 October 2018

Greetings From Iceland

Aurora borealis — or northern lights — above Mount Kirkjufell, Iceland

● Asia ● Europe ● North America ● South America

Ireland (Éire)

President
Michael D. Higgins
Took office: 11 November 2011

Prime Minister
Leo Varadkar
Took office: 14 June 2017

> **MICHAEL D. HIGGINS has published four collections of POETRY.**

Israel

President
Reuven Rivlin
Took office: 27 July 2014

Prime Minister
Binyamin Netanyahu
Took office: 31 March 2009

Italy

President Sergio Mattarella
Took office: 3 February 2015

Prime Minister
Giuseppe Conte
Took office: 1 June 2018

Jamaica

Governor General
Sir Patrick L. Allen
Took office: 26 February 2009

Prime Minister
Andrew Holness
Took office: 3 March 2016

Japan

Emperor Naruhito
Began reign: 1 May 2019

Prime Minister Shinzo Abe
Took office: 26 December 2012

Jordan

King Abdullah II
Began reign: 7 February 1999

Prime Minister
Omar al-Razzaz
Took office: 4 June 2018

> **King Abdullah II made a CAMEO APPEARANCE in a *STAR TREK: VOYAGER* episode.**

Kazakhstan

President
Kassym-Jomart Tokayev
Took office: 20 March 2019

Prime Minister
Askar Mamin
Took office: 25 February 2019

Welcome to Kenya

Zebras in Amboseli, Kenya

COLOUR KEY ● Africa ● Australia, New Zealand and Oceania

Kenya

President Uhuru Kenyatta
Took office: 9 April 2013

Kiribati

President Taneti Maamau
Took office: 11 March 2016

Kosovo

President Hashim Thaçi
Took office: 7 April 2016

Prime Minister
position vacant

HASHIM THAÇI has more than 40,000 FOLLOWERS ON INSTAGRAM.

Kuwait

Emir Sabah al-Ahmad al-Jabir al-Sabah
Began reign: 29 January 2006

Prime Minister
Jabir al-Mubarak al-Hamad al-Sabah
Took office: 30 November 2011

Kyrgyzstan

President
Sooronbay Jeenbekov
Took office: 24 November 2017

Prime Minister
Mukhammedkalyy Abylgaziev
Took office: 20 April 2018

Laos

President
Bounnyang Vorachit
Took office: 20 April 2016

Prime Minister
Thongloun Sisoulit
Took office: 20 April 2016

Latvia

President Egils Levits
Took office: 8 July 2019

Prime Minister
Krisjanis Karins
Took office: 23 January 2019

Lebanon

President Michel Awn
Took office: 31 October 2016

Prime Minister
Saad al-Hariri
Took office: 24 May 2018

Lesotho

King Letsie III
Began reign: 7 February 1996

Prime Minister
Thomas Motsoahae Thabane
Took office: 16 June 2017

Liberia

President George Weah
Took office: 22 January 2018

GEORGE WEAH was named the WORLD'S FOOTBALLER OF THE YEAR IN 1995.

Libya

Prime Minister
Fayiz al-Saraj
Took office: December 2015

Liechtenstein

Prince Hans Adam II
Began reign: 13 November 1989

Prime Minister
Adrian Hasler
Took office: 27 March 2013

Lithuania

President
Gitanas Nauseda
Took office: 12 July 2019

Prime Minister
Saulius Skvernelis
Took office: 13 December 2016

Luxembourg

Grand Duke Henri
Began reign: 7 October 2000

Prime Minister
Xavier Bettel
Took office: 4 December 2013

Madagascar

President Andry Rajoelina
Took office: 21 January 2019

Prime Minister
Christian Ntsay
Took office: 6 June 2018

Malawi

President
Arthur Peter Mutharika
Took office: 31 May 2014

Malaysia

King Sultan Abdullah Sultan Ahmad Shah
Installed: 24 January 2019

Prime Minister
Mahathir bin Mohamad
Took office: 10 May 2018

Prior to entering politics, MAHATHIR BIN MOHAMAD was a successful DOCTOR.

Maldives

President Ibrahim 'Ibu' Mohamed Solih
Took office: 17 November 2018

Mali

President
Ibrahim Boubacar Keita
Took office: 4 September 2013

Prime Minister
Boubou Cisse
Took office: 23 April 2019

Malta

President
George Vella
Took office: 4 April 2019

Prime Minister
Robert Abela
Took office: 13 January 2020

Marshall Islands

President
Hilda C. Heine
Took office: 28 January 2016

Mauritania

President Mohamed Cheikh El Ghazouani
Took office: 1 August 2019

Prime Minister
Ould Bedda Ould Cheikh Sidiya
Took office: 5 August 2019

Mauritius

President
Pritivirajsing Roopun
Took office: 2 December 2019

Prime Minister
Pravind Jugnauth
Took office: 23 January 2017

Mexico

President
Andres Manuel Lopez Obrador
Took office: 1 December 2018

Micronesia

President David W. Panuelo
Took office: 11 May 2019

Moldova

President Igor Dodon
Took office: 23 December 2016

Prime Minister Ion Chicu
Took office: 14 November 2019

Monaco

Prince Albert II
Began reign: 6 April 2005

Minister of State
Serge Telle
Took office: 1 February 2016

Mongolia

President
Khaltmaa Battulga
Took office: 10 July 2017

Prime Minister
Ukhnaa Khurelsukh
Took office: 4 October 2017

UKHNAA KHURELSUKH is a motorbike enthusiast.

Montenegro

President
Milo Djukanovic
Took office: 20 May 2018

Prime Minister
Dusko Markovic
Took office: 28 November 2016

Morocco

King Mohammed VI
Began reign: 30 July 1999

Prime Minister
Saad-Eddine al-Othmani
Took office: 17 March 2017

Mozambique

President
Filipe Jacinto Nyusi
Took office: 15 January 2015

Prime Minister
Carlos Agostinho Do Rosario
Took office: 17 January 2015

Myanmar (Burma)

President Win Myint
Took office: 30 March 2018

Namibia

President Hage Geingob
Took office: 21 March 2005

HAGE GEINGOB has a rugby stadium named after him.

Nauru

President Lionel Aingimea
Took office: 27 August 2019

Nepal

President
Bidhya Devi Bhandari
Took office: 29 October 2015

Prime Minister Khadga Prasad (KP) Sharma Oli
Took office: 15 February 2018

Netherlands

King Willem-Alexander
Began reign: 30 April 2013

Prime Minister Mark Rutte
Took office: 14 October 2010

Once a week, MARK RUTTE TEACHES DUTCH and SOCIAL STUDIES at a secondary school.

New Zealand

Governor General
Dame Patricia Lee Reddy
Took office: 28 September 2016

Prime Minister
Jacinda Ardern
Took office: 26 October 2017

JACINDA ARDERN had a baby girl eight months after becoming PRIME MINISTER.

Nicaragua

President
José Daniel Ortega Saavedra
Took office: 10 January 2007

Niger

President
Issoufou Mahamadou
Took office: 7 April 2011

Prime Minister
Brigi Rafini
Took office: 7 April 2011

Nigeria

President Maj. Gen. (ret.)
Muhammadu Buhari
Took office: 29 May 2015

North Korea

Supreme Leader
Kim Jong-un
Took office: 17 December 2011

Assembly President
Choe Ryong Hae
Took office: 11 April 2019

North Macedonia

President Stevo Pendarovski
Took office: 12 May 2019

Prime Minister Zoran Zaev
Took office: 31 May 2017

Norway

King Harald V
Began reign: 17 January 1991

Prime Minister
Erna Solberg
Took office: 16 October 2013

ERNA SOLBERG plays games on her iPad TO DE-STRESS.

Oman

Sultan
Qaboos bin Said al-Said
Began reign: 23 July 1970

Pakistan

President
Arif Alvi
Took office: 9 September 2018

Prime Minister
Imran Khan
Took office: 18 August 2018

Palau

President
Tommy Remengesau
Took office: 17 January 2013

Panama

President
Laurentino 'Nito' Cortizo Cohen
Took office: 1 July 2019

Papua New Guinea

Governor General
Grand Chief Sir Bob Dadae
Took office: 28 February 2017

Prime Minister
James Marape
Took office: 30 May 2019

Paraguay

President
Mario Abdo Benitez
Took office: 15 August 2018

Peru

President
Martin Alberto Vizcarra Cornejo
Took office: 23 March 2018

MARTIN ALBERTO VIZCARRA CORNEJO served as Peru's AMBASSADOR to CANADA.

Philippines

President
Rodrigo Duterte
Took office: 30 June 2016

Poland

President
Andrzej Duda
Took office: 6 August 2015

Prime Minister
Mateusz Morawiecki
Took office: 11 December 2017

ANDRZEJ DUDA is an accomplished SKIER.

Portugal

President
Marcelo Rebelo de Sousa
Took office: 9 March 2016

Prime Minister
António Costa
Took office: 26 November 2015

Qatar

Amir Tamim bin Hamad Al Thani
Began reign: 25 June 2013

Prime Minister Abdallah bin Nasir bin Khalifa Al Thani
Took office: 26 June 2013

Romania

President Klaus Werner Iohannis
Took office: 21 December 2014

Prime Minister Ludovic Orban
Took office: 4 November 2019

Russia

President Vladimir Vladimirovich Putin
Took office: 7 May 2012

Premier Dmitriy Anatolyevich Medvedev
Took office: 8 May 2012
Note: Russia is in both Europe and Asia, but its capital is in Europe, so it is classified here as a European country.

VLADIMIR PUTIN SWIMS LAPS and LIFTS WEIGHTS every day.

Rwanda

President Paul Kagame
Took office: 22 April 2000

Prime Minister Edouard Ngirente
Took office: 30 August 2017

Samoa

Head of State Tuimaleali'ifano Va'aletoa Sualauvi II
Took office: 21 July 2017

Prime Minister Tuila'epa Lupesoliai Sailele Malielegaoi
Took office: 23 November 1998

Tuimaleali'ifano Va'aletoa Sualauvi II is a former POLICE OFFICER.

San Marino

Co-Chiefs of State: Captain Regent Luca Boschi Captain Regent Mariella Mularoni
Took office: 1 October 2019

Secretary of State for Foreign and Political Affairs Nicola Renzi
Took office: 27 December 2016

Sao Tome and Principe

President Evaristo Carvalho
Took office: 3 September 2016

Prime Minister Jorge Bom Jesus
Took office: 3 December 2018

Saudi Arabia

King and Prime Minister Salman bin Abd al-Aziz Al Saud
Began reign: 23 January 2015

Senegal

President Macky Sall
Took office: 2 April 2012

MACKY SALL worked as a GEOLOGIST before entering politics.

Serbia

President Aleksandar Vucic
Took office: 31 May 2017

Prime Minister Ana Brnabic
Took office: 29 June 2017

Seychelles

President Danny Faure
Took office: 16 October 2016

Sierra Leone

President Julius Maada Bio
Took office: 4 April 2018

Singapore

President Halimah Yacob
Took office: 14 September 2017

Prime Minister Lee Hsien Loong
Took office: 12 August 2004

Slovakia

President Zuzana Caputova
Took office: 15 June 2019

Prime Minister Peter Pelligrini
Took office: 22 March 2018

Slovenia

President Borut Pahor
Took office: 22 December 2012

Prime Minister Marjan Sarec
Took office: 13 September 2018

Solomon Islands

Governor General David Vunagi
Took office: 8 July 2019

Prime Minister Manessah Sogavare
Took office: 24 April 2019

COLOUR KEY ● Africa ● Australia, New Zealand and Oceania

Somalia

President
Mohamed Abdullahi Mohamed 'Farmaajo'
Took office: 8 February 2017

Prime Minister
Hassan Ali Khayre
Took office: 1 March 2017

South Africa

President
Matamela Cyril Ramaphosa
Took office: 15 February 2018

South Korea

President
Moon Jae-in
Took office: 10 May 2017

Prime Minister
Lee Nak-yon
Took office: 1 June 2017

South Sudan

President
Salva Kiir Mayardit
Took office: 9 July 2011

Spain

King Felipe VI
Began reign: 19 June 2014

President of the Government
Pedro Sánchez Pérez-Castejón
Took office: 2 June 2018

PEDRO SÁNCHEZ PÉREZ-CASTEJÓN was a top BASKETBALL PLAYER in high school.

Sri Lanka

President
Gotabaya Rajapaksa
Took office: 18 November 2019

St. Kitts and Nevis

Governor General
Samuel W. T. Seaton
Took office: 2 September 2015

Prime Minister
Timothy Harris
Took office: 18 February 2015

St. Lucia

Governor General
Neville Cenac
Took office: 12 January 2018

Prime Minister
Allen Chastanet
Took office: 7 June 2016

Postcard From Singapore

The view from the top of the Singapore Flyer, one of the tallest Ferris wheels in the world

● Asia ● Europe ● North America ● South America

St. Vincent and the Grenadines

**Governor General
Susan Dougan**
Took office: 1 August 2019

**Prime Minister
Ralph E. Gonsalves**
Took office: 29 March 2001

SUSAN DOUGAN is the FIRST FEMALE governor general of St. Vincent and the Grenadines.

Sudan

**President
position vacant**

**Chairman of the Sovereignty Council:
General Abd-al-Fatah al-Burhan Abd-al-Rahman**
Took office: August 2019

Suriname

**President
Desiré Delano Bouterse**
Took office: 12 August 2010

Sweden

King Carl XVI Gustaf
Began reign: 19 September 1973

**Prime Minister
Stefan Löfven**
Took office: 3 October 2014

KING CARL XVI GUSTAF collects SPORTS CARS.

Switzerland

**President of the Swiss Confederation
Ueli Maurer**
Took office: 1 January 2019

**Federal Council members:
Viola Amherd, Guy Parmelin, Simonetta Sommaruga, Ignazio Cassis, Alain Berset, Karin Keller-Sutter**
Took office: dates vary

Syria

**President
Bashar al-Asad**
Took office: 17 July 2000

**Prime Minister
Imad Muhammad Dib Khamis**
Took office: 22 June 2016

Tajikistan

President Emomali Rahmon
Took office: 19 November 1992

**Prime Minister
Qohir Rasulzoda**
Took office: 23 November 2013

EMOMALI RAHMON has nine children — SEVEN daughters and TWO sons.

Tanzania

**President
John Magufuli**
Took office: 5 November 2015

JOHN MAGUFULI did push-ups on the campaign trail to prove his FITNESS.

Thailand

King Wachiralongkon Bodinthrathepphay-awarangkun
Began reign: 1 December 2016

**Prime Minister
General Prayut Chan-ocha**
Took office: 25 August 2014

Timor-Leste (East Timor)

**President
Francisco Guterres**
Took office: 20 May 2017

**Prime Minister
Taur Matan Ruak**
Took office: 22 June 2018

Togo

President Faure Gnassingbé
Took office: 4 May 2005

**Acting Prime Minister
Komi Klassou**
Took office: 5 June 2015

Tonga

King Tupou VI
Began reign: 18 March 2012

**Prime Minister
Pohiva Tu'i'onetoa**
Took office: 27 September 2019

Trinidad and Tobago

President Paula-Mae Weekes
Took office: 19 March 2018

Prime Minister Keith Rowley
Took office: 9 September 2015

KEITH ROWLEY is a VOLCANOLOGIST — a scientist who studies volcanoes.

COLOUR KEY ● Africa ● Australia, New Zealand and Oceania

Tunisia

**President
Kais Saied**
Took office: 23 October 2019

**Prime Minister
Youssef Chahed**
Took office: 27 August 2016

Turkey

**President
Recep Tayyip Erdogan**
Took office: 28 August 2014

Turkmenistan

**President Gurbanguly
Berdimuhamedow**
Took office: 14 February 2007

Tuvalu

**Governor General
Iakoba Taeia Italeli**
Took office: 16 April 2010

**Prime Minister
Kausea Natano**
Took office: 19 September 2019

Uganda

**President
Yoweri Kaguta Museveni**
Took office: 26 January 1986

Ukraine

**President
Volodymyr Zelenskyy**
Took office: 20 May 2019

**Prime Minister
Oleksiy Honcharuk**
Took office: 29 August 2019

A former actor, VOLODYMYR ZELENSKYY has appeared in SEVERAL FILMS.

United Arab Emirates

**President Khalifa bin Zayid
al-Nuhayyan**
Took office: 3 November 2004

**Prime Minister
Muhammad bin Rashid
al-Maktum**
Took office: 5 January 2006

MUHAMMAD BIN RASHID AL-MAKTUM has medalled in INTERNATIONAL HORSE RACES.

United Kingdom

Queen Elizabeth II
Began reign: 6 February 1952

**Prime Minister
Boris Johnson**
Took office: 24 July 2019

United States

President Donald J. Trump
Took office: 20 January 2017

Uruguay

President Luis Lacalle Pou
Took office: 1 March 2020

Uzbekistan

**President
Shavkat Mirziyoyev**
Took office: 8 September 2016

**Prime Minister
Abdulla Aripov**
Took office: 14 December 2016

Vanuatu

President Tallis Obed Moses
Took office: 6 July 2017

Prime Minister Charlot Salwai
Took office: 11 February 2016

Vatican City

**Supreme Pontiff
Pope Francis**
Took office: 13 March 2013

**Secretary of State
Cardinal Pietro Parolin**
Took office: 15 October 2013

POPE FRANCIS is a fan of TANGO DANCING.

Venezuela

**President
Nicolas Maduro Moros**
Took office: 19 April 2013

Vietnam

**President
Nguyen Phu Trong**
Took office: 21 October 2018

**Prime Minister
Nguyen Xuan Phuc**
Took office: 7 April 2016

Yemen

**President Abd Rabuh
Mansur Hadi**
Took office: 21 February 2012

**Prime Minister
Maeen Abd al-Malik Saeed**
Took office: 15 October 2018

Zambia

**President
Edgar Lungu**
Took office: 25 January 2015

Zimbabwe

**President
Emmerson Dambudzo
Mnnangagwa**
Took office: 24 November 2017

QUIZ WHIZ

Go back in time to seek the answers to this history quiz!

Write your answers on a piece of paper. Then check them below.

1. **True or false?** Ancient Egyptians lined linen bandages with honey to get them to stick to skin.

2. The city of _____ was part of the largest empire in the ancient world.
a. Timbuktu
b. Cairo
c. Alexandria
d. Troy

3. Farmers in China once discovered thousands of _____ buried in a field.
a. clay soldiers
b. diamonds
c. dinosaur bones
d. diamonds

4. **True or false?** The yeti is also known as Bigfoot.

5. What did Belgian resistance fighters use as a sneaky way to relay messages about the Germans during World War I?
a. secret scarves
b. hidden messages in songs
c. Morse code
d. carrier pigeons

Not **STUMPED** yet? Check out the *NATIONAL GEOGRAPHIC KIDS QUIZ WHIZ* collection for more crazy **HISTORY** questions!

ANSWERS: 1. True; 2. c; 3. a; 4. False. It's known as the Abominable Snowman; 5. a

HOMEWORK HELP

Brilliant Biographies

A biography is the story of a person's life. It can be a brief summary or a long book. Biographers — people who write biographies — use many different sources to learn about their subjects. You can write your own biography of a famous person you find inspiring.

Malala Yousafzai

Here's a SAMPLE BIOGRAPHY of Malala Yousafzai, a human rights advocate and the youngest ever recipient of the Nobel Peace Prize. Of course, there is so much more for you to discover and write about on your own!

How to Get Started

Choose a subject you find interesting. If you think Cleopatra is cool, you have a good chance of getting your reader interested, too. If you're bored by ancient Egypt, your reader will be snoring after your first paragraph.

Your subject can be almost anyone: an author, an inventor, a celebrity, a politician or a member of your family. To find someone to write about, ask yourself these simple questions:

1. Who do I want to know more about?
2. What did this person do that was special?
3. How did this person change the world?

Do Your Research

- Find out as much about your subject as possible. Read books, news articles and encyclopedia entries. Watch video clips and films, and search the internet. Conduct interviews, if possible.
- Take notes, writing down important facts and interesting stories about your subject.

Write the Biography

- Come up with a title. Include the person's name.
- Write an introduction. Consider asking a probing question about your subject.
- Include information about the person's childhood. When was this person born? Where did he or she grow up? Who did he or she admire?
- Highlight the person's talents, accomplishments and personal attributes.
- Describe the specific events that helped to shape this person's life. Did this person ever have a problem and overcome it?
- Write a conclusion. Include your thoughts about why it is important to learn about this person.
- Once you have finished your first draft, revise and then proofread your work.

Malala Yousafzai

Malala Yousafzai was born in Pakistan on July 12, 1997. Malala's father, Ziauddin, a teacher, made it his priority for his daughter to receive a proper education. Malala loved school. She learned to speak three languages and even wrote a blog about her experiences as a student.

Around the time Malala turned 10, the Taliban — a group of strict Muslims who believe women should stay at home — took over the region where she lived. The Taliban did not approve of Malala's outspoken love of learning. One day, on her way home from school, Malala was shot in the head by a Taliban gunman. Very badly injured, she was sent to a hospital in England.

Not only did Malala survive the shooting — she thrived. She used her experience as a platform to fight for girls' education worldwide. She began speaking out about educational opportunities for all. Her efforts gained worldwide attention, and she was eventually awarded the Nobel Peace Prize in 2014 at the age of 17. She is the youngest person to earn the prestigious prize.

Each year on 12 July, World Malala Day honours her heroic efforts to bring attention to human rights issues.

At Giant's Causeway in County Antrim, Northern Ireland, U.K., visitors climb the unique rock formations created millions of years ago by rapidly cooling lava.

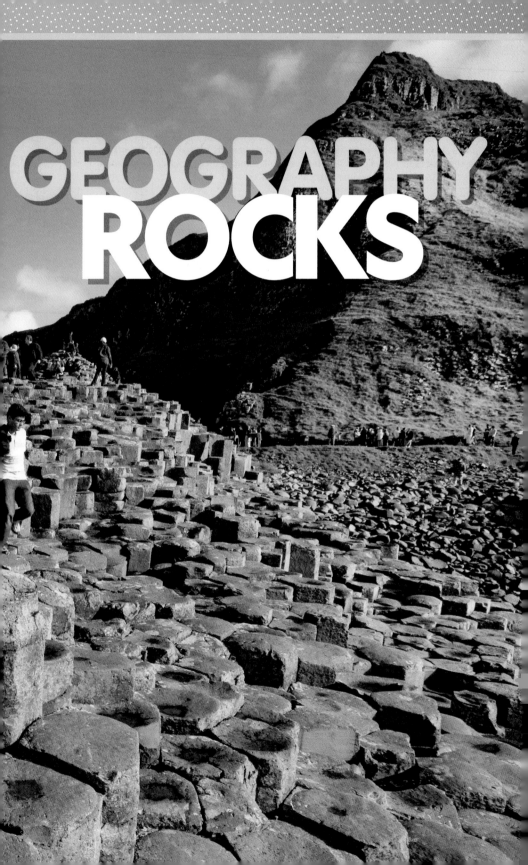

GEOGRAPHY
ROCKS

ᴛʜᴇPOLITICAL WORLD

Earth's land area is made up of seven continents, but people have divided much of the land into smaller political units called countries. Australia is a continent made up of a single country, and Antarctica is used for scientific research. But the other five continents include almost 200 independent countries. The political map shown here depicts boundaries — imaginary lines created by treaties — that separate countries. Some boundaries, such as the one between the United States and Canada, are very stable and have been recognised for many years.

See Europe map for more detail.

Winkel Tripel Projection

Other boundaries, such as the one between Sudan and South Sudan in northeast Africa, are relatively new and still disputed. Countries come in all shapes and sizes. Russia and Canada are giants; others, such as El Salvador and Qatar, are small. Some countries are long and skinny — look at Chile in South America! Still other countries — such as Indonesia and Japan in Asia — are made up of groups of islands. The political map is a clue to the diversity that makes Earth so fascinating.

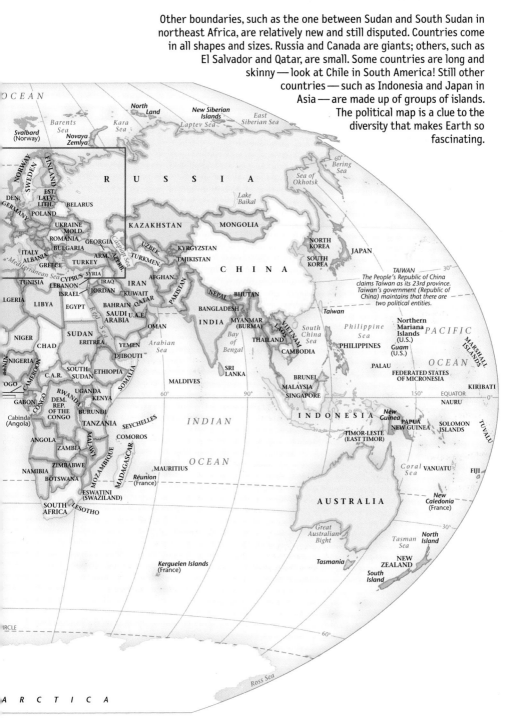

TAIWAN
The People's Republic of China claims Taiwan as its 23rd province. Taiwan's government (Republic of China) maintains that there are two political entities.

255

ᴛʜᴇPHYSICAL WORLD

Earth is dominated by large landmasses called continents — seven in all — and by an interconnected global ocean that is divided into four parts by the continents. More than 70 percent of Earth's surface is covered by oceans, and the rest is made up of land areas.

Different landforms give variety to the surface of the continents. The Rocky Mountains divide North America, the Andes mark the western edge of South America and the Himalaya tower above South Asia. The Plateau of Tibet forms the rugged core of Asia, while

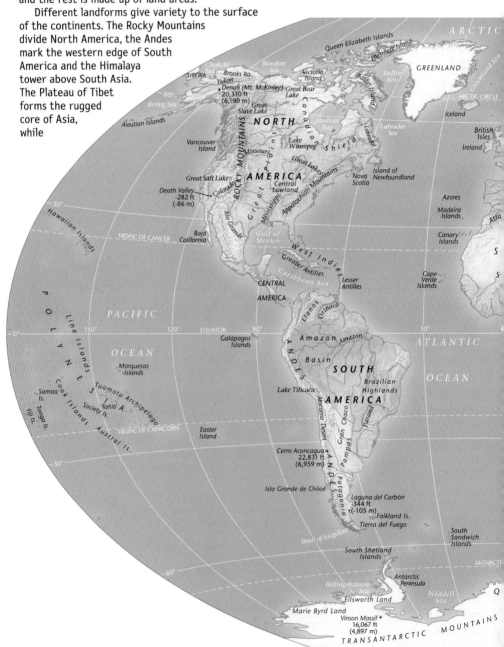

the Northern European Plain extends from the North Sea to the Ural Mountains. Much of Africa is a plateau, and dry plains cover large areas of Australia. Mountains rise more than 4,877 metres (16,000 ft) above Antarctica's massive ice sheets. Mountains and trenches make the ocean floors as varied as any continent. A mountain chain called the Mid-Atlantic Ridge runs the length of the Atlantic Ocean. In the western Pacific, trenches drop deep into the ocean floor.

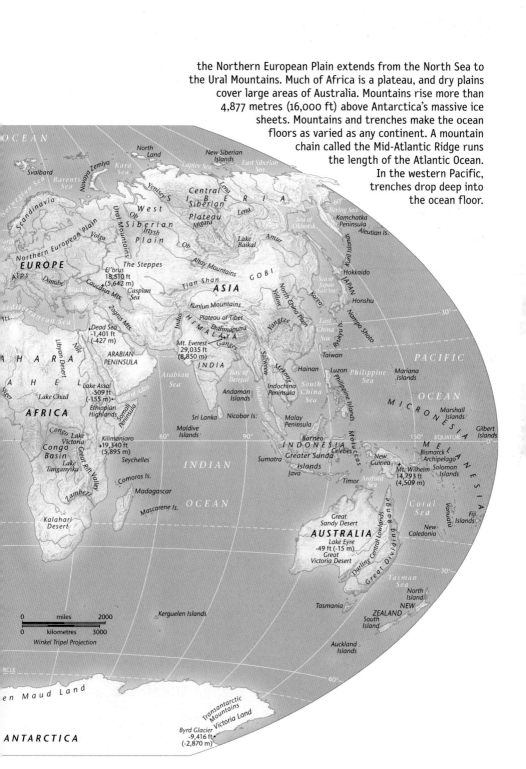

OCEAN

Svalbard
Barents Sea
Novaya Zemlya
Kara Sea
North Land
New Siberian Islands
Laptev Sea
East Siberian Sea
Norwegian Sea
Scandinavia
Yenisey S
Central
S I B E R I A
Lena
Bering Sea
North Sea
West
Ob Siberian Plateau
Lena
Angara
Kamchatka Peninsula
Sea of Okhotsk
Aleutian Is.
Ural Mountains
Volga
Ob
Irtysh
Siberian Plain
Lake Baikal
Amur
Kuril Islands
EUROPE
Alps
Danube
El'brus 18,510 ft (5,642 m)
The Steppes
Black Sea
Caucasus Mts.
Caspian Sea
Tian Shan
GOBI
Altay Mountains
Sea of Japan East Sea
JAPAN
Hokkaido
Honshu
Nampo Shoto
Mediterranean Sea
Its.
Zagros Mts.
ASIA
Kunlun Mountains
Plateau of Tibet
Yellow
North China Plain
Yangtze
East China Sea
Ryukyu Is.
Korea
Dead Sea -1,401 ft (-427 m)
ARABIAN PENINSULA
Indus
H I M A L A Y A
Brahmaputra
Mt. Everest 29,035 ft (8,850 m)
Ganges
INDIA
Salween
Taiwan
PACIFIC
SAHARA
Libyan Desert
Nile
Arabian Sea
Bay of Bengal
Mekong
Hainan
Luzon
Philippine Islands
Philippine Sea
Mariana Islands
SAHEL
Niger
Lake Chad
Lake Assal -509 ft (-155 m)
Gulf of Aden
Somali Peninsula
Ethiopian Highlands
Andaman Islands
Indochina Peninsula
South China Sea
OCEAN
MICRONESIA
Marshall Islands
AFRICA
Congo
Lake Victoria
Kilimanjaro +19,340 ft (5,895 m)
Sri Lanka
Nicobar Is.
Malay Peninsula
Maldive Islands
Borneo
Greater Sunda Islands
Celebes
Moluccas
New Guinea
Gilbert Islands
EQUATOR
MELANESIA
Congo Basin
Great Rift Valley
Lake Tanganyika
Seychelles
INDONESIA
Sumatra
Java
INDIAN
Comoros Is.
Madagascar
Mascarene Is.
OCEAN
Timor
Arafura Sea
Mt. Wilhelm 14,793 ft (4,509 m)
Bismarck Archipelago
Solomon Islands
Coral Sea
Vanuatu
Fiji Islands
Zambezi
Kalahari Desert
Great Sandy Desert
AUSTRALIA
Lake Eyre -49 ft (-15 m)
Great Victoria Desert
Central Lowlands
Darling
Great Dividing Range
New Caledonia
Tasman Sea
Kerguelen Islands
Tasmania
North Island
NEW ZEALAND
South Island
0 miles 2000
0 kilometres 3000
Winkel Tripel Projection
Auckland Islands
RCLE
en Maud Land
Transantarctic Mountains
Victoria Land
Byrd Glacier -9,416 ft (-2,870 m)
ANTARCTICA

257

KINDS OF MAPS

Maps are special tools that geographers use to tell a story about Earth. Maps can be used to show just about anything related to places. Some maps show physical features, such as mountains or vegetation. Maps can also show climates or natural hazards and other things we cannot easily see. Other maps illustrate different features on Earth — political boundaries, urban centres and economic systems.

AN IMPERFECT TOOL

Maps are not perfect. A globe is a scale model of Earth with accurate relative sizes and locations. Because maps are flat, they involve distortions of size, shape and direction. Also, cartographers — people who create maps — make choices about what information to include. Because of this, it is important to study many different types of maps to learn the complete story of Earth. Three commonly found kinds of maps are shown on this page.

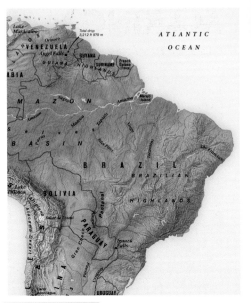

PHYSICAL MAPS. Earth's natural features — landforms, water bodies and vegetation — are shown on physical maps. The map above uses colour and shading to illustrate mountains, lakes, rivers and deserts of central South America. Country names and borders are added for reference, but they are not natural features.

POLITICAL MAPS. These maps represent characteristics of the landscape created by humans, such as boundaries, cities and place-names. Natural features are added only for reference. On the map above, capital cities are represented with a star inside a circle, while other cities are shown with black dots.

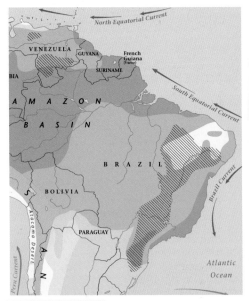

THEMATIC MAPS. Patterns related to a particular topic or theme, such as population distribution, appear on these maps. The map above displays the region's climate zones, which range from tropical wet (bright green) to tropical wet and dry (light green) to semiarid (dark yellow) to arid or desert (light yellow).

MAKING MAPS

Long ago, cartographers worked with pen and ink, carefully handcrafting maps based on explorers' observations and diaries. Today, mapmaking is a high-tech business. Cartographers use Earth data stored in 'layers' in a geographic information system (GIS) and special computer programs to create maps that can be easily updated as new information becomes available.

National Geographic staff cartographers Mike McNey and Rosemary Wardley review a map of Africa for the *National Geographic Kids World Atlas.*

Satellites in orbit around Earth act as eyes in the sky, recording data about the planet's land and ocean areas. The data is converted to numbers that are transmitted back to computers that are specially programmed to interpret the data. They record it in a form that cartographers can use to create maps.

MAP **PROJECTIONS**

To create a map, cartographers transfer an image of the round Earth to a flat surface, a process called projection. All projections involve distortion. For example, an interrupted projection (bottom map) shows accurate shapes and relative sizes of land areas, but oceans have gaps. Other types of projections are cylindrical, conic or azimuthal — each with certain advantages, but all with some distortion.

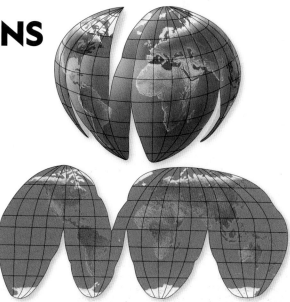

GEOGRAPHIC FEATURES

From roaring rivers to parched deserts, from underwater canyons to jagged mountains, Earth is covered with beautiful and diverse environments. Here are examples of the most common types of geographic features found around the world.

WATERFALL

Waterfalls form when a river reaches an abrupt change in elevation. The Iguazú waterfall system — on the border of Brazil and Argentina — is made up of 275 falls.

VALLEY

Valleys, cut by running water or moving ice, may be broad and flat or narrow and steep, such as the Indus River Valley (above) in Ladakh, India.

RIVER

As a river moves through flatlands, it twists and turns. Above, the Rio Los Amigos winds through a rainforest in Peru.

MOUNTAIN

Mountains are Earth's tallest landforms, and Mount Everest (above) rises highest of all, at 8,850 metres (29,035 ft) above sea level.

GLACIER

Glaciers — 'rivers' of ice — such as Hubbard Glacier (above) in Alaska, U.S.A., move slowly from mountains to the sea. Global warming is shrinking them.

CANYON

Steep-sided valleys called canyons are created mainly by running water. Buckskin Gulch (above) in Utah, U.S.A., is the deepest 'slot' canyon in the American Southwest.

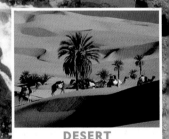

DESERT

Deserts are land features created by climate, specifically by a lack of water. Here, a camel caravan crosses the Sahara in North Africa.

THE TALLEST THING ON EARTH

MAUNA LOA

MAUNA LOA IS SO MASSIVE THAT IT ACTUALLY SUNK THE OCEAN FLOOR ABOUT 8,000 METRES (26,000 FT) IN THE SHAPE OF AN INVERTED CONE.

Think the tallest mountain on Earth is Everest? Surprise! It's Mauna Loa, an active volcano in Hawaii, U.S.A. Now, before you demand a re-measure, here's the scoop: At 17,170 metres (56,000 ft) from its peak to its base, which is depressed 7,990 metres (26,200 ft) below the ocean floor, Mauna Loa is almost twice as tall as Mount Everest's 8,850 metres (29,035 ft). So why doesn't it look like it? Because only a quarter of Mauna Loa is above water! Although Everest's summit is the highest above sea level, Mauna Loa takes the prize from top to bottom. To further bruise Everest's ego, Mauna Loa's neighbour, Mauna Kea, also towers: From the ocean floor to its summit, Mauna Kea stands at 9,750 metres (32,000 ft).

VOLCANO TYPE:
SHIELD VOLCANO*

HEIGHT BASE TO SUMMIT:
17,170 METRES (56,000 FT)

HEIGHT ABOVE SEA LEVEL:
4,170 METRES (13,680 FT)

ABOVE-WATER SURFACE AREA:
HALF OF THE BIG ISLAND OF HAWAII

ERUPTIONS SINCE 1843:
33

LAST ERUPTION:
1984

NAME'S MEANING:
'LONG MOUNTAIN'

*For more about types of volcanoes, see page 121.

AFRICA

Baobab trees from South Africa can live for 2,000 years.

Hippos show they claim a territory by yawning.

Hippopotamus

The massive continent of Africa, where humankind began millions of years ago, is second only to Asia in size. Stretching nearly as far from west to east as it does from north to south, Africa is home to both the longest river in the world (the Nile) and the largest hot desert on Earth (the Sahara).

Luanda, Angola

SPEEDY SPECIES

Some of the world's fastest animals live in Africa, such as cheetahs, pronghorn antelopes, wildebeests and lions. Each of these species can reach speeds topping 80 kilometres an hour (50 mph).

ON LOCATION

Nigeria's film industry — also known as 'Nollywood' — produces nearly 1,500 movies every year. It's the world's second largest film producer, ahead of Hollywood and behind India's Bollywood.

Great Pyramid, Great Numbers
How do the numbers for Earth's biggest pyramid stack up?

Due to erosion the pyramid is **9 metres (30 ft)** shorter than it was originally.

Weight of largest stone blocks: **14 tonnes (15 tons)**

Number of stone blocks: **2.3 million**

Number of builders: **20,000**

Angle at which the sides rise: **51°52″**

Height: **138 metres (451 ft)**

Average length of each side: **230 metres (756 ft)**

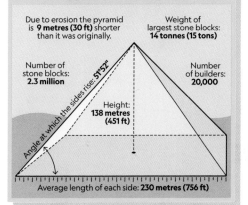

HIDDEN GEM

High atop Mount Mabu in Mozambique is a hidden rainforest where new species of snakes, butterflies, chameleons and other critters were recently found. Among the discoveries? The aptly named all-white ghost slug.

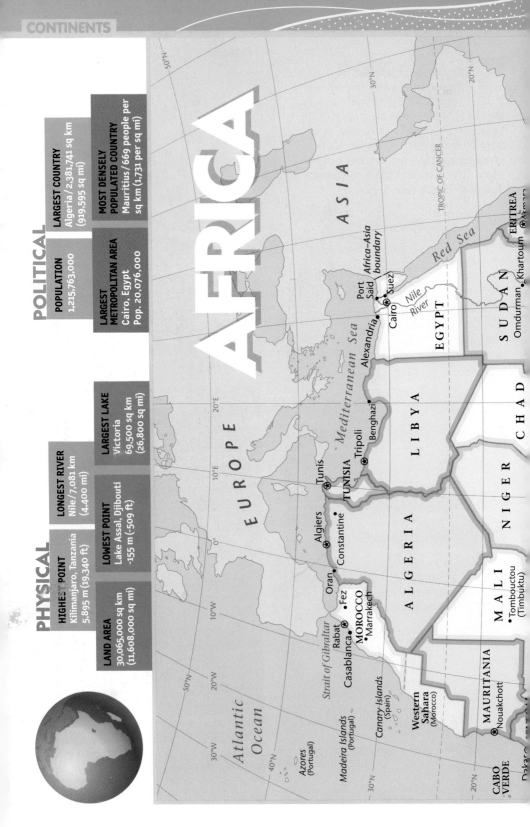

AFRICA

PHYSICAL

HIGHEST POINT Kilimanjaro, Tanzania 5,895 m (19,340 ft)	LONGEST RIVER Nile / 7,081 km (4,400 mi)
LOWEST POINT Lake Assal, Djibouti -155 m (-509 ft)	LARGEST LAKE Victoria 69,500 sq km (26,800 sq mi)
LAND AREA 30,065,000 sq km (11,608,000 sq mi)	

POLITICAL

POPULATION 1,215,763,000	LARGEST COUNTRY Algeria / 2,381,741 sq km (919,595 sq mi)
LARGEST METROPOLITAN AREA Cairo, Egypt Pop. 20,076,000	MOST DENSELY POPULATED COUNTRY Mauritius / 669 people per sq km (1,731 per sq mi)

EUROPE

ASIA

Atlantic Ocean

Mediterranean Sea

Red Sea

Azores (Portugal)

Madeira Islands (Portugal)

Canary Islands (Spain)

Strait of Gibraltar

Rabat
Casablanca
MOROCCO
Marrakech
Fez

Oran
Constantine
Algiers
Tunis
TUNISIA
Tripoli
Benghazi

LIBYA

ALGERIA

Western Sahara (Morocco)

MAURITANIA
Nouakchott

MALI
Tombouctou (Timbuktu)

NIGER

CHAD

EGYPT

Alexandria
Cairo
Port Said
Suez
Africa-Asia boundary
Nile River

SUDAN
Omdurman
Khartoum

ERITREA

CABO VERDE

Dakar

TROPIC OF CANCER

50°N
40°N
30°N
20°N
30°W
20°W
10°W
0°
10°E
20°E
30°E
50°N
30°N
20°N

264

SOMALIA
Mogadishu
Gulf of Aden
Djibouti
DJIBOUTI
SOMALILAND
Gulf of Aden
Lake Assal
(-155 m) -509 ft ▾
Addis Ababa
ETHIOPIA
SOUTH SUDAN
Juba
UGANDA
Kampala
Lake Victoria
Kisangani
RWANDA
Kigali
BURUNDI
Bujumbura
Nairobi
KENYA
Kilimanjaro
19,340 ft
(5,895 m) ▲
Mombasa
Dar es Salaam
TANZANIA
Dodoma
SEYCHELLES
Victoria ⊛
COMOROS
Moroni ⊛
MADAGASCAR
Antananarivo ⊛
MAURITIUS
Port Louis ⊛
Réunion (France)
Indian Ocean

CENTRAL AFRICAN REPUBLIC
Bangui
DEMOCRATIC REPUBLIC OF THE CONGO
Kinshasa
Mbuji-Mayi
Kananga
Lubumbashi
Kolwezi
Kitwe
ZAMBIA
Lusaka
MALAWI
Lilongwe
Harare
ZIMBABWE
MOZAMBIQUE
Mozambique Channel
N'Djamena
CAMEROON
Yaoundé
Douala
Malabo
EQUATORIAL GUINEA
GABON
Libreville
CONGO
Brazzaville
Pointe-Noire
Cabinda (Angola)
São Tomé
SAO TOME & PRINCIPE
Luanda
ANGOLA
NAMIBIA
Windhoek ⊛
BOTSWANA
Gaborone
Pretoria (Tshwane)
Johannesburg
Bloemfontein
SOUTH AFRICA
Durban
Port Elizabeth
Cape Town
Maputo
Lobamba
Mbabane
ESWATINI (SWAZILAND)
Maseru
LESOTHO

NIGERIA
Abuja
Kano
Ogbomosho
Lagos
Porto-Novo
BENIN
TOGO
Lomé
Cotonou
GHANA
Accra
Yamoussoukro
Abidjan
COTE D'IVOIRE (IVORY COAST)
LIBERIA
Monrovia
SIERRA LEONE
Freetown
GUINEA
Conakry
GUINEA-BISSAU
Bissau
Niamey
FASO
Ouagadougou
Bamako

Atlantic Ocean
St. Helena (U.K.)
Ascension (U.K.)
EQUATOR

ANTARCTICA

Gentoo penguin

Scientists found stardust in a meteorite from Antarctica.

An adult gentoo penguin makes as many as 450 dives a day looking for food.

This frozen continent may be a cool place to visit, but unless you're a penguin, you probably wouldn't want to hang out in Antarctica for long. The fact that it's the coldest, windiest and driest continent helps explain why humans never colonised this ice-covered land surrounding the South Pole.

Weddell seal

GOING THE DISTANCE

Each year, a few hundred runners from around the world compete in the Antarctica Marathon and Half-Marathon, a hilly and twisty race along the continent's icy peninsula.

A DAY TO CELEBRATE

DECEMBER
1

Signed in 1959, the Antarctic Treaty, which governs Antarctica, says that the continent should be used only for peaceful purposes. The treaty, which has now been signed by 54 countries, also established Antarctica as a scientific reserve and a place for scientific exploration. Any activities that may disrupt the natural environment are prohibited. Each year on 1 December, World Antarctica Day marks the signing of the treaty and celebrates this unique and fascinating place on Earth.

Annual Average Snowfall

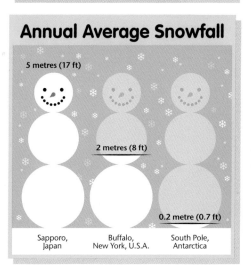

5 metres (17 ft)

2 metres (8 ft)

0.2 metre (0.7 ft)

| Sapporo, Japan | Buffalo, New York, U.S.A. | South Pole, Antarctica |

SEEING GREEN

Emerald icebergs? Only in Antarctica! Here you can spot these rare and beautiful bergs in a deep green hue. So how do these icebergs acquire their stunning shade? Experts say it could be a combo of the bluish tint of glacial ice and yellow-red glacial dust dredged up from deep below the surface.

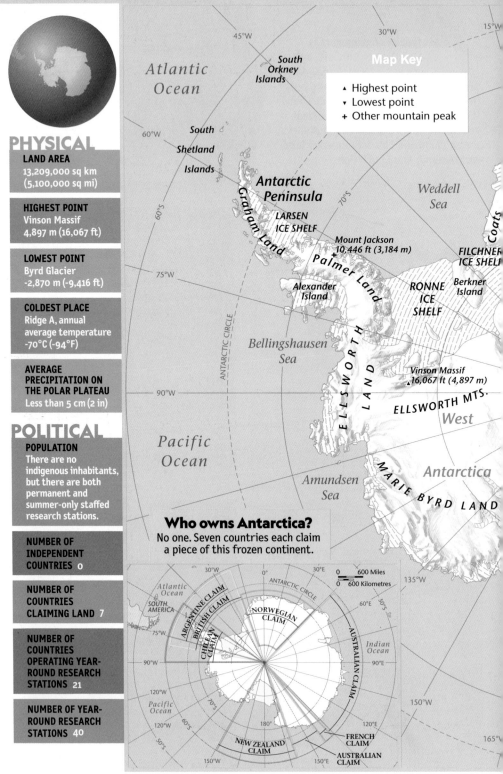

PHYSICAL

LAND AREA
13,209,000 sq km
(5,100,000 sq mi)

HIGHEST POINT
Vinson Massif
4,897 m (16,067 ft)

LOWEST POINT
Byrd Glacier
-2,870 m (-9,416 ft)

COLDEST PLACE
Ridge A, annual
average temperature
-70°C (-94°F)

**AVERAGE
PRECIPITATION ON
THE POLAR PLATEAU**
Less than 5 cm (2 in)

POLITICAL

POPULATION
There are no
indigenous inhabitants,
but there are both
permanent and
summer-only staffed
research stations.

**NUMBER OF
INDEPENDENT
COUNTRIES** 0

**NUMBER OF
COUNTRIES
CLAIMING LAND** 7

**NUMBER OF
COUNTRIES
OPERATING YEAR-
ROUND RESEARCH
STATIONS** 21

**NUMBER OF YEAR-
ROUND RESEARCH
STATIONS** 40

Map Key
▲ Highest point
▼ Lowest point
+ Other mountain peak

Atlantic Ocean

South Orkney Islands

South Shetland Islands

Antarctic Peninsula

Graham Land

LARSEN ICE SHELF

Mount Jackson
10,446 ft (3,184 m)

Weddell Sea

Coats

FILCHNER ICE SHELF

Palmer Land

Alexander Island

RONNE ICE SHELF

Berkner Island

Bellingshausen Sea

ELLSWORTH LAND

Vinson Massif
16,067 ft (4,897 m)

ELLSWORTH MTS.

West

Pacific Ocean

Antarctica

Amundsen Sea

MARIE BYRD LAND

ANTARCTIC CIRCLE

45°W 30°W 15°W
60°W
70°S
75°W
90°W

Who owns Antarctica?
No one. Seven countries each claim
a piece of this frozen continent.

Atlantic Ocean
SOUTH AMERICA
ARGENTINE CLAIM
BRITISH CLAIM
CHILEAN CLAIM
NORWEGIAN CLAIM
AUSTRALIAN CLAIM
Indian Ocean
Pacific Ocean
NEW ZEALAND CLAIM
FRENCH CLAIM
AUSTRALIAN CLAIM
ANTARCTIC CIRCLE

30°W 0° 30°E
75°W 60°E
90°W 90°E
120°W 120°E
150°W 180° 150°E
135°W
150°W
165°W

0   600 Miles
0   600 Kilometres

ANTARCTICA

FIMBUL
ICE SHELF

RIISER-LARSEN
ICE SHELF

Land

QUEEN MAUD LAND

ENDERBY
LAND

60°E

Indian
Ocean

Valkyrie
Dome

Lambert
Glacier

MacKenzie Bay

AMERY ICE SHELF

75°E

AMERICAN

HIGHLAND

WEST
ICE SHELF

TRANSANTARCTIC MOUNTAINS

Ridge A +

POLAR PLATEAU

East

South Pole

Antarctica

90°E

SHACKLETON
ICE SHELF

80°S

ROSS
ICE
SHELF

Byrd Glacier
-9,416 ft (-2,870 m)

105°E

WILKES LAND

Roosevelt
Island

Taylor
Glacier

Ross Island

Mount Erebus
12,448 ft
(3,794 m)

VICTORIA LAND

70°S

Ross
Sea

120°E

Talos
Dome

180°

60°S

Indian
Ocean

| 0 | | 600 Miles |
| 0 | | 600 Kilometres |

Azimuthal Equidistant Projection

150°E

135°E

269

ASIA

Children with a water buffalo
in Sa Pa, Vietnam

A water buffalo's wide hooves keep it from sinking in mud.

The Bengal tiger is India's national animal.

Made up of 46 countries, Asia is the world's largest continent. Just how big is it? From western Turkey to the eastern tip of Russia, Asia spans nearly half the globe! Home to more than four billion citizens — that's three out of five people on the planet — Asia's population is bigger than that of all the other continents combined.

Kuala Lumpur, Malaysia

ON THE MOVE

About a third of the population of Mongolia moves seasonally. They live in portable huts called *ger* while travelling up to 112 kilometres (70 mi) on foot to find food sources for their livestock.

FLYING HIGH

Native to Central Asia, the bar-headed goose can soar at altitudes higher than even helicopters can fly. Powerful lungs and strong wings allow these birds to cross over the Himalaya during their annual migration.

GOING BATTY

From the giant golden-crowned flying fox to the teeny-weeny bumblebee bat, Asia is home to at least 435 of the world's more than 1,300 species of bats. Indonesia has the world's largest number of species, with more than 175 different types of bats. And in Malaysia? Bats outnumber all other mammals in the country, including humans! The winged mammals help keep the ecosystem healthy, especially in Southeast Asia's forests, where the bats play a key role in spreading the seeds of trees and other plants.

World's Deepest Lakes

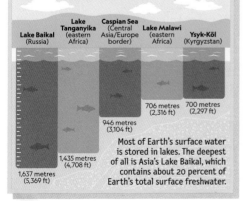

Lake Baikal (Russia)	Lake Tanganyika (eastern Africa)	Caspian Sea (Central Asia/Europe border)	Lake Malawi (eastern Africa)	Ysyk-Köl (Kyrgyzstan)
1,637 metres (5,369 ft)	1,435 metres (4,708 ft)	946 metres (3,104 ft)	706 metres (2,316 ft)	700 metres (2,297 ft)

Most of Earth's surface water is stored in lakes. The deepest of all is Asia's Lake Baikal, which contains about 20 percent of Earth's total surface freshwater.

PHYSICAL

LAND AREA
44,570,000 sq km
(17,208,000 sq mi)

HIGHEST POINT
Mount Everest,
China–Nepal
8,850 m (29,035 ft)

LOWEST POINT
Dead Sea,
Israel–Jordan
-427 m (-1,401 ft)

LONGEST RIVER
Yangtze, China
6,244 km (3,880 mi)

**LARGEST LAKE
ENTIRELY IN ASIA**
Lake Baikal, Russia
31,500 sq km
(12,200 sq mi)

POLITICAL

POPULATION
4,402,007,000

**LARGEST
METROPOLITAN AREA**
Tokyo, Japan
Pop. 37,468,000

**LARGEST COUNTRY
ENTIRELY IN ASIA**
China
9,596,960 sq km
(3,705,405 sq mi)

**MOST DENSELY
POPULATED COUNTRY**
Singapore
8,603 people
per sq km
(22,290 per sq mi)

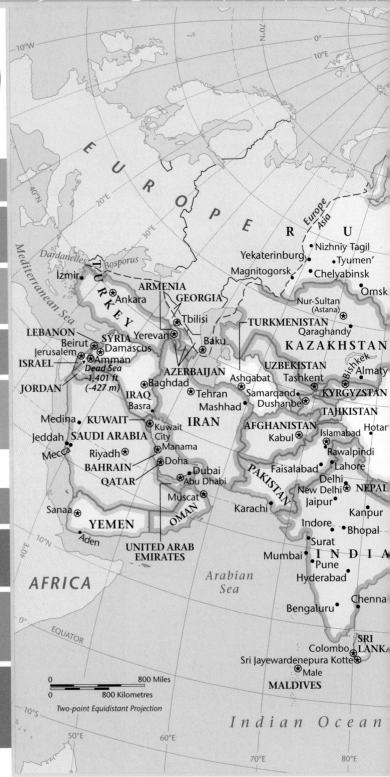

EUROPE

E R U

Europe
Asia

Nizhniy Tagil
Yekaterinburg • Tyumen'
Magnitogorsk • Chelyabinsk
Omsk

Mediterranean Sea

Dardanelles Bosporus
İzmir
ARMENIA
TURKEY
Ankara GEORGIA
Nur-Sultan
(Astana)
Tbilisi TURKMENISTAN
Qaraghandy
LEBANON SYRIA Yerevan KAZAKHSTAN
Beirut Damascus Baku
Jerusalem Amman UZBEKISTAN Bishkek
ISRAEL Dead Sea Ashgabat Tashkent Almaty
-1,401 ft AZERBAIJAN
JORDAN (-427 m) Baghdad Samarqand KYRGYZSTAN
IRAQ Tehran Dushanbe
Basra Mashhad TAJIKISTAN

Medina KUWAIT IRAN AFGHANISTAN Hotar
Jeddah Kuwait Kabul Islamabad
SAUDI ARABIA City Rawalpindi
Mecca Manama Faisalabad Lahore
Riyadh Doha Delhi
BAHRAIN Dubai New Delhi NEPAL
QATAR Abu Dhabi Jaipur
Muscat Kanpur
Sanaa Karachi Indore
YEMEN OMAN Bhopal
Aden Surat
UNITED ARAB Mumbai I N D I A
EMIRATES Pune
AFRICA Hyderabad
Arabian
Sea Chenna
Bengaluru

EQUATOR
SRI
Colombo LANKA
Sri Jayewardenepura Kotte
Male
MALDIVES

0   800 Miles
0   800 Kilometres
Two-point Equidistant Projection

I n d i a n   O c e a n

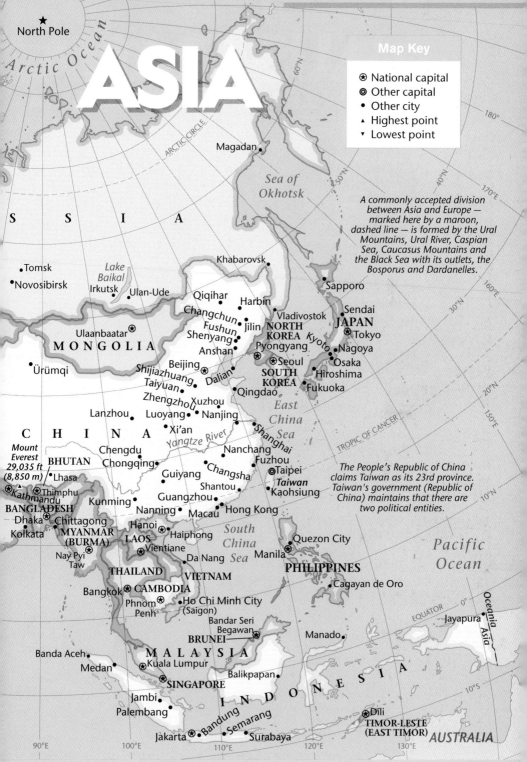

★ North Pole

Arctic Ocean

ASIA

Map Key

⊛ National capital
◉ Other capital
• Other city
▲ Highest point
▼ Lowest point

Magadan •

Sea of Okhotsk

R U S S I A

A commonly accepted division
between Asia and Europe —
marked here by a maroon,
dashed line — is formed by the Ural
Mountains, Ural River, Caspian
Sea, Caucasus Mountains and
the Black Sea with its outlets, the
Bosporus and Dardanelles.

Khabarovsk •

• Tomsk
• Novosibirsk
Lake Baikal
Irkutsk • Ulan-Ude •
Qiqihar • Harbin •
Changchun • Jilin •
Fushun •
Shenyang •
Anshan •
Vladivostok •
Sapporo •
Sendai •
JAPAN
Kyoto • Tokyo
• Nagoya

Ulaanbaatar ⊛
M O N G O L I A
NORTH KOREA
Pyongyang ◉
Seoul ⊛
SOUTH KOREA
Osaka •
Hiroshima •

• Ürümqi
Beijing ⊛
Shijiazhuang •
Taiyuan •
Dalian •
Qingdao •
Fukuoka •

East China Sea

Zhengzhou • Xuzhou •
Lanzhou • Luoyang • Nanjing •
C H I N A
Xi'an •
Yangtze River
Shanghai •

Mount Everest
29,035 ft
(8,850 m) ▲
Chengdu •
Chongqing •
Nanchang •
Fuzhou •
Taipei ◉
Taiwan
Kaohsiung •

TROPIC OF CANCER

The People's Republic of China
claims Taiwan as its 23rd province.
Taiwan's government (Republic of
China) maintains that there are
two political entities.

BHUTAN
• Lhasa
Guiyang •
Changsha •
Shantou •
Guangzhou •
Kunming •
⊛ Thimphu
⊛ Kathmandu
BANGLADESH
Dhaka ⊛
Chittagong •
Kolkata •
Nanning •
Macau •
Hong Kong •

Hanoi ⊛
Haiphong •
MYANMAR (BURMA)
LAOS
⊛ Vientiane
Da Nang •
South China Sea
Quezon City •

Nay Pyi Taw
THAILAND
VIETNAM
Manila ⊛
PHILIPPINES
Pacific Ocean

Bangkok ⊛
CAMBODIA
Phnom ⊛
Penh
Ho Chi Minh City •
(Saigon)
• Cagayan de Oro

Bandar Seri Begawan ⊛
BRUNEI
Manado •

Banda Aceh •
M A L A Y S I A
⊛ Kuala Lumpur
Balikpapan •

Medan •
⊛ **SINGAPORE**
Oceania
Asia

Jambi •
I N D O N E S I A
Jayapura •

EQUATOR

Palembang •
Dili ◉
**TIMOR-LESTE
(EAST TIMOR)**
Jakarta ⊛ Bandung •
Semarang • Surabaya •
AUSTRALIA

90°E   100°E   110°E   120°E   130°E

AUSTRALIA,
NEW ZEALAND AND OCEANIA

More than one-third of New Zealand's population lives in the city of Auckland.

Australia's last volcanic eruption was about 5,000 years ago.

Auckland Harbour in Auckland, New Zealand

G'day, mate! This vast region, covering almost 8.5 million square kilometres (3.3 million sq mi), includes Australia — the world's smallest and flattest continent — and New Zealand, as well as a fleet of mostly tiny islands scattered across the Pacific Ocean. Also known as 'down under', most of the countries in this region are in the Southern Hemisphere, south of the Equator.

Aboriginal children of Australia in ceremonial dress

COLOURFUL CRITTER

Almost half of known peacock spiders on the planet live in Western Australia. This eight-eyed spider, named for the bright blue markings on the males of the species, can jump a distance of more than 20 times its body length.

FLAT LAND

Australia has mountain ranges with low elevations compared to the other continents of the world. This makes it the flattest continent on Earth. Its highest point? Mount Kosciuszko, which is only about a quarter of the height of Mount Everest.

More Animals Than People

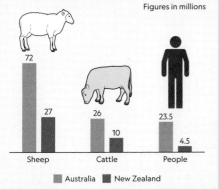

Figures in millions

	Sheep	Cattle	People
Australia	72	26	23.5
New Zealand	27	10	4.5

■ Australia ■ New Zealand

GROW ON

About 80 percent of the plants in New Zealand are not found anywhere else in the world. And some of them doubled as dinosaur snacks! Plants like the kauri — a coniferous tree — have ancestors that date back to the Jurassic period. And New Zealand's magnificent lowland forests have been nicknamed 'dinosaur forests' because of the prehistoric plants that grow there.

PHYSICAL

LAND AREA
8,490,000 sq km
(3,278,000 sq mi)

HIGHEST POINT*
Mount Wilhelm,
Papua New Guinea
4,509 m (14,793 ft)
*includes Oceania

LOWEST POINT
Lake Eyre, Australia
-15 m (-49 ft)

LONGEST RIVER
Murray-Darling,
Australia
3,672 km (2,282 mi)

LARGEST LAKE
Lake Eyre, Australia
8,884 sq km
(3,430 sq mi)

POLITICAL

POPULATION
38,004,000

**LARGEST
METROPOLITAN AREA**
Melbourne, Australia
Pop. 4,968,000

LARGEST COUNTRY
Australia
7,741,220 sq km
(2,988,901 sq mi)

**MOST DENSELY
POPULATED COUNTRY**
Nauru
476 people per sq km
(1,250 per sq mi)

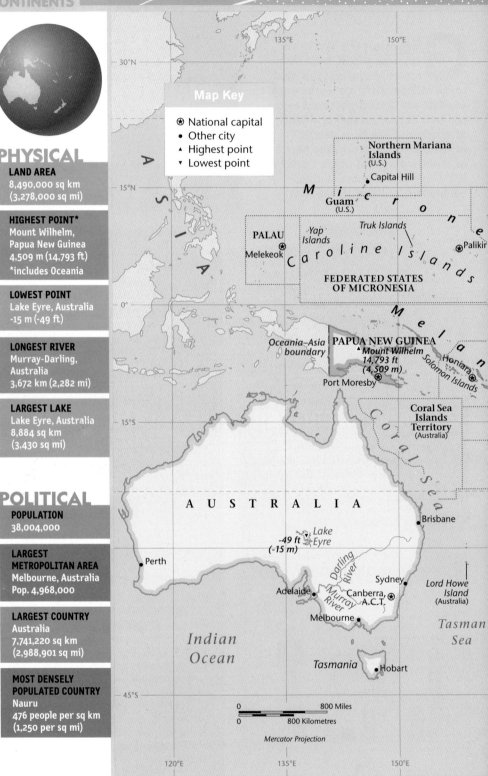

Map Key

⊗ National capital
• Other city
▲ Highest point
▼ Lowest point

Northern Mariana
Islands
(U.S.)
• Capital Hill

Guam
(U.S.)

M i c r o n e s i a

PALAU
Melekeok ⊗
Yap
Islands
Truk Islands
C a r o l i n e   I s l a n d s
Palikir ⊗

FEDERATED STATES
OF MICRONESIA

M e l a n e s i a

Oceania–Asia
boundary

PAPUA NEW GUINEA
▲ Mount Wilhelm
14,793 ft
(4,509 m)
Port Moresby ⊗

Honiara ⊗
Solomon Islands

Coral Sea
Islands
Territory
(Australia)

A S I A

Coral Sea

A U S T R A L I A

Brisbane •

-49 ft ▼ Lake
(-15 m)   Eyre

Perth •

Darling River

Murray River

Adelaide •

Sydney •
Canberra, ⊗
A.C.T.

Lord Howe
Island
(Australia)

Melbourne •

Indian
Ocean

Tasman
Sea

Tasmania   • Hobart

0   800 Miles
0   800 Kilometres

Mercator Projection

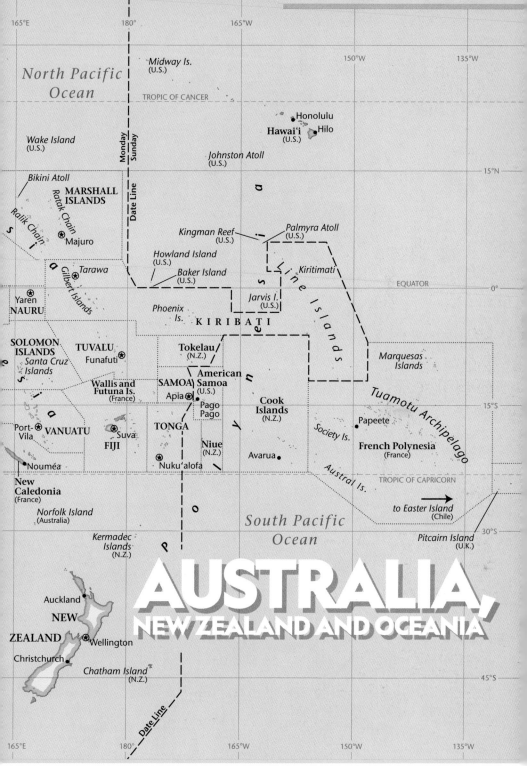

165°E   180°   165°W   150°W   135°W

North Pacific Ocean

Midway Is.
(U.S.)

TROPIC OF CANCER

Honolulu
Hawai'i • Hilo
(U.S.)

Wake Island
(U.S.)

Johnston Atoll
(U.S.)

15°N

Bikini Atoll

Monday | Sunday

MARSHALL ISLANDS

Ratak Chain

Date Line

Ralik Chain

Kingman Reef
(U.S.)

Palmyra Atoll
(U.S.)

• Majuro

Howland Island
(U.S.)

Kiritimati

Tarawa

Baker Island
(U.S.)

EQUATOR

0°

Gilbert Islands

Yaren
NAURU

Phoenix
Is.

Jarvis I.
(U.S.)

K I R I B A T I

Line Islands

SOLOMON ISLANDS

TUVALU
Funafuti

Tokelau
(N.Z.)

Marquesas
Islands

Santa Cruz
Islands

Wallis and
Futuna Is.
(France)

SAMOA

**American
Samoa**
(U.S.)

Apia •

15°S

Pago
Pago

**Cook
Islands**
(N.Z.)

Tuamotu Archipelago

Port-
Vila •

VANUATU

Suva

TONGA

Society Is.

Papeete

FIJI

Niue
(N.Z.)

Avarua •

French Polynesia
(France)

Nouméa •

Nuku'alofa

Austral Is.

TROPIC OF CAPRICORN

**New
Caledonia**
(France)

Norfolk Island
(Australia)

*South Pacific
Ocean*

to Easter Island
(Chile)

Kermadec
Islands
(N.Z.)

Pitcairn Island
(U.K.)

30°S

AUSTRALIA,
NEW ZEALAND AND OCEANIA

Auckland •

NEW

ZEALAND • Wellington

Christchurch •

Chatham Island
(N.Z.)

45°S

Date Line

165°E   180°   165°W   150°W   135°W

EUROPE

On sunny days, the Eiffel Tower in Paris, France, leans towards the shade.

You can cross the border between Spain and Portugal on a zip line.

Acrobats build human castles at the La Mercè festival in Barcelona, Spain.

278

A cluster of islands and peninsulas jutting west from Asia, Europe is bordered by the Atlantic and Arctic Oceans and more than a dozen seas. Here you'll find a variety of scenery, from mountains to countryside to coastlines. Europe is also known for its rich culture and fascinating history, which make it one of the most visited continents on Earth.

Traditional dance performed in Greece

SPOT IT

Dalmatians get their name from Dalmatia, a region of Croatia along the Adriatic Sea. The spotted canines have served as border guard dogs during conflicts in the region.

LONG REIGN

The longest reign of any European monarch was that of Afonso Henriques, who served from 1112 to 1185, first as count, then as king of Portugal. Also known as Afonso the Conqueror, this leader is credited with securing Portugal's independence from the kingdom of Leon in 1139. A close runner-up? Louis XIV, who reigned as king of France for 72 years, from 1643 until 1715.

Europe's Six Most Visited Cities

1. London, U.K.
🇬🇧 ♀♀♀♀♀♀♀♀♀♀♀♀♀♀♀♀♀♀♀♀ 20.72 million

2. Paris, France
🇫🇷 ♀♀♀♀♀♀♀♀♀♀♀♀♀♀♀♀ 16.84 million

3. Istanbul, Turkey
🇹🇷 ♀♀♀♀♀♀♀♀♀♀♀♀ 12.12 million

4. Antalya, Turkey
🇹🇷 ♀♀♀♀♀♀♀♀♀♀ 10.73 million

5. Rome, Italy
🇮🇹 ♀♀♀♀♀♀♀♀♀ 9.70 million

6. Prague, Czechia
🇨🇿 ♀♀♀♀♀♀♀ 9.04 million

Estimated international visitors in 2018
Source: Euromonitor International

OLD SHOW

Folks have been watching films at the Eden Theatre in La Ciotat, a seaside town in southern France, since 1899. The 166-seat theatre is considered one of the oldest cinemas in the world.

279

PHYSICAL

LAND AREA
9,947,000 sq km
(3,841,000 sq mi)

HIGHEST POINT
El'brus, Russia
5,642 m (18,510 ft)

LOWEST POINT
Caspian Sea
-28 m (-92 ft)

LONGEST RIVER
Volga, Russia
3,685 km
(2,290 mi)

**LARGEST LAKE
ENTIRELY IN EUROPE**
Ladoga, Russia
17,749 sq km
(6,853 sq mi)

POLITICAL

POPULATION
751,632,000

**LARGEST
METROPOLITAN AREA**
Moscow, Russia
Pop. 12,410,000

**LARGEST COUNTRY
ENTIRELY IN EUROPE**
Ukraine
603,550 sq km
(233,032 sq mi)

**MOST DENSELY
POPULATED COUNTRY**
Monaco
19,000 people per sq
km (38,000 per sq mi)

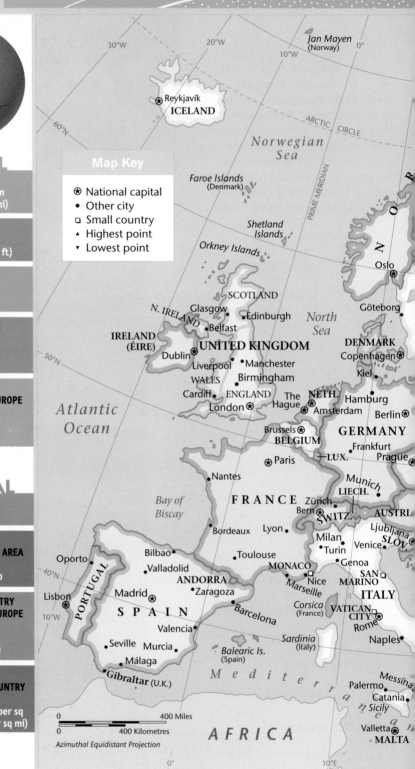

Map Key
⊛ National capital
• Other city
▫ Small country
▲ Highest point
▼ Lowest point

EUROPE

A commonly accepted division between Asia and Europe — marked here by a maroon, dashed line — is formed by the Ural Mountains, Ural River, Caspian Sea, Caucasus Mountains and the Black Sea with its outlets, the Bosporus and Dardanelles.

10°E 20°E 30°E 40°E 50°E 60°E

Barents Sea

60°N

Asia
Europe

Murmansk

N O R W A Y

S W E D E N

FINLAND

Archangel

R U S S I A

•Ufa

Lake Ladoga

Helsinki

St. Petersburg

Volga River Kazan'

Tallinn
Stockholm
ESTONIA

Yaroslavl'
Tver'
Moscow
Ryazan'

Nizhniy
Novgorod

Samara Orenburg

Baltic Sea

Rīga LATVIA

Smolensk

•Penza

50°N

LITHUANIA
Vitsyebsk•
Kaliningrad Vilnius
(Russia) Kaunas•
Gdańsk•

Bryansk

Saratov•

KAZAKHSTAN

Minsk

BELARUS

POLAND
•Łódź
Bydgoszcz
•Wrocław
Warsaw
Homyel'•

Kursk

Volgograd•

Kraków•

Kiev•
Kharkiv

CZECHIA
(CZECH REP.)
Vienna
SLOVAKIA
Bratislava
Budapest
HUNGARY
Zagreb
CROATIA
BOSNIA &
HERZEGOVINA
Sarajevo
SERBIA
MONTENEGRO
Podgorica
Tirana N. MACED.
ALBANIA

L'viv UKRAINE
Poltava•
Vinnytsya Donets'k
•Dnipropetrovs'k

Rostov

Astrakhan'

MOLDOVA
Chişinău

Boundary
claimed
by Ukraine

-92 ft
(-28 m)

Caspian Sea

ROMANIA

Odesa
CRIMEA
Simferopol'
Sevastopol'

El'brus
(5,642 m) 18,510 ft

Grozny
Sochi

Baku

Belgrade Bucharest

GEORGIA

AZERBAIJAN

40°N

Black Sea

BULGARIA
Sofia
Skopje

Varna

Bosporus

Thessaloníki Istanbul

T U R K E Y

Dardanelles

GREECE

Athens

Sea

Crete

NORTHERN CYPRUS
Nicosia
CYPRUS

20°E 30°E 40°E

NORTH AMERICA

Grand Banks, Newfoundland, Canada, is the foggiest place on Earth.

Wolves howl more often in the winter.

A grey wolf running along a forest trail during autumn in Minnesota, U.S.A.

From the Great Plains of the United States and Canada to the rainforests of Panama, North America stretches 8,850 kilometres (5,500 mi) from north to south. The third largest continent, North America can be divided into five regions: the mountainous west (including parts of Mexico and Central America's western coast), the Great Plains, the Canadian Shield, the varied eastern region (including Central America's lowlands and coastal plains) and the Caribbean.

Onlookers celebrate the opening of the Panama Canal expansion in 2016.

BIG BONES

Canada was once a hotbed of activity for dinosaurs. In fact, the skeleton of the largest *Tyrannosaurus rex* to date was recently uncovered by researchers at a site in Saskatchewan, Canada. Estimated to weigh more than an elephant, the giant dino — nicknamed 'Scotty' — stomped around some 68 million years ago.

BERRY GOOD

The United States is the world's largest producer of strawberries, with some 90 percent of the crops grown in the coastal climates of California. That's about 907 million kilograms (2 billion lb) of strawberries plucked from the state each year! Other top strawberry-producing states? Florida, Oregon, North Carolina and Washington.

International Tourist Arrivals

Cuba
4,594,000

Puerto Rico
3,797,000

Jamaica
2,353,000

Bahamas
1,439,000

International tourist arrivals, 2018 data

TAKING FLIGHT

Millions of monarchs migrate up to 4,800 kilometres (3,000 mi) to Mexico every year from the United States and Canada. They're the only butterflies to make such a massive journey.

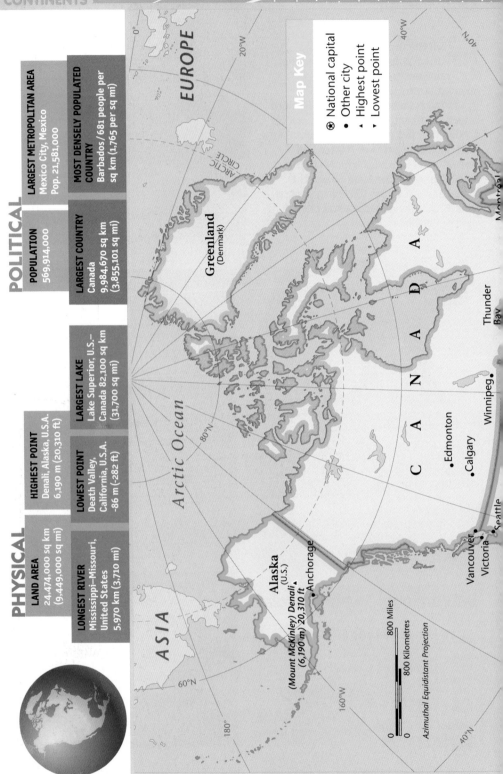

PHYSICAL

LAND AREA
24,474,000 sq km
(9,449,000 sq mi)

LONGEST RIVER
Mississippi–Missouri,
United States
5,970 km (3,710 mi)

HIGHEST POINT
Denali, Alaska, U.S.A.
6,190 m (20,310 ft)

LOWEST POINT
Death Valley,
California, U.S.A.
-86 m (-282 ft)

LARGEST LAKE
Lake Superior, U.S.–
Canada 82,100 sq km
(31,700 sq mi)

POLITICAL

POPULATION
569,914,000

LARGEST COUNTRY
Canada
9,984,670 sq km
(3,855,101 sq mi)

LARGEST METROPOLITAN AREA
Mexico City, Mexico
Pop. 21,581,000

MOST DENSELY POPULATED COUNTRY
Barbados / 681 people per
sq km (1,765 per sq mi)

Map Key

⊛ National capital
• Other city
▲ Highest point
▼ Lowest point

EUROPE

Greenland
(Denmark)

ARCTIC CIRCLE

Arctic Ocean

ASIA

Alaska
(U.S.)

(Mount McKinley) Denali ▲
(6,190 m) 20,310 ft
• Anchorage

C   A   N   A   D   A

• Edmonton
• Calgary
Winnipeg •
Thunder Bay •
Montreal

Vancouver •
Victoria • • Seattle

80°N
60°N
40°N
0°
20°W
40°W
160°W
180°

800 Miles
800 Kilometres
0
0

Azimuthal Equidistant Projection

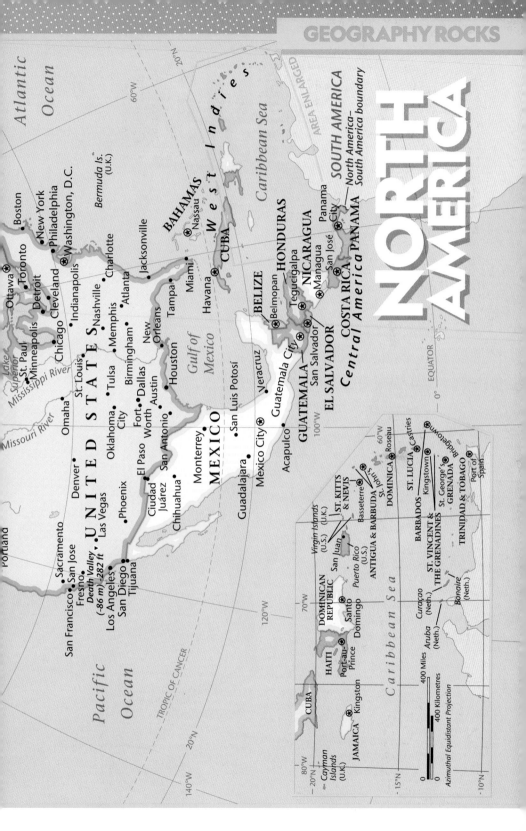

NORTH AMERICA

Atlantic Ocean

AREA ENLARGED

SOUTH AMERICA
North America–
South America boundary

Bermuda Is.
(U.K.)

West Indies

Caribbean Sea

BAHAMAS
Nassau ✪

CUBA

Boston
New York
Philadelphia
Washington, D.C. ✪
Ottawa ✪
Toronto
Detroit
Cleveland
Indianapolis
Charlotte
Jacksonville
Nashville
Atlanta
Memphis
Birmingham
New Orleans
Tampa
Miami ✪
Havana ✪

BELIZE
Belmopan ✪
HONDURAS
Tegucigalpa ✪
NICARAGUA
Managua ✪
COSTA RICA
San José ✪
Panama City ✪
PANAMA
Central America

GUATEMALA
Guatemala City ✪
EL SALVADOR
San Salvador ✪

St. Paul
Minneapolis
Chicago
Milwaukee
St. Louis
Kansas City

Lake Superior
Mississippi River
Missouri River

U N I T E D   S T A T E S

Omaha
Oklahoma City
Tulsa
Dallas
Fort Worth
Austin
San Antonio
Houston
Gulf of Mexico
Veracruz
San Luis Potosí

Denver
Las Vegas
Phoenix
El Paso
Ciudad Juárez
Chihuahua
Monterrey

MEXICO
Mexico City ✪
Acapulco
Guadalajara

Portland
Sacramento
San Jose
Fresno
San Francisco
Death Valley −282 ft
(−86 m)
Los Angeles
San Diego
Tijuana

Pacific Ocean

TROPIC OF CANCER

20°N

120°W
140°W
100°W
80°W
70°W
60°W

EQUATOR
0°

Virgin Islands
(U.S.)
ST. KITTS
& NEVIS
Basseterre ✪
ANTIGUA & BARBUDA
St. John's ✪
DOMINICA
Roseau ✪
ST. LUCIA
Castries ✪
BARBADOS
Bridgetown ✪
ST. VINCENT &
THE GRENADINES
Kingstown ✪
GRENADA
St. George's ✪
TRINIDAD & TOBAGO
Port of Spain ✪

Puerto Rico
(U.S.)
San Juan ✪
DOMINICAN
REPUBLIC
Santo Domingo ✪
HAITI
Port-au-Prince ✪

Curaçao
(Neth.)
Aruba
(Neth.)
Bonaire
(Neth.)

CUBA
JAMAICA
Kingston ✪
Cayman
Islands
(U.K.)

Caribbean Sea

400 Miles
400 Kilometres
0
Azimuthal Equidistant Projection

20°N
15°N
10°N

SOUTH AMERICA

Lasting about five minutes, Uruguay's national anthem is the world's longest in duration.

Brazil has participated in the World Cup 21 times — more than any other team.

A boy plays football in Manaus, Brazil.

South America is bordered by three major bodies of water — the Caribbean Sea, Atlantic Ocean and Pacific Ocean. The world's fourth largest continent extends over a range of climates, from tropical in the north to subarctic in the south. South America produces a rich diversity of natural resources, including nuts, fruits, sugar, grains, coffee and chocolate.

Santiago Cathedral in Santiago, Chile

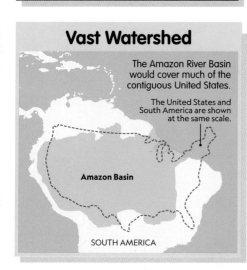

BIG BIRD

The Andean condor, which lives exclusively in the mountains and valleys of the Andes, is the largest raptor in the world and the largest flying bird in South America.

OCEANS ALL AROUND

South America is surrounded by both the Pacific and Atlantic Oceans. Experts think that the two oceans used to be one massive body of water until North and South America joined together at the Isthmus of Panama some three million years ago. That move, scientists think, divided the original ocean into two. Today, Colombia and Chile are the only two countries in South America with a coastline on each ocean.

Vast Watershed

The Amazon River Basin would cover much of the contiguous United States.

The United States and South America are shown at the same scale.

Amazon Basin

SOUTH AMERICA

ANCIENT BRIDGE

Deep in the Peruvian Andes, a suspension bridge made of handwoven grass stretches more than 30 metres (100 ft) over a rushing river. Once used to connect two villages on either side of the river, the bridge, which dates back more than 500 years, is now more of a symbolic nod to the past. Each June, the suspension bridge is rebuilt and replaced by the local indigenous community.

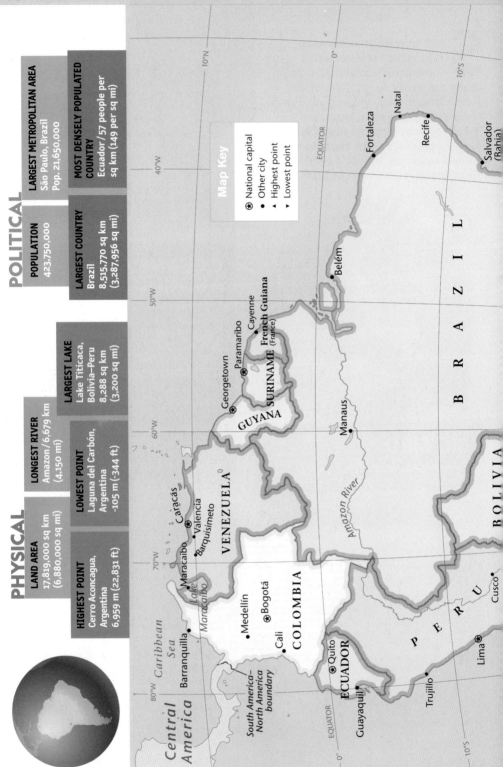

PHYSICAL

LAND AREA
17,819,000 sq km
(6,880,000 sq mi)

HIGHEST POINT
Cerro Aconcagua,
Argentina
6,959 m (22,831 ft)

LOWEST POINT
Laguna del Carbón,
Argentina
-105 m (-344 ft)

LONGEST RIVER
Amazon / 6,679 km
(4,150 mi)

LARGEST LAKE
Lake Titicaca,
Bolivia–Peru
8,288 sq km
(3,200 sq mi)

POLITICAL

POPULATION
423,750,000

LARGEST COUNTRY
Brazil
8,515,770 sq km
(3,287,956 sq mi)

LARGEST METROPOLITAN AREA
São Paulo, Brazil
Pop. 21,650,000

MOST DENSELY POPULATED COUNTRY
Ecuador / 57 people per
sq km (149 per sq mi)

Map Key

⊛ National capital
• Other city
▲ Highest point
▼ Lowest point

Central America

Caribbean Sea

South America–North America boundary

Barranquilla
Maracaibo
Lake Maracaibo
Caracás
Valencia
Barquisimeto
VENEZUELA
Medellín
Bogotá
Cali
COLOMBIA
Quito
ECUADOR
Guayaquil
Trujillo
Lima
Cusco
P E R U
BOLIVIA
Georgetown
GUYANA
Paramaribo
SURINAME
Cayenne
French Guiana
(France)
Manaus
Amazon River
B R A Z I L
Belém
Fortaleza
Natal
Recife
Salvador
(Bahia)

EQUATOR

10°N
0°
10°S

40°W
50°W
60°W
70°W
80°W

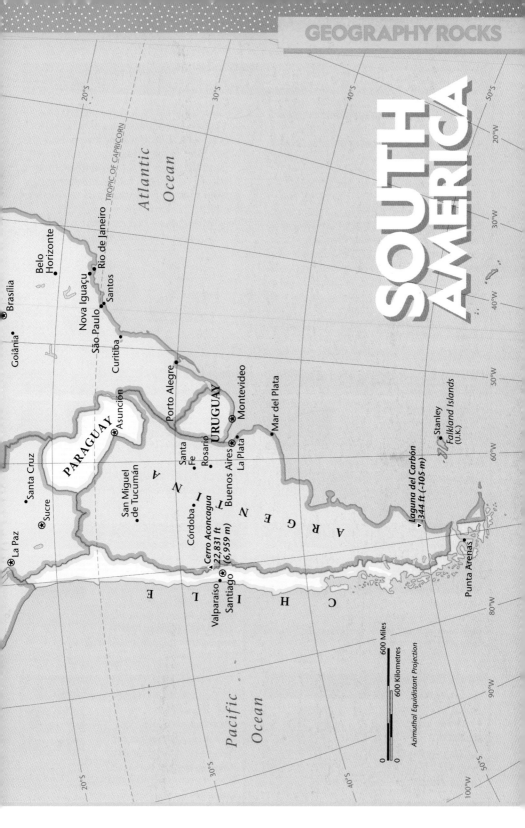

SOUTH
AMERICA

Atlantic
Ocean

TROPIC OF CAPRICORN

20°S

30°S

40°S

50°S

20°W

30°W

40°W

50°W

60°W

Brasília

Belo
Horizonte

Goiânia

Rio de Janeiro

Nova Iguaçu

Santos

São Paulo

Curitiba

Porto Alegre

PARAGUAY

Asunción

Santa Cruz

Sucre

La Paz

San Miguel
de Tucumán

Córdoba

Cerro Aconcagua
22,831 ft
(6,959 m)

Valparaíso
Santiago

Santa
Fe

Rosario

URUGUAY

Montevideo

Buenos Aires

La Plata

Mar del Plata

ARGENTINA

CHILE

Laguna del Carbón
−344 ft (−105 m)

Stanley
Falkland Islands
(U.K.)

Punta Arenas

Pacific
Ocean

600 Miles

600 Kilometres

Azimuthal Equidistant Projection

0

0

20°S

30°S

40°S

50°S

80°W

90°W

100°W

289

COUNTRIES OF THE WORLD

The following pages present a general overview of all 195 independent countries recognised by the National Geographic Society, including the newest nation, South Sudan, which gained independence in 2011.

The flags of each independent country symbolise diverse cultures and histories. The statistical data cover highlights of geography and demography and provide a brief overview of each country. They present general characteristics and are not intended to be comprehensive. For example, not every language spoken in a specific country can be listed. Thus, languages shown are the most representative of that area. This is also true of the religions mentioned.

A country is defined as a political body with its own independent government, geographical space and, in most cases, laws, military and taxes.

Disputed areas such as Northern Cyprus and Taiwan, and dependencies of independent nations, such as Bermuda and Puerto Rico, are not included in this listing.

Note the colour key at the bottom of the pages and the locator map below, which assign a colour to each country based on the continent on which it is located. Some capital city populations include that city's metro area. All information is accurate as of press time.

Colour Key by Continent

Afghanistan

Area: 652,230 sq km (251,827 sq mi)
Population: 34,941,000
Capital: Kabul, pop. 4,012,000
Currency: afghani
Religions: Sunni Muslim, Shia Muslim
Languages: Afghan Persian (Dari), Pashto, Uzbek, Turkmen

Albania

Area: 28,748 sq km (11,100 sq mi)
Population: 3,057,000
Capital: Tirana, pop. 476,000
Currency: lek
Religions: Muslim, Roman Catholic, Orthodox
Languages: Albanian, Greek, Vlach, Romani, Slavic dialects

Algeria

Area: 2,381,741 sq km (919,595 sq mi)
Population: 41,657,000
Capital: Algiers, pop. 2,694,000
Currency: Algerian dinar
Religion: Sunni Muslim
Languages: Arabic, French, Berber dialects

Andorra

Area: 468 sq km (181 sq mi)
Population: 86,000
Capital: Andorra la Vella, pop. 23,000
Currency: euro
Religion: Roman Catholic
Languages: Catalan, French, Castilian, Portuguese

Angola

Area: 1,246,700 sq km (481,353 sq mi)
Population: 30,356,000
Capital: Luanda, pop. 7,774,000
Currency: kwanza
Religions: Roman Catholic, Protestant, indigenous beliefs
Languages: Portuguese, Umbundu, other African languages

Antigua and Barbuda

Area: 443 sq km (171 sq mi)
Population: 96,000
Capital: St. John's, pop. 21,000
Currency: East Caribbean dollar
Religions: Anglican, Methodist, other Protestant, Roman Catholic
Languages: English, Antiguan creole

Argentina

Area: 2,780,400 sq km
(1,073,518 sq mi)
Population: 44,694,000
Capital: Buenos Aires,
pop. 14,967,000
Currency: Argentine peso
Religion: Roman Catholic
Languages: Spanish, Italian, English, German, French

Armenia

Area: 29,743 sq km
(11,484 sq mi)
Population: 3,038,000
Capital: Yerevan,
pop. 1,080,000
Currency: Armenian dram
Religions: Armenian Apostolic, other Christian
Languages: Armenian, Russian

Australia

Area: 7,741,220 sq km
(2,988,901 sq mi)
Population: 23,470,000
Capital: Canberra, A.C.T.,
pop. 423,000
Currency: Australian dollar
Religions: Anglican, Roman Catholic, other Christian
Language: English

Austria

Area: 83,871 sq km (32,383 sq mi)
Population: 8,793,000
Capital: Vienna, pop. 1,901,000
Currency: euro
Religions: Roman Catholic, Protestant, Muslim
Languages: German, Turkish, Serbian, Croatian,
Slovene, Hungarian

Azerbaijan

Area: 86,600 sq km
(33,436 sq mi)
Population: 10,047,000
Capital: Baku, pop. 2,286,000
Currency: Azerbaijani manat
Religions: Muslim, Russian Orthodox
Languages: Azerbaijani (Azeri), Russian, Armenian

Bahamas

Area: 13,880 sq km
(5,359 sq mi)
Population: 333,000
Capital: Nassau, pop. 280,000
Currency: Bahamian dollar
Religions: Baptist, Anglican, Pentecostal,
Roman Catholic
Languages: English, Creole

Bahrain

Area: 760 sq km (293 sq mi)
Population: 1,443,000
Capital: Manama, pop. 565,000
Currency: Bahraini dinar
Religions: Muslim (Shia and Sunni), Christian
Languages: Arabic, English, Farsi, Urdu

Bangladesh

Area: 148,460 sq km
(57,321 sq mi)
Population: 159,453,000
Capital: Dhaka, pop. 19,578,000
Currency: taka
Religions: Muslim, Hindu
Language: Bangla (Bengali)

3 cool things about BANGLADESH

1. Hailstones the size of grapefruits once hammered the Gopalganj district of Bangladesh. Weighing 1 kilogram (2 lb), they are the heaviest hailstones on record.

2. Bangladesh provides plenty of the world's fruit, including mangoes, guavas, papayas, lemons, pineapples and watermelons. The jackfruit, which can weigh as much as a 12-year-old, also comes from the country.

3. Much of the remaining Bengal tiger population prowls around the area of Bangladesh known as the Sundarban. It's estimated that fewer than 200 tigers roam the area, the world's only coastal habitat for the big cats.

Barbados

Area: 430 sq km (166 sq mi)
Population: 293,000
Capital: Bridgetown, pop. 89,000
Currency: Barbadian dollar
Religions: Protestant, Roman Catholic
Languages: English, Bajan

Bhutan

Area: 38,394 sq km (14,824 sq mi)
Population: 766,000
Capital: Thimphu, pop. 203,000
Currencies: ngultrum, Indian rupee
Religions: Lamaistic Buddhist,
Indian- and Nepalese-influenced Hindu
Languages: Sharchhopka, Dzongkha, Lhotshamkha

Belarus

Area: 207,600 sq km
(80,155 sq mi)
Population: 9,528,000
Capital: Minsk, pop. 2,005,000
Currency: Belarusian ruble
Religions: Eastern Orthodox, Roman Catholic
Languages: Russian, Belarusian

Bolivia

Area: 1,098,581 sq km (424,164 sq mi)
Population: 11,306,000
Capitals: La Paz, pop. 1,814,000;
Sucre, pop. 278,000
Currency: boliviano
Religions: Roman Catholic, Protestant
Languages: Spanish, Quechua, Aymara

Belgium

Area: 30,528 sq km (11,787 sq mi)
Population: 11,571,000
Capital: Brussels, pop. 2,050,000
Currency: euro
Religions: Roman Catholic, Muslim,
Protestant
Languages: Dutch, French, German

Bosnia and Herzegovina

Area: 51,197 sq km
(19,767 sq mi)
Population: 3,850,000
Capital: Sarajevo, pop. 343,000
Currency: convertible mark
Religions: Muslim, Orthodox, Roman Catholic
Languages: Bosnian, Serbian, Croatian

Belize

Area: 22,966 sq km (8,867 sq mi)
Population: 386,000
Capital: Belmopan, pop. 23,000
Currency: Belize dollar
Religions: Roman Catholic, Protestant
(includes Pentecostal, Seventh-Day Adventist,
Mennonite, Methodist)
Languages: English, Spanish, Creole, Maya

Botswana

Area: 581,730 sq km
(224,607 sq mi)
Population: 2,249,000
Capital: Gaborone, pop. 269,000
Currency: pula
Religions: Christian, Badimo
Languages: Setswana, Sekalanga, Sekgalagadi, English

Benin

Area: 112,622 sq km (43,484 sq mi)
Population: 11,341,000
Capitals: Porto-Novo, pop. 285,000;
Cotonou, pop. 685,000
Currency: Communauté Financière Africaine franc
Religions: Muslim, Roman Catholic, Protestant, Vodoun
Languages: French, Fon, Yoruba, tribal languages

Brazil

Area: 8,515,770 sq km
(3,287,956 sq mi)
Population: 208,847,000
Capital: Brasília, pop. 4,470,000
Currency: Brazilian real
Religions: Roman Catholic, Protestant
Language: Portuguese

Brunei

Area: 5,765 sq km (2,226 sq mi)
Population: 451,000
Capital: Bandar Seri Begawan, pop. 241,000
Currency: Brunei dollar
Religions: Muslim, Christian, Buddhist, indigenous beliefs
Languages: Malay, English, Chinese

Burkina Faso

Area: 274,200 sq km (105,869 sq mi)
Population: 19,743,000
Capital: Ouagadougou, pop. 2,531,000
Currency: Communauté Financière Africaine franc
Religions: Muslim, Catholic, animist
Languages: French, African languages

Bulgaria

Area: 110,879 sq km (42,811 sq mi)
Population: 7,058,000
Capital: Sofia, pop. 1,272,000
Currency: Bulgarian lev
Religions: Eastern Orthodox, Muslim
Languages: Bulgarian, Turkish, Romany

Burundi

Area: 27,830 sq km (10,745 sq mi)
Population: 11,845,000
Capital: Bujumbura, pop. 899,000
Currency: Burundi franc
Religions: Roman Catholic, Protestant, Muslim
Languages: Kirundi, French, Swahili

SNAPSHOT
Bhutan

A sacred site, Paro Taktsang — or Tiger's Nest Monastery — sits at the edge of a cliff some 915 metres (3,000 ft) above Paro, Bhutan.

● Asia ● Europe ● North America ● South America

Cabo Verde

Area: 4,033 sq km (1,557 sq mi)
Population: 568,000
Capital: Praia, pop. 168,000
Currency: Cape Verdean escudo
Religions: Roman Catholic, Protestant
Languages: Portuguese, Crioulo

Cameroon

Area: 475,440 sq km (183,568 sq mi)
Population: 25,641,000
Capital: Yaoundé, pop. 3,412,000
Currency: Communauté Financière Africaine franc
Religions: Roman Catholic, Protestant, Muslim, animist
Languages: African languages, English, French

Cambodia

Area: 181,035 sq km (69,898 sq mi)
Population: 16,450,000
Capital: Phnom Penh, pop. 1,952,000
Currency: riel
Religion: Buddhist
Language: Khmer

Canada

Area: 9,984,670 sq km (3,855,101 sq mi)
Population: 35,882,000
Capital: Ottawa, pop. 1,363,000
Currency: Canadian dollar
Religions: Roman Catholic, Protestant
Languages: English, French

SNAPSHOT Colombia

A long-tailed sylph hummingbird feeds on a tropical flower in Colombia.

Central African Republic

Area: 622,984 sq km (240,535 sq mi)
Population: 5,745,000
Capital: Bangui, pop. 851,000
Currency: Communauté Financière Africaine franc
Religions: indigenous beliefs, Protestant, Roman Catholic, Muslim
Languages: French, Sangho, tribal languages

Chad

Area: 1,284,000 sq km (495,755 sq mi)
Population: 15,833,000
Capital: N'Djamena, pop. 1,323,000
Currency: Communauté Financière Africaine franc
Religions: Muslim, Protestant, Roman Catholic, animist
Languages: French, Arabic, Sara, indigenous languages

Chile

Area: 756,102 sq km (291,932 sq mi)
Population: 17,925,000
Capital: Santiago, pop. 6,680,000
Currency: Chilean peso
Religions: Roman Catholic, Protestant
Languages: Spanish, English, indigenous languages

China

Area: 9,596,960 sq km (3,705,405 sq mi)
Population: 1,384,689,000
Capital: Beijing, pop. 19,618,000
Currency: yuan
Religions: folk religion, Buddhist, Christian
Languages: Standard Chinese or Mandarin, Yue or Cantonese, Wu, Minbei, Minnan, Xiang, Gan, Hakka dialects

Colombia

Area: 1,138,910 sq km (439,735 sq mi)
Population: 48,169,000
Capital: Bogotá, pop. 10,574,000
Currency: Colombian peso
Religions: Roman Catholic, Protestant
Language: Spanish

Comoros

Area: 2,235 sq km (863 sq mi)
Population: 821,000
Capital: Moroni, pop. 62,000
Currency: Comoran franc
Religion: Sunni Muslim
Languages: Arabic, French, Shikomoro

Congo

Area: 342,000 sq km (132,047 sq mi)
Population: 5,062,000
Capital: Brazzaville, pop. 2,230,000
Currency: Communauté Financière Africaine franc
Religions: Christian, animist, Muslim
Languages: French, Lingala, local languages

Costa Rica

Area: 51,100 sq km (19,730 sq mi)
Population: 4,987,000
Capital: San José, pop. 1,358,000
Currency: Costa Rican colón
Religions: Roman Catholic, Evangelical
Languages: Spanish, English

Côte d'Ivoire (Ivory Coast)

Area: 322,463 sq km (124,504 sq mi)
Population: 26,261,000
Capitals: Abidjan, pop. 4,921,000; Yamoussoukro, pop. 231,000
Currency: Communauté Financière Africaine franc
Religions: Muslim, Christian, indigenous beliefs
Languages: French, Dioula, native dialects

Croatia

Area: 56,594 sq km (21,581 sq mi)
Population: 4,270,000
Capital: Zagreb, pop. 686,000
Currency: kuna
Religions: Roman Catholic, Orthodox
Languages: Croatian, Serbian

Cuba

Area: 110,860 sq km
(42,803 sq mi)
Population: 11,116,000
Capital: Havana, pop. 2,136,000
Currencies: Cuban peso, peso convertible
Religion: Roman Catholic
Language: Spanish

Cyprus

Area: 9,251 sq km (3,572 sq mi)
Population: 1,237,000
Capital: Nicosia, pop. 269,000
Currency: euro
Religions: Greek Orthodox, Muslim
Languages: Greek, Turkish, English

3 cool things about CYPRUS

1. There were once so many snakes in the country that it was known as Ophiussa, or 'abode of snakes'. Today, the sight of one of the reptiles slithering around is fairly rare.

2. The earliest evidence of a pet cat was unearthed in an ancient village in Cyprus. Dating back some 9,500 years, the cat's remains were found in a grave next to human bones of the same age, suggesting they were buried together.

3. A massive ferry that sank off the coast of Cyprus in 1980 is now a top spot for scuba divers. The M.S. *Zenobia* wreckage is so popular that divers even decorate it during the holidays.

Czechia (Czech Republic)

Area: 78,867 sq km (30,451 sq mi)
Population: 10,686,000
Capital: Prague, pop. 1,292,000
Currency: Czech koruny
Religions: Roman Catholic, Protestant
Languages: Czech, Slovak

Democratic Republic of the Congo

Area: 2,344,858 sq km
(905,354 sq mi)
Population: 85,281,000
Capital: Kinshasa, pop. 13,171,000
Currency: Congolese franc
Religions: Roman Catholic, Protestant, Kimbanguist, Muslim
Languages: French, Lingala, Kingwana, Kikongo, Tshiluba

Denmark

Area: 43,094 sq km
(16,639 sq mi)
Population: 5,810,000
Capital: Copenhagen, pop. 1,321,000
Currency: Danish krone
Religions: Evangelical Lutheran, Muslim
Languages: Danish, Faroese, Greenlandic

Djibouti

Area: 23,200 sq km
(8,958 sq mi)
Population: 884,000
Capital: Djibouti, pop. 562,000
Currency: Djiboutian franc
Religions: Muslim, Christian
Languages: French, Arabic, Somali, Afar

Dominica

Area: 751 sq km (290 sq mi)
Population: 74,000
Capital: Roseau, pop. 15,000
Currency: East Caribbean dollar
Religions: Roman Catholic, Protestant
Languages: English, French patois

Dominican Republic

Area: 48,670 sq km
(18,792 sq mi)
Population: 10,299,000
Capital: Santo Domingo,
pop. 3,172,000
Currency: Dominican peso
Religion: Roman Catholic
Language: Spanish

Ecuador

Area: 283,561 sq km (109,483 sq mi)
Population: 16,499,000
Capital: Quito, pop. 1,822,000
Currency: U.S. dollar
Religions: Roman Catholic, Evangelical
Languages: Spanish, Quechua, other Amerindian languages

Egypt

Area: 1,001,450 sq km (386,662 sq mi)
Population: 99,413,000
Capital: Cairo, pop. 20,076,000
Currency: Egyptian pound
Religions: Muslim (mostly Sunni), Coptic Christian
Languages: Arabic, English, French

El Salvador

Area: 21,041 sq km (8,124 sq mi)
Population: 6,187,000
Capital: San Salvador, pop. 1,107,000
Currencies: U.S. dollar, El Salvador colón
Religions: Roman Catholic, Protestant
Languages: Spanish, Nawat

Equatorial Guinea

Area: 28,051 sq km (10,831 sq mi)
Population: 797,000
Capital: Malabo, pop. 297,000
Currency: Communauté Financière Africaine franc
Religions: Roman Catholic, pagan practices
Languages: Spanish, French, Fang, Bubi

Eritrea

Area: 117,600 sq km (45,406 sq mi)
Population: 5,971,000
Capital: Asmara, pop. 896,000
Currency: nakfa
Religions: Muslim, Coptic Christian, Roman Catholic
Languages: Tigrigna (Tigrinya), Arabic, English, Tigre, Kunama, Afar, other Cushitic languages

Estonia

Area: 45,228 sq km (17,463 sq mi)
Population: 1,244,000
Capital: Tallinn, pop. 437,000
Currency: euro
Religions: Lutheran, Orthodox
Languages: Estonian, Russian

Eswatini (Swaziland)

Area: 17,364 sq km (6,704 sq mi)
Population: 1,087,000
Capitals: Mbabane, pop. 68,000; Lobamba, pop. 5,800
Currency: lilangeni
Religions: Christian, Muslim
Languages: English, siSwati

Ethiopia

Area: 1,104,300 sq km (426,372 sq mi)
Population: 108,386,000
Capital: Addis Ababa, pop. 4,400,000
Currency: Ethiopian birr
Religions: Ethiopian Orthodox, Muslim, Protestant
Languages: Oromo, Amharic, Somali, Tigrigna (Tigrinya)

Fiji

Area: 18,274 sq km (7,056 sq mi)
Population: 926,000
Capital: Suva, pop. 178,000
Currency: Fiji dollar
Religions: Protestant, Hindu, Roman Catholic, Muslim
Languages: English, Fijian, Hindustani

Finland

Area: 338,145 sq km (130,558 sq mi)
Population: 5,537,000
Capital: Helsinki, pop. 1,279,000
Currency: euro
Religion: Lutheran
Languages: Finnish, Swedish

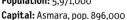 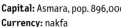 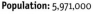

France

Area: 643,801 sq km
(248,573 sq mi)
Population: 67,364,000
Capital: Paris, pop. 10,901,000
Currency: euro
Religions: Roman Catholic, Protestant, Muslim, Jewish
Language: French

Gambia

Area: 11,300 sq km (4,363 sq mi)
Population: 2,093,000
Capital: Banjul, pop. 437,000
Currency: dalasi
Religions: Muslim, Christian
Languages: English, Mandinka, Wolof, Fula, other indigenous vernaculars

Gabon

Area: 267,667 sq km (103,347 sq mi)
Population: 2,119,000
Capital: Libreville, pop. 813,000
Currency: Communauté Financière Africaine franc
Religions: Christian, Muslim
Languages: French, Fang, Myene, Nzebi, Bapounou/Eschira, Bandjabi

Georgia

Area: 69,700 sq km (26,911 sq mi)
Population: 4,003,000
Capital: Tbilisi, pop. 1,077,000
Currency: lari
Religions: Orthodox Christian, Muslim, Armenian Apostolic
Languages: Georgian, Azeri, Armenian

SNAPSHOT
Ghana

A cheerful fisherman repairs a net in Accra, Ghana.

Germany

Area: 357,022 sq km (137,847 sq mi)
Population: 80,458,000
Capital: Berlin, pop. 3,563,000
Currency: euro
Religions: Roman Catholic, Protestant, Muslim
Language: German

Ghana

Area: 238,533 sq km (92,098 sq mi)
Population: 28,102,000
Capital: Accra, pop. 2,439,000
Currency: Ghana cedi
Religions: Christian, Muslim, traditional beliefs
Languages: Asante, Ewe, Fante, Boron (Brong), Dagomba, Dangme, Dagarte (Dagaba), Kokomba, English

Greece

Area: 131,957 sq km (50,949 sq mi)
Population: 10,762,000
Capital: Athens, pop. 3,156,000
Currency: euro
Religions: Greek Orthodox, Muslim
Language: Greek

Grenada

Area: 344 sq km (133 sq mi)
Population: 112,000
Capital: St. George's, pop. 39,000
Currency: East Caribbean dollar
Religions: Roman Catholic, Pentacostal, other Protestant
Languages: English, French patois

Guatemala

Area: 108,889 sq km (42,042 sq mi)
Population: 16,581,000
Capital: Guatemala City, pop. 2,851,000
Currency: quetzal
Religions: Roman Catholic, Protestant, indigenous Maya beliefs
Languages: Spanish, Amerindian languages

Guinea

Area: 245,857 sq km (94,926 sq mi)
Population: 11,855,000
Capital: Conakry, pop. 1,843,000
Currency: Guinean franc
Religions: Muslim, Christian, indigenous beliefs
Languages: French, African languages

Guinea-Bissau

Area: 36,125 sq km (13,948 sq mi)
Population: 1,833,000
Capital: Bissau, pop. 558,000
Currency: Communauté Financière Africaine franc
Religions: Muslim, Christian, indigenous beliefs
Languages: Crioulu, Portuguese, Pular, Mandingo

Guyana

Area: 214,969 sq km (83,000 sq mi)
Population: 741,000
Capital: Georgetown, pop. 110,000
Currency: Guyanese dollar
Religions: Protestant, Hindu, Roman Catholic, Muslim
Languages: English, Guyanese Creole, Amerindian languages, Caribbean Hindustani

Haiti

Area: 27,750 sq km (10,714 sq mi)
Population: 10,788,000
Capital: Port-au-Prince, pop. 2,637,000
Currencies: gourde, U.S. dollar
Religions: Roman Catholic, Protestant, vodou
Languages: French, Creole

Honduras

Area: 112,090 sq km (43,278 sq mi)
Population: 9,183,000
Capital: Tegucigalpa, pop. 1,363,000
Currency: lempira
Religions: Roman Catholic, Protestant
Languages: Spanish, Amerindian dialects

Hungary
Area: 93,028 sq km (35,918 sq mi)
Population: 9,826,000
Capital: Budapest, pop. 1,759,000
Currency: forint
Religions: Roman Catholic, Calvinist, Lutheran
Language: Hungarian

Iraq
Area: 438,317 sq km (169,235 sq mi)
Population: 40,194,000
Capital: Baghdad, pop. 6,634,000
Currency: Iraqi dinar
Religions: Shiite Muslim, Sunni Muslim
Languages: Arabic, Kurdish, Turkmen, Syriac, Armenian

Iceland
Area: 103,000 sq km (39,769 sq mi)
Population: 344,000
Capital: Reykjavík, pop. 216,000
Currency: Icelandic krona
Religions: Lutheran, Roman Catholic
Languages: Icelandic, English, Nordic languages

Ireland (Éire)
Area: 70,273 sq km (27,133 sq mi)
Population: 5,068,000
Capital: Dublin (Baíle Átha Cliath), pop. 1,201,000
Currency: euro
Religions: Roman Catholic, Church of Ireland
Languages: English, Irish (Gaelic)

India
Area: 3,287,263 sq km (1,269,219 sq mi)
Population: 1,296,834,000
Capital: New Delhi, pop. 28,514,000
Currency: Indian rupee
Religions: Hindu, Muslim, Christian, Sikh
Languages: Hindi, Bengali, Telugu, Marathi, Tamil, Urdu, Gujarati, Kannada, Malayalam, Oriya, Panjabi, Assamese, Maithili, English

Israel
Area: 20,770 sq km (8,019 sq mi)
Population: 8,425,000
Capital: Jerusalem, pop. 907,000
Currency: new Israeli sheqel
Religions: Jewish, Muslim
Languages: Hebrew, Arabic, English

Indonesia
Area: 1,904,569 sq km (735,358 sq mi)
Population: 262,787,000
Capital: Jakarta, pop. 10,517,000
Currency: Indonesian rupiah
Religions: Muslim, Protestant, Roman Catholic, Hindu
Languages: Bahasa Indonesia (modified form of Malay), English, Dutch, Javanese, local dialects

Italy
Area: 301,340 sq km (116,348 sq mi)
Population: 62,247,000
Capital: Rome, pop. 4,210,000
Currency: euro
Religion: Roman Catholic
Languages: Italian, German, French, Slovene

Iran
Area: 1,648,195 sq km (636,371 sq mi)
Population: 83,025,000
Capital: Tehran, pop. 8,896,000
Currency: Iranian rial
Religions: Shiite Muslim, Sunni Muslim
Languages: Persian (Farsi), Azeri, Turkic dialects, Kurdish, Gilaki and Mazandarani, Luri, Baluchi, Arabic

Jamaica
Area: 10,991 sq km (4,244 sq mi)
Population: 2,812,000
Capital: Kingston, pop. 589,000
Currency: Jamaican dollar
Religions: Protestant, Roman Catholic
Languages: English, English patois

Japan

Area: 377,915 sq km (145,914 sq mi)
Population: 126,168,000
Capital: Tokyo, pop. 37,468,000
Currency: yen
Religions: Shinto, Buddhist
Language: Japanese

Kazakhstan

Area: 2,724,900 sq km (1,052,089 sq mi)
Population: 18,745,000
Capital: Nur-Sultan, pop. 1,068,000
Currency: tenge
Religions: Muslim, Russian Orthodox
Languages: Kazakh (Qazaq), Russian

Jordan

Area: 89,342 sq km (34,495 sq mi)
Population: 10,458,000
Capital: Amman, pop. 2,065,000
Currency: Jordanian dinar
Religions: Sunni Muslim, Christian
Languages: Arabic, English

Kenya

Area: 580,367 sq km (224,081 sq mi)
Population: 48,398,000
Capital: Nairobi, pop. 4,386,000
Currency: Kenyan shilling
Religions: Protestant, Roman Catholic, Muslim, indigenous beliefs
Languages: English, Kiswahili, many indigenous languages

SNAPSHOT
Jamaica

Children dance in Kingston, Jamaica, wearing yellow, green and black — Jamaica's national colours.

● Asia ● Europe ● North America ● South America

Kiribati

Area: 811 sq km (313 sq mi)
Population: 109,000
Capital: Tarawa, pop. 64,000
Currency: Australian dollar
Religions: Roman Catholic, Protestant
Languages: I-Kiribati, English

Kuwait

Area: 17,818 sq km (6,880 sq mi)
Population: 2,916,000
Capital: Kuwait City, pop. 2,989,000
Currency: Kuwaiti dinar
Religions: Sunni Muslim, Shiite Muslim, Christian
Languages: Arabic, English

Kosovo

Area: 10,887 sq km (4,203 sq mi)
Population: 1,908,000
Capital: Pristina, pop. 207,062
Currencies: euro, Serbian dinar
Religions: Muslim, Roman Catholic, Serbian Orthodox
Languages: Albanian, Serbian, Bosnian

Kyrgyzstan

Area: 199,951 sq km (77,201 sq mi)
Population: 5,849,000
Capital: Bishkek, pop. 996,000
Currency: som
Religions: Muslim, Russian Orthodox
Languages: Kyrgyz, Uzbek, Russian

SNAPSHOT
Luxembourg

Pretzel from Grevenmacher, Luxembourg

Laos

Area: 236,800 sq km
(91,429 sq mi)
Population: 7,234,000
Capital: Vientiane, pop. 665,000
Currency: Lao kip
Religions: Buddhist, animist
Languages: Lao, French, English,
various ethnic languages

Libya

Area: 1,759,540 sq km
(679,362 sq mi)
Population: 6,755,000
Capital: Tripoli, pop. 1,158,000
Currency: Libyan dinar
Religions: Sunni Muslim, Christian
Languages: Arabic, Italian, English, Berber

Latvia

Area: 64,589 sq km
(24,938 sq mi)
Population: 1,924,000
Capital: Riga, pop. 637,000
Currency: euro
Religions: Lutheran, Orthodox
Languages: Latvian, Russian

Liechtenstein

Area: 160 sq km (62 sq mi)
Population: 39,000
Capital: Vaduz, pop. 5,000
Currency: Swiss franc
Religions: Roman Catholic, Protestant
Languages: German, Italian

Lebanon

Area: 10,400 sq km (4,015 sq mi)
Population: 6,100,000
Capital: Beirut, pop. 2,385,000
Currency: Lebanese pound
Religions: Muslim, Christian
Languages: Arabic, French, English, Armenian

Lithuania

Area: 65,300 sq km
(25,212 sq mi)
Population: 2,793,000
Capital: Vilnius, pop. 536,000
Currency: euro
Religions: Roman Catholic, Russian Orthodox
Languages: Lithuanian, Russian, Polish

Lesotho

Area: 30,355 sq km (11,720 sq mi)
Population: 1,962,000
Capital: Maseru, pop. 202,000
Currencies: loti, rand
Religions: Protestant, Roman Catholic
Languages: Sesotho, English, Zulu, Xhosa

Luxembourg

Area: 2,586 sq km (998 sq mi)
Population: 606,000
Capital: Luxembourg,
pop. 120,000
Currency: euro
Religion: Roman Catholic
Languages: Luxembourgish,
German, French, Portuguese

Liberia

Area: 111,369 sq km
(43,000 sq mi)
Population: 4,810,000
Capital: Monrovia,
pop. 1,418,000
Currency: Liberian dollar
Religions: Christian, Muslim, indigenous beliefs
Languages: English, indigenous languages

Madagascar

Area: 587,041 sq km
(226,658 sq mi)
Population: 25,684,000
Capital: Antananarivo,
pop. 3,058,000
Currency: Malagasy ariary
Religions: Christian, indigenous beliefs, Muslim
Languages: French, Malagasy, English

Malawi

Area: 118,484 sq km (45,747 sq mi)
Population: 19,843,000
Capital: Lilongwe, pop. 1,030,000
Currency: Malawian kwacha
Religions: Christian, Muslim
Languages: Chichewa, Chinyanja, Chiyao, Chitumbuka, Chisena, Chilomwe, Chitonga, English

Malaysia

Area: 329,847 sq km (127,355 sq mi)
Population: 31,810,000
Capital: Kuala Lumpur, pop. 7,564,000
Currency: Malaysian ringgit
Religions: Muslim, Buddhist, Christian, Hindu
Languages: Bahasa Malaysia (Malay), English, Chinese, Tamil, Telugu, Malayalam, Panjabi, Thai

Maldives

Area: 298 sq km (115 sq mi)
Population: 392,000
Capital: Male, pop. 177,000
Currency: rufiyaa
Religion: Sunni Muslim
Languages: Dhivehi, English

Mali

Area: 1,240,192 sq km (478,841 sq mi)
Population: 18,430,000
Capital: Bamako, pop. 2,447,000
Currency: Communauté Financière Africaine franc
Religions: Muslim, Christian, animist
Languages: French, Bambara, African languages

Malta

Area: 316 sq km (122 sq mi)
Population: 449,000
Capital: Valletta, pop. 213,000
Currency: euro
Religion: Roman Catholic
Languages: Maltese, English

Marshall Islands

Area: 181 sq km (70 sq mi)
Population: 76,000
Capital: Majuro, pop. 31,000
Currency: U.S. dollar
Religions: Protestant, Roman Catholic, Mormon
Languages: Marshallese, English

3 cool things about the MARSHALL ISLANDS

1. At just 35 years old, the Marshall Islands is one of the world's youngest nations. The chain of some 1,200 islands and atolls gained its independence from the United States in 1986.

2. There are some 47 sunken ships and 270 aeroplanes dating back to World War II at the bottom of the Pacific Ocean off the coast of the Marshall Islands. This is a popular spot for scuba divers, who flock to the tropical waters to explore the submerged ships and planes some 30 metres (100 ft) below.

3. First debuted in 1946, the bikini is named for the Marshall Islands' Bikini Atoll. The designer of the two-piece bathing suit gave it the unique name as a nod to the ring-shaped reef, which was in the news at the time during World War II.

Mauritania

Area: 1,030,700 sq km (397,955 sq mi)
Population: 3,840,000
Capital: Nouakchott, pop. 1,205,000
Currency: ouguiya
Religion: Muslim
Languages: Arabic, Pulaar, Soninke, Wolof, French, Hassaniya

Mauritius

Area: 2,040 sq km (788 sq mi)
Population: 1,364,000
Capital: Port Louis, pop. 149,000
Currency: Mauritius rupee
Religions: Hindu, Roman Catholic, Muslim, other Christian
Languages: Creole, Bhojpuri, French, English

Mexico

Area: 1,964,375 sq km
(758,449 sq mi)
Population: 125,959,000
Capital: Mexico City,
pop. 21,581,000
Currency: Mexican peso
Religions: Roman Catholic, Protestant
Languages: Spanish, indigenous languages

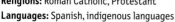

The CHIHUAHUA, the WORLD'S SMALLEST DOG, is named for a STATE in MEXICO.

Micronesia

Area: 702 sq km (271 sq mi)
Population: 104,000
Capital: Palikir, pop. 7,000
Currency: U.S. dollar
Religions: Roman Catholic, Protestant
Languages: English, Chuukese, Kosrean, Pohnpeian, Yapese, other indigenous languages

Moldova

Area: 33,851 sq km
(13,070 sq mi)
Population: 3,438,000
Capital: Chișinău,
pop. 510,000
Currency: Moldovan leu
Religion: Eastern Orthodox
Languages: Moldovan, Russian, Gagauz

Monaco

Area: 2 sq km (1 sq mi)
Population: 38,000
Capital: Monaco, pop. 38,000
Currency: euro
Religion: Roman Catholic
Languages: French, English, Italian, Monegasque

Mongolia

Area: 1,564,116 sq km
(603,908 sq mi)
Population: 3,103,000
Capital: Ulaanbaatar,
pop. 1,520,000
Currency: tugrik
Religions: Buddhist, Muslim, Shamanist, Christian
Languages: Mongolian, Turkic, Russian

Montenegro

Area: 13,812 sq km
(5,333 sq mi)
Population: 614,000
Capital: Podgorica, pop. 177,000
Currency: euro
Religions: Orthodox, Muslim, Roman Catholic
Languages: Serbian, Montenegrin, Bosnian, Albanian

Morocco

Area: 446,550 sq km
(172,414 sq mi)
Population: 34,314,000
Capital: Rabat, pop. 1,847,000
Currency: Moroccan dirham
Religion: Muslim
Languages: Arabic, Tamazight, other Berber languages, French

Mozambique

Area: 799,380 sq km
(308,642 sq mi)
Population: 27,234,000
Capital: Maputo, pop. 1,102,000
Currency: Mozambique metical
Religions: Christian, Muslim
Languages: Emakhuwa, Portuguese, Xichangana, Cisena, Elomwe, Echuwabo, other local languages

Myanmar (Burma)

Area: 676,578 sq km
(261,228 sq mi)
Population: 55,623,000
Capital: Nay Pyi Taw,
pop. 1,176,000
Currency: kyat
Religions: Buddhist, Christian, Muslim
Languages: Burmese, ethnic languages

Namibia

Area: 824,292 sq km
(318,261 sq mi)
Population: 2,533,000
Capital: Windhoek, pop. 404,000
Currencies: Namibian dollar,
South African rand
Religion: Christian
Languages: Indigenous languages, Afrikaans, English

Nepal

Area: 147,181 sq km
(56,827 sq mi)
Population: 29,718,000
Capital: Kathmandu, pop. 1,330,000
Currency: Nepalese rupee
Religions: Hindu, Buddhist, Muslim, Kirant
Languages: Nepali, Maithali, Bhojpuri, Tharu,
Tamang, Newar, Magar, Bajjika, Awadhi

Nauru

Area: 21 sq km (8 sq mi)
Population: 10,000
Capital: Yaren, pop. 1,000
Currency: Australian dollar
Religions: Protestant, Roman Catholic
Languages: Nauruan, English

Netherlands

Area: 41,543 sq km
(16,040 sq mi)
Population: 17,151,000
Capitals: Amsterdam, pop. 1,132,000;
The Hague, pop. 685,000
Currency: euro
Religions: Roman Catholic, Protestant, Muslim
Languages: Dutch, Frisian

SNAPSHOT Norway

The brightly painted buildings along
the Nidelva River in Trondheim,
Norway, date back to the 18th century.

COLOUR KEY ● Africa ● Australia, New Zealand and Oceania

New Zealand

Area: 268,838 sq km
(103,799 sq mi)
Population: 4,546,000
Capital: Wellington, pop. 411,000
Currency: New Zealand dollar
Religions: Protestant, Roman Catholic,
Hindu, Buddhist, Maori Christian
Languages: English, Maori

Nicaragua

Area: 130,370 sq km
(50,336 sq mi)
Population: 6,085,000
Capital: Managua, pop. 1,048,000
Currency: córdoba oro
Religions: Roman Catholic, Protestant
Languages: Spanish, Miskito

Niger

Area: 1,267,000 sq km (489,191 sq mi)
Population: 19,866,000
Capital: Niamey, pop. 1,214,000
Currency: Communauté
Financière Africaine franc
Religion: Muslim
Languages: French, Hausa, Djerma

Nigeria

Area: 923,768 sq km
(356,669 sq mi)
Population: 203,453,000
Capital: Abuja, pop. 2,919,000
Currency: naira
Religions: Muslim, Christian, indigenous beliefs
Languages: English, Hausa, Yoruba, Igbo (Ibo), Fulani

North Korea

Area: 120,538 sq km
(46,540 sq mi)
Population: 25,381,000
Capital: Pyongyang,
pop. 3,038,000
Currency: North Korean won
Religions: Buddhist, Confucianist, some Christian
and syncretic Chondogyo
Language: Korean

North Macedonia

Area: 25,713 sq km
(9,928 sq mi)
Population: 2,119,000
Capital: Skopje, pop. 584,000
Currency: denar
Religions: Macedonian Orthodox, Muslim
Languages: Macedonian, Albanian, Turkish, Romany,
Aromanian, Serbian

Norway

Area: 323,802 sq km
(125,021 sq mi)
Population: 5,372,000
Capital: Oslo, pop. 1,012,000
Currency: Norwegian krone
Religion: Lutheran
Languages: Bokmal Norwegian, Nynorsk
Norwegian, Sami, Finnish

Oman

Area: 309,500 sq km
(119,499 sq mi)
Population: 3,494,000
Capital: Muscat, pop. 1,447,000
Currency: Omani rial
Religions: Muslim, Christian, Hindu
Languages: Arabic, English, Baluchi,
Urdu, Indian dialects

Pakistan

Area: 796,095 sq km
(307,374 sq mi)
Population: 207,863,000
Capital: Islamabad, pop. 1,061,000
Currency: Pakistani rupee
Religions: Sunni Muslim, Shiite Muslim
Languages: Punjabi, Sindhi, Saraiki, Pashto, Urdu,
Baluchi, Hindko, Brahui, English, Burushaski

Palau

Area: 459 sq km (177 sq mi)
Population: 22,000
Capital: Melekeok
(on Babelthuap), pop. 299
Currency: U.S. dollar
Religions: Roman Catholic, Protestant, Modekngei
Languages: Palauan, Filipino, English, Chinese

Panama

Area: 75,420 sq km (29,120 sq mi)
Population: 3,801,000
Capital: Panama City, pop. 1,783,000
Currency: U.S. dollar
Religions: Roman Catholic, Protestant
Languages: Spanish, English

Papua New Guinea

Area: 462,840 sq km (178,703 sq mi)
Population: 7,027,000
Capital: Port Moresby, pop. 367,000
Currency: kina
Religions: Protestant, Roman Catholic
Languages: Tok Pisin, English, Hiri Motu, other indigenous languages

Paraguay

Area: 406,752 sq km (157,048 sq mi)
Population: 7,026,000
Capital: Asunción, pop. 3,222,000
Currency: guaraní
Religions: Roman Catholic, Protestant
Languages: Spanish, Guarani

Peru

Area: 1,285,216 sq km (496,224 sq mi)
Population: 31,331,000
Capital: Lima, pop. 10,391,000
Currency: sol
Religions: Roman Catholic, Evangelical
Languages: Spanish, Quechua, Aymara, Ashaninka, other indigenous languages

Philippines

Area: 300,000 sq km (115,831 sq mi)
Population: 105,893,000
Capital: Manila, pop. 13,482,000
Currency: Philippine peso
Religions: Roman Catholic, Protestant, Muslim
Languages: Filipino (Tagalog), English

Poland

Area: 312,685 sq km (120,728 sq mi)
Population: 38,421,000
Capital: Warsaw, pop. 1,768,000
Currency: zloty
Religion: Roman Catholic
Language: Polish

Portugal

Area: 92,090 sq km (35,556 sq mi)
Population: 10,355,000
Capital: Lisbon, pop. 2,927,000
Currency: euro
Religion: Roman Catholic
Languages: Portuguese, Mirandese

Qatar

Area: 11,586 sq km (4,473 sq mi)
Population: 2,364,000
Capital: Doha, pop. 633,000
Currency: Qatari rial
Religions: Muslim, Christian
Languages: Arabic, English

Romania

Area: 238,391 sq km (92,043 sq mi)
Population: 21,457,000
Capital: Bucharest, pop. 1,821,000
Currency: Romanian leu
Religions: Eastern Orthodox, Protestant, Roman Catholic
Languages: Romanian, Hungarian, Romany

Russia

Area: 17,098,242 sq km (6,601,665 sq mi)
Population: 142,123,000
Capital: Moscow, pop. 12,410,000
Currency: Russian ruble
Religions: Russian Orthodox, Muslim
Languages: Russian, Tatar, other local languages

Note: Russia is in both Europe and Asia, but its capital is in Europe, so it is classified here as a European country.

COLOUR KEY   ● Africa   ● Australia, New Zealand and Oceania

Rwanda

Area: 26,338 sq km (10,169 sq mi)
Population: 12,187,000
Capital: Kigali, pop. 1,058,000
Currency: Rwandan franc
Religions: Protestant, Roman Catholic, Muslim
Languages: Kinyarwanda, French, English, Kiswahili (Swahili)

San Marino

Area: 61 sq km (24 sq mi)
Population: 34,000
Capital: San Marino, pop. 4,000
Currency: euro
Religion: Roman Catholic
Language: Italian

Samoa

Area: 2,831 sq km (1,093 sq mi)
Population: 201,000
Capital: Apia, pop. 36,000
Currency: tala
Religions: Protestant, Roman Catholic, Mormon
Languages: Samoan (Polynesian), English

Sao Tome and Principe

Area: 964 sq km (372 sq mi)
Population: 204,000
Capital: São Tomé, pop. 80,000
Currency: dobra
Religions: Roman Catholic, Protestant
Languages: Portuguese, Forro

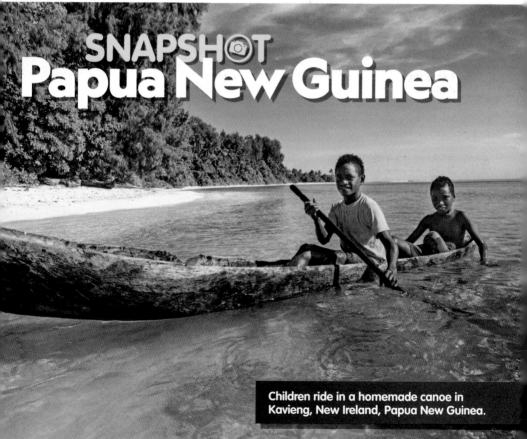

SNAPSHOT
Papua New Guinea

Children ride in a homemade canoe in Kavieng, New Ireland, Papua New Guinea.

● Asia ● Europe ● North America ● South America

Saudi Arabia

Area: 2,149,690 sq km (830,000 sq mi)
Population: 33,091,000
Capital: Riyadh, pop. 6,907,000
Currency: Saudi riyal
Religion: Muslim
Language: Arabic

Singapore

Area: 697 sq km (269 sq mi)
Population: 5,996,000
Capital: Singapore, pop. 5,792,000
Currency: Singapore dollar
Religions: Buddhist, Christian, Muslim, Taoist, Hindu
Languages: English, Mandarin, Malay, Tamil

Senegal

Area: 196,722 sq km (75,955 sq mi)
Population: 15,021,000
Capital: Dakar, pop. 2,978,000
Currency: Communauté Financière Africaine franc
Religions: Muslim, Roman Catholic
Languages: French, Wolof, Pulaar, Jola, Mandinka

Slovakia

Area: 49,035 sq km (18,933 sq mi)
Population: 5,445,000
Capital: Bratislava, pop. 430,000
Currency: euro
Religions: Roman Catholic, Protestant, Greek Catholic
Languages: Slovak, Hungarian, Romany

Serbia

Area: 77,474 sq km (29,913 sq mi)
Population: 7,078,000
Capital: Belgrade, pop. 1,389,000
Currency: Serbian dinar
Religions: Serbian Orthodox, Roman Catholic, Protestant
Languages: Serbian, Hungarian, Bosniak, Romany

Slovenia

Area: 20,273 sq km (7,827 sq mi)
Population: 2,102,000
Capital: Ljubljana, pop. 286,000
Currency: euro
Religions: Roman Catholic, Muslim, Orthodox
Languages: Slovene, Serbo-Croatian, Italian, Hungarian

Seychelles

Area: 455 sq km (176 sq mi)
Population: 95,000
Capital: Victoria, pop. 28,000
Currency: Seychelles rupee
Religions: Roman Catholic, Protestant, Hindu, Muslim
Languages: Seychellois Creole, English, French

3 cool things about SLOVENIA

1. Some 54 percent of Slovenia's land is forest. Kočevje, a town that is made up of about 90 percent forest, is also known as Slovenia's Bear Forest, as it's home to much of the country's 500-strong brown bear population.

2. There are about 10,000 caves in Slovenia, including Postojna Cave, which has 24 kilometres (15 mi) of passages, galleries and chambers that started forming some three million years ago.

3. A 360-metre (1,181-ft)-tall chimney soars above the city of Trbovlje, Slovenia. The tallest chimney in Europe, it's part of the old Trbovlje Power Station and is a destination for climbers, who scale the more than 50-year-old tower.

Sierra Leone

Area: 71,740 sq km (27,699 sq mi)
Population: 6,312,000
Capital: Freetown, pop. 1,136,000
Currency: leone
Religions: Muslim, Christian
Languages: English, Mende, Temne, Krio

Solomon Islands

Area: 28,896 sq km (11,157 sq mi)
Population: 660,000
Capital: Honiara, pop. 82,000
Currency: Solomon Islands dollar
Religions: Protestant, Roman Catholic
Languages: Melanesian pidgin, English, indigenous languages

Somalia

Area: 637,657 sq km (246,201 sq mi)
Population: 11,259,000
Capital: Mogadishu, pop. 2,082,000
Currency: Somali shilling
Religion: Sunni Muslim
Languages: Somali, Arabic, Italian, English

South Africa

Area: 1,219,090 sq km (470,693 sq mi)
Population: 55,380,000
Capitals: Pretoria (Tshwane), pop. 2,378,000; Cape Town, pop. 4,430,000; Bloemfontein, pop. 465,000
Currency: rand
Religions: Christian, indigenous religions
Languages: isiZulu, isiXhosa, Afrikaans, Sepedi, Setswana, English, Sesotho, Xitsonga, siSwati, Tshivenda isiNdebele

South Korea

Area: 99,720 sq km (38,502 sq mi)
Population: 51,418,000
Capital: Seoul, pop. 9,963,000
Currency: won
Religions: Christian, Buddhist
Languages: Korean, English

South Sudan

Area: 644,329 sq km (248,777 sq mi)
Population: 10,205,000
Capital: Juba, pop. 369,000
Currency: South Sudanese pound
Religions: animist, Christian
Languages: English, Arabic, Dinke, Nuer, Bari, Zande, Shilluk

Spain

Area: 505,370 sq km (195,124 sq mi)
Population: 49,331,000
Capital: Madrid, pop. 6,497,000
Currency: euro
Religion: Roman Catholic
Languages: Castilian Spanish, Catalan, Galician, Basque

Sri Lanka

Area: 65,610 sq km (25,332 sq mi)
Population: 22,577,000
Capitals: Colombo, pop. 600,000; Sri Jayewardenepura Kotte, pop. 103,000
Currency: Sri Lankan rupee
Religions: Buddhist, Muslim, Hindu, Christian
Languages: Sinhala, Tamil

St. Kitts and Nevis

Area: 261 sq km (101 sq mi)
Population: 53,000
Capital: Basseterre, pop. 14,000
Currency: East Caribbean dollar
Religions: Protestant, Roman Catholic
Language: English

St. Lucia

Area: 616 sq km (238 sq mi)
Population: 166,000
Capital: Castries, pop. 22,000
Currency: East Caribbean dollar
Religions: Roman Catholic, Protestant, Rastafarian
Languages: English, French patois

St. Vincent and the Grenadines

Area: 389 sq km (150 sq mi)
Population: 102,000
Capital: Kingstown, pop. 27,000
Currency: East Caribbean dollar
Religions: Protestant, Roman Catholic
Languages: English, Vincentian Creole English, French patois

Sudan

Area: 1,861,484 sq km
(718,723 sq mi)
Population: 43,121,000
Capital: Khartoum,
pop. 5,534,000
Currency: Sudanese pound
Religions: Sunni Muslim, Christian
Languages: Arabic, English, Nubian, Ta BedawieFur

Syria

Area: 185,180 sq km (71,498 sq mi)
Population: 19,454,000
Capital: Damascus, pop. 2,320,000
Currency: Syrian pound
Religions: Sunni Muslim, other Muslim
(includes Alawite), Christian, Druze
Languages: Arabic, Kurdish, Armenian, Aramaic,
Circassian, French

Suriname

Area: 163,820 sq km (63,251 sq mi)
Population: 598,000
Capital: Paramaribo, pop. 239,000
Currency: Suriname dollar
Religions: Protestant, Hindu,
Roman Catholic, Muslim
Languages: Dutch, English, Sranang Tongo, Caribbean
Hindustani, Javanese

Tajikistan

Area: 144,100 sq km
(55,637 sq mi)
Population: 8,605,000
Capital: Dushanbe,
pop. 873,000
Currency: somoni
Religions: Sunni Muslim, Shia Muslim
Languages: Tajik, Uzbek

Some 90 percent of SURINAME is covered in UNINHABITED RAINFOREST.

Tanzania

Area: 947,300 sq km (365,754 sq mi)
Population: 55,451,000
Capitals: Dar es Salaam, pop.
6,048,000; Dodoma, pop. 262,000
Currency: Tanzanian shilling
Religions: Christian, Muslim, indigenous beliefs
Languages: Kiswahili (Swahili), Kiunguja (Swahili in
Zanzibar), English, Arabic, local languages

Sweden

Area: 450,295 sq km
(173,860 sq mi)
Population: 10,041,000
Capital: Stockholm,
pop. 1,583,000
Currency: Swedish krona
Religion: Lutheran
Languages: Swedish, Sami, Finnish

More than 1.5 MILLION WILDEBEESTS migrate through TANZANIA each year.

Switzerland

Area: 41,277 sq km
(15,937 sq mi)
Population: 8,293,000
Capital: Bern, pop. 422,000
Currency: Swiss franc
Religions: Roman Catholic, Protestant, Muslim
Languages: German, French, Italian, English, Romansh

Thailand

Area: 513,120 sq km
(198,117 sq mi)
Population: 68,616,000
Capital: Bangkok, pop. 10,156,000
Currency: baht
Religions: Buddhist, Muslim, Christian
Languages: Thai, English, ethnic dialects

Timor-Leste (East Timor)

Area: 14,874 sq km
(5,743 sq mi)
Population: 1,322,000
Capital: Díli, pop. 281,000
Currency: U.S. dollar
Religions: Roman Catholic, Protestant
Languages: Tetum, Portuguese, Indonesian, English

Togo

Area: 56,785 sq km (21,925 sq mi)
Population: 8,176,000
Capital: Lomé, pop. 1,746,000
Currency: Communauté Financière Africaine franc
Religions: indigenous beliefs, Christian, Muslim
Languages: French, Ewe, Mina, Kabye, Dagomba

Tonga

Area: 747 sq km (288 sq mi)
Population: 106,000
Capital: Nuku'alofa
(on Tongatapu), pop. 23,000
Currency: pa'anga
Religions: Protestant, Church of Latter Day Saints, Roman Catholic
Languages: Tongan, English

Trinidad and Tobago

Area: 5,128 sq km (1,980 sq mi)
Population: 1,216,000
Capital: Port of Spain
(on Trinidad), pop. 544,000
Currency: Trinidad and Tobago dollar
Religions: Protestant, Roman Catholic, Hindu, Muslim
Languages: English, Creole, Caribbean Hindustani

Tunisia

Area: 163,610 sq km
(63,170 sq mi)
Population: 11,516,000
Capital: Tunis, pop. 2,291,000
Currency: Tunisian dinar
Religion: Muslim
Languages: Arabic, French, Berber (Tamazight)

Turkey

Area: 783,562 sq km
(302,535 sq mi)
Population: 81,257,000
Capital: Ankara, pop. 4,919,000
Currency: Turkish lira
Religion: Muslim
Languages: Turkish, Kurdish, other minority languages

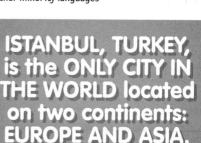

ISTANBUL, TURKEY, is the ONLY CITY IN THE WORLD located on two continents: EUROPE AND ASIA.

Turkmenistan

Area: 488,100 sq km
(188,456 sq mi)
Population: 5,411,000
Capital: Ashgabat, pop. 810,000
Currency: Turkmenistan new manat
Religions: Muslim, Eastern Orthodox
Languages: Turkmen, Russian, Uzbek

Tuvalu

Area: 26 sq km (10 sq mi)
Population: 11,000
Capital: Funafuti
(on Funafuti Atoll), pop. 7,000
Currency: Australian dollar
Religions: Protestant, Baha'i
Languages: Tuvaluan, English, Samoan, Kiribati

Uganda

Area: 241,038 sq km
(93,065 sq mi)
Population: 40,854,000
Capital: Kampala, pop. 2,986,000
Currency: Ugandan shilling
Religions: Protestant, Roman Catholic, Muslim
Languages: English, Ganda (Luganda), other local languages, Swahili, Arabic

Ukraine

Area: 603,550 sq km
(233,032 sq mi)
Population: 43,952,000
Capital: Kiev, pop. 2,957,000
Currency: hryvnia
Religions: Ukrainian Orthodox, Ukrainian Greek Catholic, Roman Catholic, Protestant, Jewish
Languages: Ukrainian, Russian

United Arab Emirates

Area: 83,600 sq km
(32,278 sq mi)
Population: 9,701,000
Capital: Abu Dhabi,
pop. 1,420,000
Currency: United Arab Emirates dirham
Religions: Muslim, Christian, Hindu
Languages: Arabic, Persian, English, Hindi, Urdu

Some 105 metres (350 ft) **underground, the Arsenalna Metro Station in KIEV, UKRAINE, is the WORLD'S DEEPEST UNDERGROUND STOP.**

United Kingdom

Area: 243,610 sq km
(94,058 sq mi)
Population: 65,105,000
Capital: London, pop. 9,046,000
Currency: pound sterling
Religions: Anglican, Roman Catholic, Presbyterian, Methodist, Muslim, Hindu
Languages: English, Scottish Gaelic, Welsh, Irish

SNAPSHOT
Vietnam

Outdoor market in the streets of Hoi An, Vietnam

United States

Area: 9,833,517 sq km
(3,796,741 sq mi)
Population: 329,256,000
Capital: Washington, D.C.,
pop. 5,207,000
Currency: U.S. dollar
Religions: Protestant, Roman Catholic, Jewish
Languages: English, Spanish, Native American languages

Uruguay

Area: 176,215 sq km
(68,037 sq mi)
Population: 3,369,000
Capital: Montevideo, pop. 1,737,000
Currency: Uruguayan peso
Religions: Roman Catholic, Protestant
Language: Spanish

Uzbekistan

Area: 447,400 sq km
(172,742 sq mi)
Population: 30,024,000
Capital: Tashkent,
pop. 2,464,000
Currency: Uzbekistan sum
Religions: Muslim (mostly Sunni), Eastern Orthodox
Languages: Uzbek, Russian, Tajik

Vanuatu

Area: 12,189 sq km (4,706 sq mi)
Population: 288,000
Capital: Port Vila, pop. 53,000
Currency: Vatu
Religions: Protestant, Roman Catholic,
other indigenous beliefs
Languages: Bislama, English, French, local languages

Vatican City

Area: .44 sq km (.17 sq mi)
Population: 1,000
Capital: Vatican City, pop. 1,000
Currency: euro
Religion: Roman Catholic
Languages: Italian, Latin, French

Venezuela

Area: 912,050 sq km
(352,144 sq mi)
Population: 31,689,000
Capital: Caracas, pop. 2,935,000
Currency: bolívar soberano
Religion: Roman Catholic
Languages: Spanish, numerous indigenous dialects

Vietnam

Area: 331,210 sq km
(127,881 sq mi)
Population: 97,040,000
Capital: Hanoi, pop. 1,064,000
Currency: dong
Religions: Buddhist, Roman Catholic, Hoa Hao, Cao Dai,
Protestant, Muslim
Languages: Vietnamese, English, French, Chinese, Khmer

Yemen

Area: 527,968 sq km
(203,850 sq mi)
Population: 28,667,000
Capital: Sanaa, pop. 2,779,000
Currency: Yemeni rial
Religion: Muslim
Language: Arabic

Zambia

Area: 752,618 sq km
(290,587 sq mi)
Population: 16,445,000
Capital: Lusaka, pop. 2,524,000
Currency: Zambian kwacha
Religions: Protestant, Roman Catholic
Languages: Bemba, Nyanja, Tonga, Lozi, Chewa, Nsenga,
Tumbuka, English

Zimbabwe

Area: 390,757 sq km
(150,872 sq mi)
Population: 14,030,000
Capital: Harare, pop. 1,515,000
Currency: Zimbabwe dollar
Religions: Protestant, Roman Catholic,
indigenous beliefs
Languages: Shona, Ndebele, English

EUROPE
A VIEW FROM SPACE

POLITICAL EUROPE

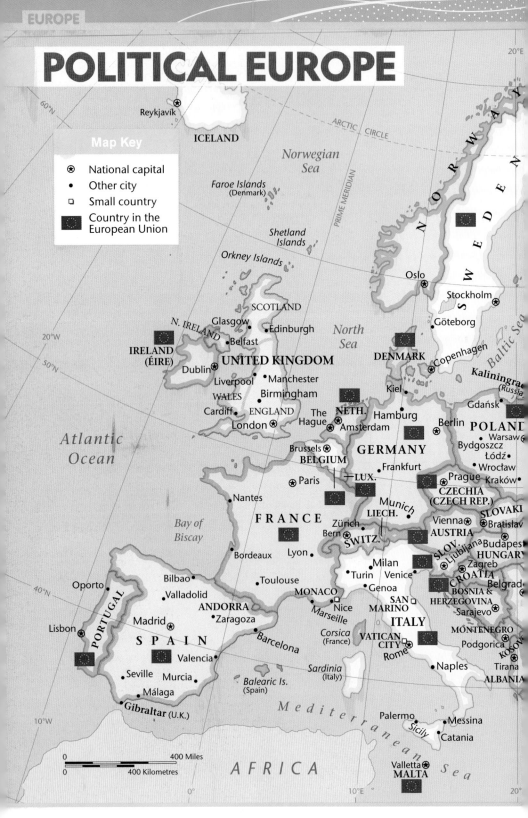

Map Key

⊛ National capital
• Other city
▢ Small country
▮ Country in the European Union

Reykjavík
ICELAND
Norwegian Sea
ARCTIC CIRCLE
PRIME MERIDIAN
Faroe Islands (Denmark)
Shetland Islands
Orkney Islands
SCOTLAND
Glasgow • Edinburgh
N. IRELAND
Belfast
IRELAND (ÉIRE)
Dublin
UNITED KINGDOM
Liverpool • Manchester
WALES • Birmingham
Cardiff • ENGLAND
London ⊛
The Hague
NETH.
Amsterdam
Brussels ⊛
BELGIUM
Paris ⊛
LUX.
Nantes •
FRANCE
Bordeaux •
Lyon •
Bay of Biscay
Atlantic Ocean
Oporto •
PORTUGAL
Bilbao •
Valladolid •
ANDORRA • Zaragoza
Madrid ⊛
Lisbon •
SPAIN
Valencia •
Seville • Murcia •
Málaga •
Gibraltar (U.K.)
Toulouse •
MONACO
Barcelona
Nice •
Marseille •
Corsica (France)
Balearic Is. (Spain)
Sardinia (Italy)
North Sea
Oslo ⊛
NORWAY
SWEDEN
Stockholm ⊛
Göteborg •
DENMARK
Copenhagen ⊛
Kiel •
Hamburg •
Berlin ⊛
GERMANY
Frankfurt •
Munich •
LIECH.
Zürich •
Bern ⊛
SWITZ.
Milan •
Turin • Venice •
Genoa •
SAN MARINO
ITALY
VATICAN CITY ▢
Rome ⊛
Naples •
Baltic Sea
Kaliningrad (Russia)
Gdańsk •
POLAND
Warsaw ⊛
Bydgoszcz •
Łódź •
Wrocław •
Prague ⊛ Kraków •
CZECHIA (CZECH REP.)
SLOVAKIA
Vienna ⊛ • Bratislava
AUSTRIA
SLOV. Budapest ⊛
Ljubljana ⊛ HUNGARY
Zagreb ⊛
CROATIA Belgrade •
BOSNIA & HERZEGOVINA
Sarajevo •
MONTENEGRO
Podgorica •
KOSOVO
Tirana ⊛
ALBANIA
Palermo •
Sicily
Messina •
Catania •
Mediterranean Sea
Valletta ⊛
MALTA
AFRICA

0 — 400 Miles
0 — 400 Kilometres

20°E
60°N
20°W
50°N
40°N
10°W
0°
10°E

Barents Sea

• Murmansk

A S I A

R U S S I A

• Archangel

A commonly accepted division between Asia and Europe — marked here by a maroon, dashed line — is formed by the Ural Mountains, Ural River, Caspian Sea, Caucasus Mountains and the Black Sea with its outlets, the Bosporus and Dardanelles.

F I N L A N D

• Ufa

• Helsinki

• St. Petersburg

Tallinn ⊛
ESTONIA

Yaroslavl'

Kazan'

Tver'
• Nizhniy Novgorod

Rīga
LATVIA

Moscow ⊛
Ryazan'

Samara
• Orenburg

LITHUANIA

Vitsyebsk

• Penza

Kaunas ⊛ • Vilnius

Smolensk

Minsk

• Bryansk

Saratov

BELARUS

Homyel'

• Kursk

KAZAKHSTAN

• Kiev

Volgograd

L'viv **U K R A I N E**
Poltava • Kharkiv
Vinnytsya
Donets'k
Astrakhan'

MOLDOVA
Chişinău
Dnipropetrovs'k
Rostov

Boundary claimed by Ukraine

ROMANIA
Odesa
CRIMEA
Simferopol'
Sevastopol'

Groznyy

Caspian Sea

Baku ⊛

Bucharest

ERBIA

Black Sea

GEORGIA

AZERBAIJAN

ristina
BULGARIA
Varna
Sofia

Bosporus

Skopje
N. MACED.

• Thessaloníki

Istanbul

T U R K E Y

Dardanelles

REECE

Athens

NORTHERN CYPRUS

Crete

Nicosia ⊛

CYPRUS

CRIMEA
Russia invaded Crimea in 2014 and, after secession from Ukraine was approved in a disputed and boycotted referendum held in Crimea, the Russian parliament voted to annex Crimea into the Russian Federation. The United Nations General Assembly subsequently adopted a nonbinding resolution declaring the annexation invalid and affirming Ukraine's territorial jurisdiction. As of 2019, Russia administers and controls all aspects of the peninsula, while Ukraine continues to maintain that Crimea is its sovereign territory.

30°E   40°E

PHYSICAL EUROPE

Iceland

Norwegian Sea

ARCTIC CIRCLE

PRIME MERIDIAN

30°W

60°N

Faroe Islands

Shetland Islands

SCANDINAVIA

Gulf of

Outer Hebrides

Orkney Islands

Highlands

20°W

50°N

Ireland

North Sea

Jutland

Zealand

Baltic

Irish Sea

Great Britain

British Isles

Celtic

Thames

N O R T H E R

Vistula

Atlantic Ocean

Sea

English Channel

Ruhr Valley

Elbe

Oder

Rhine

Brittany

Seine

Loire

Danube

Bay of Biscay

Massif Central

Mt. Blanc 15,781 ft (4,810 m)

A L P S

Po

40°N

Cantabrian Mts.

Douro

Pyrenees

Rhône

Riviera

Ligurian Sea

Apennines

Adriatic Sea

Iberian

Tagus

Ebro

Corsica

Peninsula

Balearic Sea

Sardinia

Baetic Mts.

Balearic Is.

Tyrrhenian Sea

Ionian Sea

Strait of Gibraltar

10°W

Sicily

Etna 10,899 ft (3,322 m)

M e d i t e r r a n e a n   S e a

0   400 Miles

0   400 Kilometres

A F R I C A

0°

10°E

20

10°E

20°E

320

North Cape

30°E 40°E 50°E 70°E

Barents Sea

Pechora

60°N

A S I A

Kola Peninsula

White Sea

PLAND

VIA

Bothnia

Northern Dvina

Lake Region

Lake Onega

Lake Ladoga

60°N

Kama

U R A L   M O U N T A I N S

Gulf of Finland

Western Dvina

Sea

N   E U R O P E A N   P L A I N

60°E

Europe Asia

50°N

Central Russian Upland

Don

Volga

Ural

Dnieper

rpathian Mts.

Dniester

Don

Volga

-92 ft (-28 m) Lowest point in Europe (at water level)

El'brus 18,510 ft (5,642 m) Highest point in Europe

Caspian Sea

Sea of Azov

Crimea

CAUCASUS MOUNTAINS ✛

40°N

Danube

Balkan Mts.

Balkan

Black Sea

Bosporus

Peninsula

Sea of Marmara

Dardanelles

Aegean Sea

A commonly accepted division between Asia and Europe — marked here by a maroon, dashed line — is formed by the Ural Mountains, Ural River, Caspian Sea, Caucasus Mountains and the Black Sea with its outlets, the Bosporus and Dardanelles.

Peloponnesus

Crete

30°E

Cyprus

40°E

Map Key

✛ Mountain peak

FINLAND

ESTONIA

LATVIA

LITHUANIA

KALININGRAD (RUSSIA)

POLAND

SWEDEN

NORWAY

BALTIC SEA

Shetland Islands

Orkney Islands

Rockall (UNITED KINGDOM)

Inverness

SCOTLAND
Aberdeen
Perth
Dundee
Edinburgh

Glasgow
Londonderry (Derry)
NORTHERN IRELAND
Belfast

UNITED KINGDOM
Newcastle
Sunderland
Leeds
Kingston upon Hull
ENGLAND

Isle of Man

IRELAND (ÉIRE)
Liverpool
Limerick
Dublin
Waterford
Cork
Manchester
Birmingham
Nottingham
WALES
Cardiff
London

Outer Hebrides
Inner Hebrides

IRISH SEA

CELTIC SEA

Bristol
Plymouth

AREA ENLARGED OPPOSITE PAGE

NORTH SEA

DENMARK

Kiel
Rostock
Lübeck
Hamburg
Berlin
Bremen
Hannover
Magdeburg
Leipzig
Dresden
Chemnitz

Oldenburg
Groningen
NETHERLANDS
Amsterdam
Utrecht
The Hague
Bielefeld
Essen
Köln
Erfurt
GERMANY
Frankfurt

Frisian Islands

Brugge
Antwerp
Brussels
BELGIUM
Lille
Charleroi
LUXEMBOURG

CZECHIA (CZECH REP.)

SLOVAKIA

Vienna

AUSTRIA

ATLANTIC OCEAN

ENGLISH CHANNEL
Channel Islands (U.K.)

Brest

Le Havre
Amiens
Rouen
Reims
Metz
Nancy
Paris
Orléans
Mainz
Mannheim
Nürnberg
Stuttgart
Strasbourg
Freiburg
Munich
Salzburg
Linz
Graz
Innsbruck
Bolzano
Trento
Trieste

Rennes
Angers
Le Mans
Tours
Nantes

FRANCE

Limoges
Clermont-Ferrand
Vichy
Lyon
Mont Blanc 15,781 ft 4,810 m

MASSIF CENTRAL

Bordeaux
Toulouse
PYRENEES
ANDORRA
Andorra
Perpignan

Besançon
Dijon
Lausanne
Geneva
Basel
Bern
SWITZERLAND
Zürich
LIECHTENSTEIN
SLOVENIA
Verona
Padova
Venice
Milan
Turin
Genoa
Modena
Bologna
Florence
Pisa
Perugia
SAN MARINO
Ancona

BAY OF BISCAY

Donostia-San Sebastián
Bilbao
Santander
Gijón
A Coruña
Oviedo
Vigo
Santiago de Compostela
León
Braga
Bragança
Oporto
Viseu
Coimbra
PORTUGAL
Lisbon
Setúbal

Vitoria-Gasteiz
Pamplona
Burgos
Valladolid
Zaragoza
Lleida
Sabadell
Mataró
Barcelona

SERBIA

BOSNIA & HERZEGOVINA

CROATIA

ADRIATIC SEA

MONTENEGRO

APENNINES

ITALY
Rome
VATICAN CITY
Naples
Vesuvius 4,203 ft 1,281 m

Pescara
Foggia
Bari
Lecce
Taranto
Gulf of Taranto

LIGURIAN SEA

Nice
Toulon
Marseille

CORSICA
Ajaccio
Bastia

SARDINIA
Sassari
Cagliari

TYRRHENIAN SEA

Cosenza
Messina
Reggio di Calabria
Palermo
Marsala
SICILY
Taormina
Catania
Syracuse

Montpellier
Nîmes
Avignon

Salamanca
Madrid
Toledo
SPAIN
Badajoz
Valencia
Albacete
Castelló de la Plana

Duero
Tajo
Tagus
Guadiana

BALEARIC SEA

Minorca

Palma de Mallorca
Majorca

BALEARIC ISLANDS

SIERRA MORENA
Córdoba
Jaén
Murcia
Alicante
Cartagena
Granada
Seville
Málaga
Almería
Huelva
Jerez
Cádiz
Algeciras
GIBRALTAR (U.K.)
Ceuta (SPAIN)
ALBORAN SEA
Strait of Gibraltar
Melilla (SPAIN)

MEDITERRANEAN SEA

Valletta
MALTA

TUNISIA

MOROCCO

ALGERIA

Map Key	
⊛	Country capital
⊙	Internal capital
•••	City or town
·····	Country boundary

0   200 miles
0   300 kilometres

WESTERN EUROPE

SPOTLIGHT ON THE UNITED KINGDOM AND IRELAND

The **UNITED KINGDOM** is made up of four countries: England, Northern Ireland, Scotland and Wales. The flag of the United Kingdom, known as the Union Flag, or Union Jack, combines the three crosses of the patron saints of England (St. George), Scotland (St. Andrew) and Ireland (St. Patrick).

First used in 1848, **IRELAND's** tricolour flag was officially adopted when Ireland became independent in 1922. Today, Ireland has a population of almost 5.1 million.

England's flag features the red cross of St. George on a white background. The English have been using it since the 12th century. England, by far the largest country in the United Kingdom, has around 55.3 million people.

Northern Ireland flies the Union Flag. It has a population of 1.8 million people.

Scotland's flag shows a diagonal white cross on a blue field, known as The Saltire, or St. Andrew's Cross. The English and Scottish flags were combined in 1606 as the flag for the union of England and Scotland. Scotland has a population of about 5.4 million people.

Wales was conquered by England in the 13th century. Considered a principality, not a kingdom, its red dragon flag is not part of the United Kingdom flag. Wales is mountainous, and most of its 3.1 million people live along the coast.

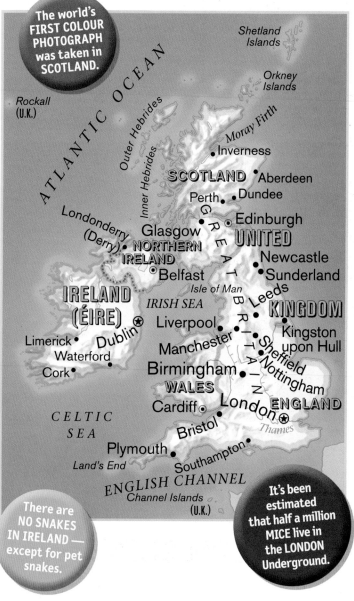

The world's FIRST COLOUR PHOTOGRAPH was taken in SCOTLAND.

There are NO SNAKES IN IRELAND — except for pet snakes.

It's been estimated that half a million MICE live in the LONDON Underground.

323

EASTERN EUROPE

200 miles
300 kilometres

Map Key

⊛ Country capital
•••• City or town
••••• Country boundary

RUSSIA

LATVIA

LITHUANIA

KALININGRAD (RUSSIA)

GERMANY

Western Dvina

Vitsyebsk
Orsha
Barysaw
Mahilyow
Babruysk
⊛ Minsk
Homyel'
Baranavichy
Hrodna
Pinsk
Brest

BELARUS

Pinsk Marshes

Dnieper
Mazyr

Chernihiv

Sumy

Kharkiv
Poltava

Lys'ychans'k
Luhans'k
Alchevs'k
Krasnyy Luch
Krasnodon
Yenakiyeve
Makiyivka
Berdyans'k

SEA OF AZOV

Slov'yans'k
Kramators'k
Kostyantynivka
Horlivka
Donets'k
Zaporizhzhya
Nikopol'
Melitopol'
Kherson
Mariupol'

Boundary claimed by Ukraine

CRIMEA

BLACK SEA

Kremenchuk
Dniprodzerzhyns'k
Dnipropetrovs'k
Kryvyy Rih
Dnipro

Chernobyl'

⊛ Kiev

Dnieper

Oleksandriya
Kirovohrad

Cherkasy

UKRAINE

Zhytomyr
Rivne
Luts'k
L'viv
Ternopil'
Khmel'nyts'kyy
Ivano-Frankivs'k
Chernivtsi

Bila Tserkva

Vinnytsya

Kam'yanets'-Podil's'kyy

Odesa
Mykolayiv

Chișinău
Tiraspol'
Bălți

MOLDOVA

Prut

Dniester

POLAND

Białystok
⊛ Warsaw
Lublin
Rzeszów
Kielce
Radom
Kraków
Tarnów
Łódź
Kalisz
Częstochowa
Katowice
Tychy
Bytom
Wrocław
Legnica
Opole
Zielona Góra
Poznań
Gorzów Wielkopolski
Bydgoszcz
Toruń
Olsztyn
Gdańsk
Gdynia
Szczecin
Wałbrzych

Vistula
Oder

Košice
Uzhhorod

CARPATHIAN MOUNTAINS

SLOVAKIA
Bratislava ⊛
Olomouc
Brno
Ostrava

CZECHIA (CZECH REP.)
⊛ Prague
Plzeň
Liberec
České Budějovice

Nyíregyháza
Debrecen
Miskolc

HUNGARY
Budapest ⊛
Győr
Székesfehérvár
Pécs
Szeged

Tisza
Drava
Danube

ROMANIA

SERBIA

BOSNIA AND HERZEGOVINA

CROATIA

SLOVENIA

AUSTRIA

Dniester

CRIMEA

Russia invaded Crimea in 2014 and, after secession from Ukraine was approved in a disputed and boycotted referendum held in Crimea, the Russian parliament voted to annex Crimea into the Russian Federation. The United Nations General Assembly subsequently adopted a nonbinding resolution declaring the annexation invalid and affirming Ukraine's territorial jurisdiction. As of 2019, Russia administers and controls all aspects of the peninsula, while Ukraine continues to maintain that Crimea is its sovereign territory.

324

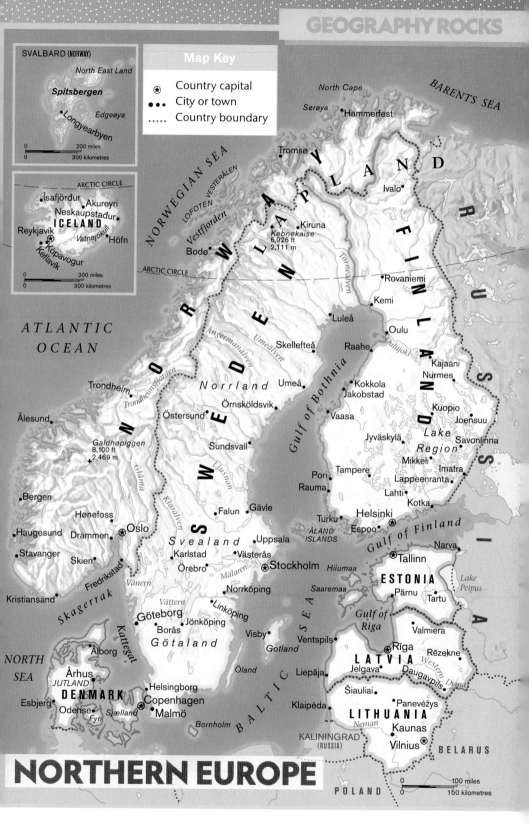

NORTHERN EUROPE

THE BALKANS

Map Key

- ✪ Country capital
- ••• City or town
- ····· Country boundary

0   100 miles

0   100 kilometres

Former Yugoslavia, 1991

Yugoslavia, or 'Land of the Southern Slavs', was created in 1918 as a country of many ethnic groups, but it started coming apart when Slovenia and Croatia became independent in 1991. Yugoslavia ceased to exist in 2003, when the country changed its name to Serbia and Montenegro. In 2006, Montenegro declared independence, as did Kosovo in 2008.

Former Yugoslavia ▬▬▬
Border (1991)

NORTHERN CYPRUS
(recognised only by Turkey)

✪ Nicosia
CYPRUS
• Limassol

Same Scale as Main Map

Map Key

⊛ Country capital
•• City or town
···· Country boundary

0   200 miles
0   300 kilometres

NORWAY

BARENTS SEA

Murmansk   Kolguyev I.

Kola
Peninsula   Vorkuta

Kanin Peninsula   ARCTIC CIRCLE   Ob

SWEDEN   Usinsk

FINLAND   WHITE SEA   Pechora   EUROPE-ASIA
                                                     BOUNDARY
Severodvinsk •Archangel   Sosnogorsk
                              Ukhta

Petrozavodsk   Zheleznodorozhnyy

Gulf of Bothnia   Northern Dvina   Syktyvkar

Lake   Lake   Sukhona
Ladoga   Onega   Kotlas

St. Petersburg   Berezniki

Gulf of Finland

ESTONIA   Cherepovets   Perm'

Lake   Velikiy   Vologda   Kirov
Peipus   Novgorod

•Pskov   Rybinsk Reservoir

LATVIA   Velikiye   Rybinsk   Izhevsk
          Luki   Yaroslavl'   Kama

KALININGRAD   Tver' Ivanovo Nizhniy
(RUSSIA) LITHUANIA   Novgorod   Kazan'   Naberezhnyye
                                                               Chelny
          Moscow⊛ Vladimir   Ufa
BALTIC SEA   Smolensk   Cheboksary Ul'yanovsk Magnitogorsk
                                                       Sterlitamak
POLAND   Kaluga Ryazan'   Volga
         •Tula   Saransk Syzran' Tol'yatti
BELARUS   Belaya
                    Oka Penza Samara Novotroitsk
Bryansk Orel Lipetsk   Balakovo Orenburg Orsk
         Kursk Tambov   Engels
         Voronezh Saratov
         Belgorod
                    Kamyshin   KAZAKHSTAN
CRIMEA   Don
Russia invaded Crimea in 2014 and, after   Ural
secession from Ukraine was approved in a
disputed and boycotted referendum held in   Volga
Crimea, the Russian parliament voted to annex
Crimea into the Russian Federation. The United   Volgograd Volzhskiy
Nations General Assembly subsequently
adopted a nonbinding resolution declaring the   Shakhty   CASPIAN DEPRESSION
annexation invalid and affirming Ukraine's
territorial jurisdiction. As of 2019, Russia   UKRAINE
administers and controls all aspects of the   Don
peninsula, while Ukraine continues to maintain   Rostov
that Crimea is its sovereign territory.   Taganrog   Astrakhan'

ROMANIA   SEA OF   Krasnodar
          CRIMEA   AZOV   Stavropol'
Simferopol'   Maykop Pyatigorsk   CASPIAN
Sevastopol' Boundary   El'brus   CHECHNYA
             claimed   18,510 ft
BULGARIA   by Ukraine   5,642 m Groznyy
          BLACK   Sochi   Vladikavkaz Makhachkala
          SEA   CAUCASUS MOUNTAINS
                              GEORGIA   SEA

TURKEY   ARMENIA AZERBAIJAN

IRAN

EUROPEAN RUSSIA

Bet You Didn't Know!

10 fast facts about

2

Karaoke, which means 'empty orchestra' in Japanese, originated in Japan in the early 1970s.

Japan is the only country with an **emperor** and an **empress.** **1**

3 Japan has the highest number of **vending machines** per capita in the world, with some **5.5 million machines.**

Japan's Akashi Kaikyō Bridge can handle up to 290-kilometre-an-hour (180-mph) winds **and withstand earthquakes.** **4**

A bullet train speeds past Mount Fuji in Japan.

Japan

5 There are more than **100 active volcanoes** in Japan.

7 In Japan, it's possible to buy **watermelons** shaped like **pyramids.**

6 About **73 percent** of Japan is covered with **mountains.**

8 Japanese kids start the school year in **April,** at about the time when the cherry blossoms bloom.

9 Japan's bullet trains, called **Shinkansen,** carry passengers at speeds of **320 kilometres an hour** (200 mph).

10 A 2011 earthquake in Japan was so powerful, it moved the entire **island of Honshu** as much as **4.7 metres** (15 ft).

EXTREME
WEIRDNESS

VADER RULES THE SKY

WHAT León International Balloon Festival

WHERE León, Mexico

DETAILS This might be the Rebels' worst nightmare. Participants at this festival soared across the sky in giant hot-air balloons, such as this one shaped like Darth Vader's mask. More than a hundred balloons fly each year — anything from pandas to bees to scarecrows. But don't worry. This Vader's only full of hot air.

THE FORCE IS STRONG WITH THIS ONE.

DON'T MOW THIS GRASS.

WEAR YOUR LAWN

WHAT Grass-covered flip-flops

WHERE New South Wales Coast, Australia

DETAILS Want to feel the grass between your toes? Just plant your feet in these grass-topped flip-flops, designed to give you the sensation of being outdoors any time. Don't worry about watering the sandals — the grass is actually a layer of artificial turf. You'll have some happy feet!

YOU'RE IN THE COLD SEAT.

ICE CUBE ON WHEELS

WHAT Truck made of ice

WHERE Hensall, Canada

DETAILS It's going to be an icy ride. This functioning truck has a body made of 4,990 kilograms (11,000 lb) of ice. Built over a base frame with wheels, the icy exterior covers a real engine, brakes and a steering wheel. It runs on a battery that's specially designed to start in frigid conditions that would keep most cars from revving up. The car can only go short distances — but what a great place to chill!

COOL
INVENTIONS

A SUPERSMART BUILDING
THAT COULD CHANGE YOUR LIFE

THE STRAWSCRAPER »

For some people, a windy day means a bad hair day. But for the folks designing this odd-looking building, a windy day is a *good* hair day. For them, windy days will mean the hairy fibres on their building are capturing loads of free energy. A Swedish architectural firm is working on plans to transform an existing Stockholm building into a futuristic, 40-floor skyscraper that will create energy. The design for this project, known as the Strawscraper, encloses the building in a casing covered with long, flexible straws that turn wind motion into electrical energy. From gentle breezes to strong winds, the friction on the straws will produce and store electricity much like a wind power plant does. The Strawscraper will be much quieter than a wind turbine, though, and will be bird-friendly, too.

Plans include a restaurant and a viewing platform in the Strawscraper.

THIS or THAT?

CHOOSE THIS:

Stack monuments all the way to the moon's surface.

or

CHOOSE THAT:

Stack hamsters to the height of a famous monument.

If you CHOSE THIS

You're reaching for the stars if you try to get to the moon by stacking Eiffel Towers on top of each other. Not counting its antennas, the height of the Eiffel Tower in Paris, France, is 300 metres (986 ft). The distance from the Earth's surface to the moon at its closest is about 360,010 kilometres (223,700 mi). If you were to stack Eiffel Tower upon Eiffel Tower all the way to the moon, it would require more than 1.1 million monuments! Be sure to build an elevator while you're at it.

If you CHOSE THAT

You've got quite a **balancing act** if you try to stack hamsters to the top of the Statue of Liberty in New York City, U.S.A. The height of the monument—from base to torch—is about 46 metres (151 ft). The average height of a hamster standing on its hind legs is 15 centimetres (6 in). That means if you created a tower of hamsters that reached the top of Lady Liberty, you'd need 302 hamsters in all! It would stink to be the hamster on the bottom, wouldn't it?

BONUS FACT

If you lined up 45 crocodiles tail to snout, they'd stretch as long as one side of the Great Pyramid at Giza.

THIS OR THAT? 3
EVEN MORE

CHECK OUT THIS BOOK!

WILD VACATION

ENTER HERE!

SLEEP HERE!

Tree Hotel
NESTLING INTO NATURE

WHERE Dalat, Vietnam

HOW MUCH About £36 to £94 a night

WHY IT'S COOL One look at this hotel and you'll understand its nickname: 'Crazy House'. The bizarre lodging is designed to resemble a giant tree stump from the outside. The structure's cosy interior is filled with twisting passageways and 10 cavelike rooms, each with a different animal, insect or plant theme. Visitors can unwind next to a fireplace shaped like a kangaroo or drift to sleep while staring at the stars through skylights in the Gourd Room. Guests can also wander through the garden, where eerie metal spiderwebs hang. More daring individuals can climb the winding walkways to the roof of the building and take in views of the surrounding city. From top to bottom, this hotel is insanely awesome.

COOL THINGS ABOUT VIETNAM

About 40 percent of the people in Vietnam have the last name Nguyen.

Grilled squid teeth are a popular snack in the country's coastal towns.

Vietnam is only 48 kilometres (30 mi) wide at its narrowest point.

THINGS TO DO IN VIETNAM

Explore the bustling Cai Rang floating market, where boats are colourfully packed with fruits and vegetables for sale.

Sample traditional noodle soup called pho (pronounced FUH) from shops in Hanoi, the country's capital city.

Discover the palaces of former emperors inside the walls of the Hue Citadel, along the Perfume River.

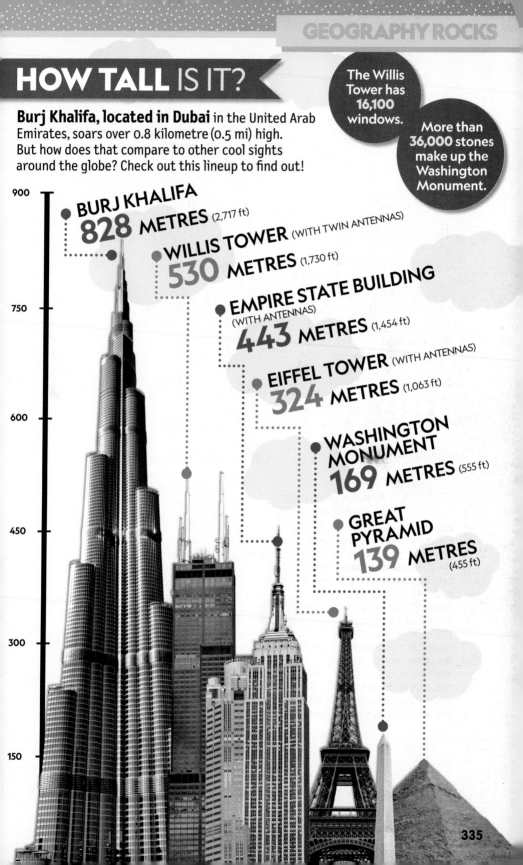

HOW TALL IS IT?

Burj Khalifa, located in Dubai in the United Arab Emirates, soars over 0.8 kilometre (0.5 mi) high. But how does that compare to other cool sights around the globe? Check out this lineup to find out!

The Willis Tower has **16,100** windows.

More than **36,000** stones make up the Washington Monument.

BURJ KHALIFA
828 METRES (2,717 ft)

WILLIS TOWER (WITH TWIN ANTENNAS)
530 METRES (1,730 ft)

EMPIRE STATE BUILDING (WITH ANTENNAS)
443 METRES (1,454 ft)

EIFFEL TOWER (WITH ANTENNAS)
324 METRES (1,063 ft)

WASHINGTON MONUMENT
169 METRES (555 ft)

GREAT PYRAMID
139 METRES (455 ft)

900
750
600
450
300
150

QUIZ WHIZ

Is your geography knowledge off the map? Quiz yourself to find out!

Write your answers on a piece of paper. Then check them below.

1 You'd have to stack _____ Eiffel Towers on top of each other to reach the moon.
a. 111
b. 1,100
c. 11,100
d. 1.1 million

2 Besides being the tallest mountain on Earth, what else is unique about Mauna Loa?
a. It's an active volcano.
b. It's a glacier.
c. It's entirely underwater.
d. It's an ancient burial ground.

3 What's the bikini bathing suit named after?
a. Bikini, Germany
b. Bikini Atoll in the Marshall Islands
c. Bikini, California, U.S.A.
d. Bikini Island in Hawaii, U.S.A.

4 **True or false?** Bullet trains in Japan travel at speeds of 320 kilometres an hour (200 mph).

5 There's a _____ at the top of Mount Mabu in Mozambique.
a. crater
b. rainforest
c. village
d. desert

Not **STUMPED** yet? Check out the *NATIONAL GEOGRAPHIC KIDS QUIZ WHIZ* collection for more crazy **GEOGRAPHY** questions!

ANSWERS:
1. d; 2. a; 3. b; 4. True; 5. b

Finding Your Way Around

Every map has a story to tell, but first you have to know how to read one. Maps represent information by using a language of symbols. Knowing how to read these symbols provides access to a wide range of information. Look at the scale and compass rose or arrow to understand distance and direction (see box below).

To find out what each symbol on a map means, you must use the key. It's your secret decoder — identifying information by each symbol on the map.

Latitude

Longitude

90°N (North Pole)
75°N
60°N
45°N
30°N
15°N
0° (Equator)
15°S
30°S
45°S

LATITUDE AND LONGITUDE

Latitude and longitude lines (above) help us determine locations on Earth. Every place on Earth has a special address called absolute location. Imaginary lines called lines of latitude run west to east, parallel to the Equator. These lines measure distance in degrees north or south from the Equator (0° latitude) to the North Pole (90° N) or to the South Pole (90° S). One degree of latitude is approximately 113 kilometres (70 mi).

Lines of longitude run north to south, meeting at the poles. These lines measure distance in degrees east or west from 0° longitude (prime meridian) to 180° longitude. The prime meridian runs through Greenwich, England.

SCALE AND DIRECTION

The scale on a map can be shown as a fraction, as words or as a line or bar. It relates distance on the map to distance in the real world. Sometimes the scale identifies the type of map projection. Maps may include an arrow or compass rose to indicate north on the map.

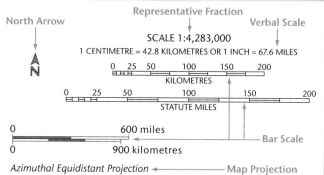

North Arrow

Representative Fraction

Verbal Scale

SCALE 1:4,283,000
1 CENTIMETRE = 42.8 KILOMETRES OR 1 INCH = 67.6 MILES

0 25 50 100 150 200
KILOMETRES

0 25 50 100 150 200
STATUTE MILES

0   600 miles
0   900 kilometres

Bar Scale

Azimuthal Equidistant Projection ◄— Map Projection

337

GAME ANSWERS

We Gave It a Swirl
page 136

1. flamingo, 2. chameleon, 3. koala,
4. cow, 5. fish

What in the World?
page 137

Top row: pineapples, garlands, coconut
Middle row: Hawaiian shirt, sea turtle
Bottom row: volcano, surfboard, ukulele

Galaxy Quest
pages 138–139

Bark Park
page 141

What in the World?
page 142

Top row: jumpers, rainbow, sprinkles
Middle row: coloured pencils, umbrella, toothbrushes
Bottom row: liquorice, towels, feathers

Undersea Stars
page 144

Find the Hidden Animals
page 146

1. D, 2. C, 3. B, 4. F, 5. A, 6. E

Signs of the Times
page 149

Sign #2 is fake.

Windy Jumble
page 150

Eleanor, A; Sam, J; Nicole, E; Steve, H;
Carlos, F; Zak, B; Ava, C; Jill, I; Isabel, G;
Daniel, D

Want to Learn More?

Find more information about the topics in this book in these National Geographic Kids resources.

Absolute Expert series

Weird But True! series

Just Joking series

5,000 Awesome Facts (About Everything!) series

Bet You Didn't Know! series

Make This!
Ella Schwartz
February 2019

Don't Read This Book Before Dinner
Anna Claybourne
July 2019

Nerd A to Z
T. J. Resler
August 2019

Sharks vs. Sloths
Julie Beer
September 2019

The Big Book of Bling
Rose Davidson
September 2019

Surprising Stories Behind Everyday Stuff
Stephanie Warren Drimmer
September 2019

Encyclopedia of American Indian History and Culture
Cynthia O'Brien
October 2019

It's a Numbers Game! Basketball
James Buckley, Jr.
February 2020

1,000 Facts About Dinosaurs, Fossils, and Prehistoric Life
Patricia Daniels
February 2020

Abbreviations:
AL: Alamy Stock Photo
DRMS: Dreamstime
GI: Getty Images
IS: iStockphoto
MP: Minden Pictures
NGIC: National Geographic Image Collection
SS: Shutterstock

All Maps
By National Geographic unless otherwise noted

All Illustrations & Charts
By Stuart Armstrong unless otherwise noted

Front Cover
(llama), Jeff Goulden/IS/GI; (diver), Mark D. Conlin; (robot), Julian Stratenschulte/dpa/GI

Spine
(llama), Jeff Goulden/IS/GI

Back Cover
(Earth), ixpert/SS; (puffin), Mlenny/E+/GI; (satellite), NASA/JPL; (frog), kuritafsheen/RooM/GI; (pyramids), Yann Arthus-Bertrand/GI Plus/GI; (explorer), Edward Selfe; (butterfly), Steven Russell Smith/AL

Front Matter (2-7)
2-3, Dave Fleetham/Perspectives/GI; 5 (Your World), Benoit Tessier/Reuters; 5 (Awesome Exploration), Jennifer Adler/NGIC; 5 (Amazing Animals), Ron Kimball/Kimball Stock; 5 (Wonders of Nature, LE), Preto_perola/GI; 5 (Wonders of Nature, RT), SpectrumPhotofile.com; 6 (Space and Earth, LE), NASA/JPL; 6 (Space and Earth, RT), Sven Sjöström/EyeEm/GI; 6 (Fun and Games, LE), David Madison/GI; 6 (Fun and Games, RT), Dan Sipple; 6 (Science and Technology), Alexander Miridonov/Kommersant Photo/Polaris/Newscom; 6 (Culture Connection, LE), Stefano Gentile/EyeEm/GI; 6 (Culture Connection, RT), Dinodia/GI; 7 (Going Green), Rana Sajid Hussain/Pacific Press/LightRocket/GI; 7 (History Happens), David Lazar/GI; 7 (Geography Rocks), Layne Kennedy/GI

Your World 2021 (8-17)
8-9, Benoit Tessier/Reuters; 10 (UP LE), Nicola Maplres and Sean Kelly; 10 (CTR RT), Dr. Luiz Rocha; 10 (CTR LE), Tim Laman/GI; 10 (LO RT), Ron Santiago, BioWeb PUCE; 11 (UP), HUBBLESITE; 11 (CTR), Kazuhiro Nogi/AFP/GI; 11 (LO), Kazuhiro Nogi/AFP/GI; 12 (UP), Joel Sartore/NGIC; 12 (LO), Fabio Pupin/MP; 13 (UP), AP Images/Carolyn Thompson; 13 (LO), Aflac Worldwide; 14 (UP), Photo courtesy of K-9 Country Inn; 14 (CTR), Photo courtesy of K-9 Country Inn; 14 (LO), Susan Schmitz/SS; 14 (LO), John Lund/GI; 15 (UP LE), Wildlife Reserves Singapore; 15 (UP RT), Wildlife Reserves Singapore; 15 (LO), Rothy's/photo by Mark Thiessen and Becky Hale/NGP Staff; 16 (UP RT), a_v_d/SS; 16 (UP CTR RT), Daniel Thornberg/DRMS; 16 (CTR LE), stanley45/IS; 16 (CTR RT), Melinda Nagy/SS; 16 (LO CTR LE), Kabayan Mark/500px/GI; 16 (LO LE),

MariaKovaleva/SS; 16 (LO LE), markgoddard/GI; 16 (LO RT), Ascent Xmedia/Taxi/GI; 17 (UP), Compass Pools UK; 17 (CTR), National Weather Service/AP Images/SS; 17 (LO), Michael Sewell Visual Pursuit/GI

Awesome Exploration (18-35)
18-19, Jennifer Adler/NGIC; 20 (LE), Tyler Roemer; 20 (inset), Tyler Roemer; 20 (LO RT), courtesy Rainforest Connection; 21 (UP LE), Jacqueline Faherty/NGIC; 21 (LO LE), Randall Scott/NGIC; 21 (UP RT), Randall Scott/NGIC; 21 (LO RT), jeep2499/SS; 22 (LE), Ali Cansino, courtesy Jamal Galves; 22 (UP RT), Mark Thiessen, NGP Staff; 22 (LO), Celeshia Guy, courtesy Jamal Galves; 23, Vladimir Wrangel/SS; 24, University of Georgia Marketing & Communications. All rights reserved.; 25 (UP LE), Pixel-Shot/Adobe Stock; 25 (UP RT), Chones/SS; 25 (CTR), Arthur Tilley/GI; 25 (LO CTR LE), Strekoza64/SS; 25 (LO CTR RT), EasternLightcraft/iStock/GI; 25 (LO), PBorowka/IS/GI; 26-27 (UP), Brian J. Skerry/NGIC; 26 (LO), Brian J. Skerry/NGIC; 27 (CTR), Mark D. Conlin/NGIC; 27 (LO), Brian J. Skerry/NGIC; 28 (UP LE), Pictures Colour Library/Newscom; 28 (UP RT), jarino47/istock/GI; 28 (LO LE), Channi Anand/AP Photo; 28 (LO RT), Bigfoot Hostel/Barcroft Media/GI; 29 (UP LE), Michael Clark/AL; 29 (UP RT), EPA/Newscom; 29 (CTR), Anthony Devlin/PA Images/AL; 29 (LO), Adam Pretty/GI; 30 (UP), courtesy Colin O'Brady; 30 (CTR LE), photo by Samuel A. Harrison, courtesy Colin O'Brady; 30 (CTR RT), courtesy Colin O'Brady; 30 (LO LE), courtesy Louis Rudd; 30 (LO RT), courtesy Louis Rudd; 31 (UP), Tony Campbell/SS; 31 (LO), SS; 32 (UP), Annie Griffiths; 32 (LO), Annie Griffiths; 33 (UP), Annie Griffiths; 33 (CTR LE), Annie Griffiths; 33 (CTR RT), Annie Griffiths; 33 (LO), Annie Griffiths; 34 (UP RT), Vladimir Wrangel/SS; 34 (UP LE), Brian J. Skerry/NGIC; 34 (CTR RT), Bigfoot Hostel/Barcroft Media/GI; 34 (LO LE), Annie Griffiths; 35, Grady Reese/IS

Amazing Animals (36-89)
36-37, Ron Kimball/Kimball Stock; 38-39, PhonlamaiPhoto/IS; 40-41 (UP), Alexandra Young; 40 (CTR LE), Kreatiw/DRMS; 40 (LO RT), Action Sports Photography/SS; 40 (LO LE), OrangeGroup/SS; 41 (UP), Özlem Pınar Iva cu; 41 (LO RT), Stefan Rousseau/PA Wire/AP Images; 41 (LO), Express Newspapers Via AP Images; 42 (UP), Zara Palmer, Marketing Specialist - Toucan Rescue Ranch; 42 (LO), Michael Sharkey; 43 (UP), Mark Ralston/AFP/GI; 43 (LO), RSPCA Trading Ltd./RSPCA Photolibrary; 44 (UP), Grahm S. Jones/Columbus Zoo and Aquarium; 44 (LO), Taneile Hoare; 45 (UP), Leondra Schere; 45 (LO), Farm Sanctuary; 46 (UP), lifegallery/iStock/GI; 46 (CTR), DioGen/SS; 46 (LO), Nick Garbutt; 47 (UP LE), EyeEm/GI; 47 (UP RT), reptiles4all/SS; 47 (CTR LE), Hiroya Minakuchi/MP; 47 (CTR RT), FP media/SS; 47 (LO), Aleksandar Dickov/SS; 48 (UP CTR LE), Ingo Arndt/naturepl.com; 48 (UP CTR RT), Dr. James L. Castner/Visuals Unlimited, Inc.; 48 (LO CTR), Alex Hyde/naturepl.com; 48 (LO LE), NHPA/

SuperStock; 48 (LO RT), Chris Mattison/FLPA/MP; 48 (UP), Cosmin Manci/SS; 49 (UP LE), Alex Hyde/naturepl.com/GI; 49 (UP RT), PREMAPHOTOS/naturepl.com; 49 (RT CTR), Kazuo Unno/Nature Production/MP; 49 (LE CTR), Christopher Smith/AL; 49 (LO), NH/SS; 50 (UP), Schafer & Hill/GI; 50 (LO LE), Chuck Graham; 50 (LO RT), Mel Melcon/GI; 51 (UP), Chuck Graham; 51 (CTR), Chuck Graham; 51 (LO), Chuck Graham; 52 (UP), Abby Wood/Smithsonian's National Zoo; 52 (LO), Anna Gowthorpe/PA Images via GI; 53 (LO LE), saad315/SS; 53 (UP LE), Andrea Izzotti/SS; 53 (UP RT), Sylvain Cordier/GI; 53 (LO RT), Dr. Axel Gebauer/Nature Picture Library; 54, Eric Baccega/NPL/MP; 55 (LO), Jordi Galbany/Dian Fossey Gorilla Fund International; 55 (UP LE), Stone Sub/GI; 55 (CTR RT), courtesy Dallas Zoo; 55 (UP RT), Martin Hale/FLPA/MP; 56 (UP), Klein and Hubert/MP; 56 (LO LE), Stephen Dalton/MP; 56 (LO RT), Christian Ziegler/MP; 57 (LO LE), Juan Carlos Muñoz/GI; 57 (UP RT), Paul Souders/GI; 57 (UP CTR), Ingo Arndt/MP; 57 (LO CTR LE), Ingo Arndt/MP; 57 (UP CTR LE), Ingo Arndt/MP; 57 (UP LE), Ingo Arndt/MP; 58 (UP), James Gourley/SS; 58 (CTR LE), Peter Murphy; 58 (LO LE), Kevin Schafer/GI; 58 (LO RT), Tom Reichner/SS; 58 (CTR RT), Purestock/GI; 59 (LO), Min-Soo Ahn/EyeEm/GI; 59 (UP), madmonkey0328/SS; 59 (UP CTR), LIMDQ/SS; 59 (CTR LE), AL-Travelpicture/iStock/GI; 59 (CTR RT), Alex Snyder; 60 (LO RT), 20th Century Fox/Entertainment Pictures/ZUMA PRESS; 60 (LO LE), Maria Diekmann/REST; 60 (LO CTR LE), Jamie Trueblood/©Columbia Pictures/Courtesy Everett Collection; 60 (LO CTR RT), Suzi Eszterhas/MP; 61 (LO CTR LE), imageBROKER/AL; 61 (UP), Christian Boix/Africa Geographic; 61 (UP CTR LE), J Dennis Nigel/GI; 61 (UP CTR RT), J Dennis Nigel/GI; 61 (LO CTR), © Walt Disney Studios Motion Pictures/Courtesy Everett Collection; 61, Everett Collection, Inc.; 62 (UP), Design Pics Inc/AL; 62 (LO), mauritius images GmbH/AL; 63 (UP LE), Kathryn Jeffs/Nature Picture Library; 63 (UP RT), Tony Wu/Nature Picture Library;63 (LO), Design Pics Inc/AL; 63 (CTR RT), Design Pics Inc/AL; 64 (UP LE), Donald M Jones/MP; 64 (LO LE), Doc White/Nature Picture Library; 64 (LO RT), Enrique R Aguirre Aves/GI; 64 (UP RT), Milo Burcham/Design Pics INC/AL; 65 (UP), John C. Lewis/SeaPics.com; 65 (LE CTR), Gary Bell/oceanwideimages.com; 65 (RT CTR), Gary Bell/oceanwideimages.com; 65 (LO LE), Jeff Rotman/SeaPics.com; 65 (LO RT), Doug Perrine/SeaPics.com; 66 (UP), Norbert Wu/MP; 66 (LO), Claudio Contreres/NPL/MP; 67 (UP), Doug Perrine/naturepl.com; 67 (CTR), SA Team/Foto Nature/MP; 67 (LO LE), Claudio Contreras/Nature Picture Library; 67 (LO RT), Doug Perrine/naturepl.com; 68 (UP), TLWilsonPhotography/SS; 68 (LO), Yuri Smityuk/TASS/AL Live News; 69 (LO LE), Action Sports Photography/SS; 69 (RT LO), Andrew Porter/SS; 69 (UP LE), Rudi Hulshhof/GI; 70 (UP), Photoshot License Ltd/AL; 70 (LO), Steve Winter/NGIC; 71 (LO LE), Tom Brakefield/CORBIS/GI; 71 (RT), James Kaiser;

72 (UP), Chris Butler/Science Photo Library/ Photo Researchers, Inc.; 72 (CTR), Publiphoto/ Photo Researchers, Inc.; 72 (LO), Pixeldust Studios/NGIC; 73 (B), Laurie O'Keefe/Photo Researchers, Inc.; 73 (C), Chris Butler/Photo Researchers, Inc.; 73 (D), Publiphoto/Photo Researchers, Inc.; 73 (A), Publiphoto/Photo Researchers, Inc.; 73 (E), image courtesy of Project Exploration; 74 (LO), Andrea Meyer/ SS; 75 (UP LE), Andrey Atuchin; 75 (UP RT), Mark Witton; 75 (LO), Jorge Gonzalez; 76 (UP), Franco Tempesta; 76 (CTR), Franco Tempesta; 76 (LO), Photo by Roderick Mickens, © American Museum of Natural History; 77 (LO LE), Julius Csotonyi; 77 (UP LE), Franco Tempesta; 77 (UP RT), Franco Tempesta; 77 (LO RT), Franco Tempesta; 78 (UP), Franco Tempesta; 78 (LO), Franco Tempesta; 79 (UP), Catmando/SS; 79 (CTR), Franco Tempesta; 79 (LO), Leonello Calvetti/SS; 80 (UP), Pete Oxford/MP; 80 (LO), Tui De Roy/MP; 81 (UP), Bernd von Jutrczenk/GI; 81 (LO LE), David Evison/SS; 81 (LO RT), Marion Vollborn/MP; 82 (LO LE), Piotr Naskrecki/MP; 82 (UP LE), Old Dog Photography/GI; 82 (RT), Keren Su/ CORBIS; 83 (UP), Vicki Jauron/Moment RF/GI; 83 (LO), Ruaridh Connellan/BarcroftImages/ GI; 84 (UP), Lubos Kovalik/GI; 84 (LO), Norbert Wu/MP; 85 (UP LE), Stephen Barnes/SS; 85 (UP RT), Jim Cumming/GI; 85 (LO LE), Mark Kostich/GI; 85 (LO RT), Ellende/GI; 86 (UP RT), Jonathan Androwski/GI; 86 (LO), Amanda Edwards/GI; 86 (UP LE), Patrick Endres/AGE Fotostock; 87 (UP), Kryssia Campos/GI; 87 (LO), Frank Lukasseck/GI; 88 (UP LE), Rudi Hulshof/GI; 88 (UP RT), James Gourley/SS; 88 (LO RT), John C. Lewis/SeaPics.com; 88 (LO LE), Design Pics Inc/AL; 89, GOLFX/SS

Wonders of Nature (90–111)

90–91, Preto_perola/GI; 92–93 (UP), Jason Edwards/NGIC; 92 (LO LE), cbpix/SS; 92 (LO RT), Mike Hill/Photographer's Choice/ GI; 93 (LO LE), Wil Meinderts/Buiten-beeld/ MP; 93 (LO RT), Paul Nicklen/NGIC; 94–95, wildestanimal/GI; 96 (UP), AVTG/IS; 96 (LO), Brad Wynnyk/SS; 97 (UP LE), Rich Carey/SS; 97 (UP RT), Richard Walters/ IS; 97 (LO LE), Karen Graham/IS; 97 (LO RT), Michio Hoshino/MP/NGIC; 98, Margarita Alshina; 99 (UP), Stephanie Sawyer/GI; 99 (LO), Grant Dixon/MP; 100 (UP), SS; 100 (LO RT), Spectrum Photofile.com; 100 (LO LE), Photo Researchers RM/GI; 101 (UP), U.S. Navy photo; 101 (LO LE), Sygma/Corbis; 101 (LO RT), AP Images; 101 (CTR), Jim Damaske/ St. Petersburg Times/ZUMAPRESS.com/ Newscom.com; 102 (UP), Stuart Armstrong; 102 (LO), Franco Tempesta; 103 (LO), Richard Peterson/SS; 103 (UP LE), Leonid Tit/SS; 103 (UP RT), Lars Christensen/SS; 103 (CTR LE), Frans Lanting/NGIC; 103 (CTR RT), Daniel Loretto/SS; 104–105, 3dmotus/SS; 106, Galen Rowell/CORBIS/GI; 107 (UP LE), Lori Mehmen/ Associated Press; 107 (LO LE), Jim Reed; 107 (UP RT), Susan Law Cain/SS; 107 (UP CTR), Brian Nolan/IS; 107 (RT CTR), Susan Law Cain/ SS; 107 (LE CTR), Judy Kennamer/SS; 107 (LO

RT), jam4travel/SS; 107 (LO CTR), jam4travel/ SS; 108 (LE), Jeff Hill; 108 (UP RT), Jeff Hill; 108 (LO RT), Jeff Hill; 109 (UP), John Amis/ EPA-EFE/SS; 109 (LO), Zoltán Csipke/AL; 110 (UP RT), Karen Graham/IS; 110 (UP LE), Galen Rowell/GI; 110 (LO RT), Jim Reed; 110 (LO LE), Wil Meinderts/Buiten-beeld/MP

Space and Earth (112–133)

112–113, NASA/JPL; 114 (UP),NGIC; 115 (UP), Ralph Lee Hopkins/NGIC; 115 (UP LE and RT), Visuals Unlimited/GI; 115 (UP CTR), Visuals Unlimited/Corbis; 115 (CTR RT), Dirk Wiersma/ Photo Researchers, Inc.; 115 (LO LE), Charles D. Winters/Photo Researchers, Inc.; 115 (LO RT), Theodore Clutter/Photo Researchers, Inc.; 116 (UP LE), raiwa/IS; 116 (LO LE), Albert Russ/SS; 116 (UP RT), MarcelC/IS; 116 (CTR RT), SS; 116 (LO RT), IS; 117 (UP RT), didyk/IS; 117 (UP RT), Mark A. Schneider/Science Source; 117 (LO LE), Ben Johnson/Science Source; 117 (LO CTR LE), Kazakovmaksim/DRMS; 117 (LO RT), oldeez/DRMS; 117 (LO CTR RT), Ingemar Magnusson/DRMS; 117 (UP CTR), Joel Arem/ Science Source; 117 (UP LE), Meetchum/ DRMS; 117 (UP CTR LE), Albertruss/DRMS; 117 (UP RT), 123dartist/DRMS; 117 (UP CTR RT), Igorkali/DRMS; 118–119 (BACKGROUND), GIPhotoStock/Science Source/GI; 119 (LE), Richard D. Norris; 119 (RT), Sven Sjöström/ EyeEm/GI; 120, Illustration © Frank Ippolito; 121 (UP LE), All Canada Photos/AL; 121 (CTR LE), NASA; 121 (CTR RT), Diane Cook & Len Jenshel/NGIC; 121 (LO LE), Image Science and Analysis Laboratory, NASA-Johnson Space Center. "The Gateway to Astronaut Photography of Earth."; 121 (LO RT), Douglas Peebles Photography/AL; 122–123, Naeblys/ SS; 124–125 (CTR), Mark Garlick/Science Photo Library; 124 (LO), NASA/CXC/IOA/A FABIAN ETAL/Science Photo Library; 125 (UP), NASA, ESA and M.J. Jee (Johns Hopkins University); 125 (LO), M. MARKEVITCH/CXC/CFA/NASA/ Science Photo Library; 126–127 (UP), David Aguilar; 128 (UP), David Aguilar; 128 (LO RT), NASA/JHUAPL/SwRI; 129 (UP), JPL/NASA; 129 (LO RT), Sommersby/DRMS; 129 (LO LE), Age FotoStock/SuperStock; 130 (CTR RT), Tony & Daphne Hallas/Photo Researchers, Inc.; 130 (BACKGROUND), Alexxandar/GI; 130 (UP RT), Walter Myers/Stocktrek Images/Corbis/ GI; 130, Don Smith/GI; 131 (UP), NASA/Science Faction/SuperStock; 131 (LO), NASA; 132 (UP), NASA; 132 (CTR), IS; 132 (LO), All Canada Photos/AL; 133, pixhook/IS

Fun and Games (134–153)

134–135, David Madison/GI; 136 (UP LE), Jak Wonderly; 136 (UP RT), Image99/Jupiter Images; 136 (CTR), gillmar/SS; 136 (LO LE), Erik Sampers/Jupiter Images; 136 (LO RT), Comstock/Jupiter Images; 137 (UP LE), Eising FoodPhotography/StockFood; 137 (UP RT), BananaStock/Jupiter Images; 137 (LE CTR), BananaStock/Jupiter Images; 137 (CTR), PhotoObjects.net/Jupiter Images; 137 (RT CTR), Stephen Frink Collection/AL; 137 (LO LE), James L. Amos/NGIC; 137 (LO CTR), Douglas

Peebles/eStock Photo; 137 (LO RT), Siede Preis/GI; 138–139, Clayton Hanmer; 140, Dan Sipple; 141, James Yamasaki; 142 (A), DRMS; 142 (B), DRMS; 142 (C), DRMS; 142 (D), DRMS; 142 (E), DRMS; 142 (F), DRMS; 142 (G), DRMS; 142 (H), DRMS; 142 (I), DRMS; 143 (UP), Pierluigi .Palazzi/SS; 143 (CTR), Konrad Wothe/naturepl .com; 143 (LO RT), S & D & K Maslowski/MP; 143 (RT CTR), Bradley Mason/GI; 144, James Yamasaki; 145 (UP LE), Gary Fields; 145 (UP RT), Gary Fields; 145 (CTR RT), Chris Ware; 145 (LO LE), Pat Moriarty; 145 (LO RT), Gary Fields; 146 (UP LE), Gerry Ellis/MP; 146 (UP RT), Michael & Patricia Fogden/MP; 146 (CTR RT), Fred Bavendam/MP; 146 (CTR LE), Julie Larsen Maher © Wildlife Conservation Society; 146 (LO LE), Gary K. Smith/MP; 146 (LO RT), Wild Wonders of Europe/Widstrand/ Nature Picture Library; 147, Marty Bauman; 148, kuritafsheen/GI; 148 (RT CTR), Larry Lilac/AL; 148 (LO LE), GK Hart/Vikki Hart/ GI; 148 (LE CTR), Stockbyte/GI; 149 (UP LE), David Wall/AL; 149 (LO LE), David Brownell/ AL; 149 (CTR RT), Alexandr Grey/AL; 149 (LO RT), Thinkstock/Jupiter Images; 149 (UP RT), Index Stock/Jupiter Images/GI; 149 (UP CTR LE), Thinkstock/Jupiter Images; 149 (LO CTR LE), Medioimages/Jupiter Images; 150, James Yamasaki; 151 (UP), Suzi Eszterhas/ MP; 151 (LO LE), Suzi Eszterhas/MP; 151 (RT CTR), Fotosearch/SuperStock; 151 (LO CTR), Stephen Dalton/NHPA/Collection/ Photoshot; 151 (LO RT), Stephen Dalton/ NHPA/Collection/Photoshot; 152–153, Strika Entertainment

Science and Technology (154–179)

154–155, Alexander Miridonov/Kommersant Photo/Polaris/Newscom; 156 (UP), Mark Thiessen, NGP Staff; 156 (CTR), courtesy Wild Blue Media; 156 (LO), courtesy Wild Blue Media; 157 (UP), courtesy Wild Blue Media; 157 (CTR), courtesy Wild Blue Media; 157 (LO LE), courtesy Wild Blue Media; 157 (LO RT), courtesy Wild Blue Media; 158–159, Visual China Group/GI; 160–161, Mondolithic Studios; 162–163, Mondolithic Studios; 164, Ted Kinsman/Science Source; 165 (F), sgame/ SS; 165 (A), Sebastian Kaulitzki/SS; 165 (B), Steve Gschmeissner/Photo Researchers, Inc.; 165 (C), Volker Steger/Christian Bardele/ Photo Researchers, Inc.; 165 (LO CTR LE), ancelpics/GI; 165 (LE), puwanai/SS; 165 (LO RT), kwest/SS; 166 (UP), FotograFFF/SS; 166 (LO), Craig Tuttle/Corbis/GI; 167 (UP), Dave Bevan/AL; 167 (CTR), Brain light/AL; 167 (UP), Steven Russell Smith/AL; 167 (CTR RT), © Joseph Lacy/AL; 168 (UP), SS; 168 (LO), SS; 169, MedusArt/SS; 170 (LO), cobalt88/SS; 170 (UP), Cynthia Turner; 171 (LO), bgblue/IS/GI; 171 (CTR), Heritage Image Partnership Ltd/AL; 172 (UP), Roger Harris/Science Source; 172 (LO), Shaber/SS; 173, Tim Vernon/SPL/Science Source; 174 (UP LE), Dimarion/SS; 174 (LO LE), Microfield Scientific Ltd./Science Source; 174 (CTR), mrfiza/SS; 174 (LO), iLexx/IS; 174 (UP RT), Eraxion/IS; 175 (UP), Jani Bryson/

IS; 175 (CTR), MyImages - Micha/SS; 175 (LO), RapidEye/IS; 176, Matthew Rakola; 177 (UP LE), Matthew Rakola; 177 (LO LE), Matthew Rakola; 177 (LO RT), Matthew Rakola; 178 (UP LE), courtesy Wild Blue Media; 178 (UP RT), Brain light/AL; 178, kwest/SS; 178 (LO RT), MedusArt/SS; 179, Klaus Vedfelt/GI

Culture Connection (180–203)

180-181, Stefano Gentile/EyeEm/GI; 182 (UP), Dan Bergeron; 182 (LO), Xinhua/eyevine/Redux; 182 (UP LE), Rex Features via AP Images; 182 (UP RT), epa european press-photo agency b.v./AL; 183 (CTR LE), oakok; 183 (LO LE), Rex Features via AP Images; 183 (CTR RT), Evening Standard/eyevine/Redux; 183 (LO RT), Mariusz Switulski/SS; 184-185, taveesak srisomthavil/SS; 186-187 (UP), fotohunter/SS; 186 (UP LE), CreativeNature.nl/SS; 186 (LO LE), Tubol Evgeniya/SS; 186 (UP CTR), pattarastock/SS; 186 (LO RT), imageBROKER/AL; 187 (LO RT), wacpan/SS; 187 (RT CTR), Zee/AL; 187 (CTR), Dinodia/GI; 188 (LO LE), Timothy A. Clary/AFP/GI; 188 (LO LE), Splash News/NewsCom; 188 (LO RT), Timothy A. Clary/AFP/GI; 188 (UP RT), Fuse/GI; 189, Chonnanit/SS; 190 (UP), Rebecca Hale, NGP Staff; 190-191 (LO), Rebecca Hale, NGP Staff; 191 (UP), Jay Talbott, NGP Staff; 192 (LO RT), Ninette Maumus/AL; 192 (UP LE), Ivan Vdovin/AL; 192 (CTR LE), iStock/Mlenny; 192 (UP LE), maogg/GI; 192 (CTR RT), Jack Guez/AFP/GI; 192 (UP RT), Paul Poplis/GI; 192 (LO LE), Courtesy of The Banknote Book; 193 (LO CTR RT), D. Hurst/AL; 193 (UP RT), Comstock/GI; 193 (LO CTR LE), Splash News/Newscom; 193 (LO RT), Kelley Miller/NGP Staff; 193 (LO LE), 'Money Dress' with 'Colonial Dress' behind. Paper currency and frame, Lifesize ©Susan Stockwell 2010. ©photo Colin Hampden-White 2010.; 193 (UP CTR LE), Igor Stramyk/SS; 193 (UP LE), Tony Baggett/SS; 195 (RT), Oreolife/AL; 195 (UP LE), Subbotina Anna/SS; 196 (UP LE), John Hazard; 196 (UP LE), Jose Ignacio Soto/SS; 196 (LO), SS; 197 (UP LE), Corey Ford/DRMS; 197 (UP RT), Photosani/SS; 198, Christina Balit; 199, Christina Balit; 200 (UP), Randy Olson; 200 (LO LE), Martin Gray/NGIC; 200 (LO RT), Sam Panthaky/AFP/GI; 201 (LO LE), Reza/NGIC; 201 (LO RT), Richard Nowitz/NGIC; 201 (UP), Thierry Falise/LightRocket/GI; 202 (UP), Chonnanit/SS; 202 (CTR), Splash News/Newscom; 202 (LO), Christina Balit; 203 (UP LE), spatuletail/SS; 203 (UP RT), PictureLake/GI; 203 (CTR), cifotart/SS; 203 (LO), zydesign/SS

204-205, Rana Sajid Hussain/Pacific Press/LightRocket/GI; 206-207, Rich Carey/SS; 208 (LE), Martin Fowler/SS; 209 (RT), AccentAlaska.com/AL; 210, Cn0ra/GI; 211 (UP), Rich Carey/SS; 211 (LO), Jimmy Cumming/GI; 212-213 (ALL), Mark Thiessen/NGP Staff; 214 (CTR), Sean Pavone/DRMS; 214 (UP), Scanrail/DRMS; 214 (LO), Rodrigo Kristensen/SS; 215 (UP RT), Jamie Squire/GI; 215 (CTR),

Joao Sabino/Solent News/REX/SS; 215 (LO LE), Dirty Sugar Photography; 215 (LO RT), Courtesy of Austin-Mergold;215 (LE), Caters News Agency; 217 (UP), James Stone/Chasing Light/GI; 217 (LO), James Balog/NGIC; 218, Martin Fowler/SS; 218, AccentAlaska.com/AL; 218 (LO), James Balog/NGIC

220-221, David Lazar/GI; 222-223, Tom Till/GI; 224 (LE), National Geographic; 224 (RT), The Print Collector/GI; 224-225, National Geographic; 225 (LO RT), © Look and Learn/Giovannini, Ruggero (1922-1983)/Italian/Bridgeman Images; 226, Wang da Gang; 227 (UP LE), O. Louis Mazzatenta/NGIC; 227 (LO LE), Wang da Gang; 227 (UP RT), O. Louis Mazzatenta/NGIC; 227 (RT CTR), O. Louis Mazzatenta/NGIC; 227 (LO RT), O. Louis Mazzatenta/NGIC; 228-229, Pius Lee/SS; 229 (UP LE), © Providence Pictures; 229 (UP RT), HOPE PRODUCTIONS/Yann Arthus Bertrand/GI; 229 (LO RT), Hulton Archive/GI; 230 (UP RT), Christian Darkin/Science Source; 230, Arabes/DRMS; 230 (UP RT), Popperfoto/GI; 230 (LO CTR), Mark Newman/FLPA/MP; 230-231, paladin13/iStock/GI; 231 (CTR RT), William S. Kuta/AL; 231 (LO), Stock Montage/GI; 231 (UP LE), Khaled Desouki/AFP/GI; 232 (UP), Hilary Andrews/NGP Staff; 232 (UP LE), Leemage/GI; 232 (LO LE), Kaesler Media/SS; 232 (LO RT), Erlo Brown/SS; 233 (UP LE), spline_x/SS; 233 (UP LE), Photos.com/GI; 233 (UP RT), Margouillat/DRMS; 233 (CTR LE), revers/SS; 233 (LO CTR), Iakov Kalinin/SS; 233 (LO LE), Gtranquillity/SS; 233 (LO LE), Yvdavyd/DRMS; 233 (CTR RT), Hilary Andrews/NGP Staff; 233 (LO RT), Hilary Andrews/NG Staff; 234 (King William), Leemage/Universal Images Group/GI; 234 (square gold frame), Iakov Filimonov/SS; 234 (King John Lackland), The Granger Collection, New York/The Granger Collection; 234 (oval detailed frame), NinaMalyna/SS; 235 (Queen Elizabeth I), Nikreates/AL; 235 (square detailed frame), Ninell/SS; 235 (Queen Victoria), William Essex/The Bridgeman Art Library/GI; 235 (King Henry VIII), Hans the Younger Holbein/The Bridgeman Art Library/GI; 235 (Queen Elizabeth II), Chris Jackson/GI; 238, Jozev/IS; 241, February/GI; 242, Anton Petrus/GI; 247, Pavol Kmeto/DRMS; 250 (UP), © Look and Learn/Giovannini, Ruggero (1922-1983)/Italian/Bridgeman Images; 250 (CTR), O. Louis Mazzatenta/NGIC; 250 (LO), Erlo Brown/SS; 251, Christopher Furlong/GI

252-253, Layne Kennedy/GI; 259, NASA; 259 (UP), Lori Epstein/NGP Staff; 260 (CTR CTR), Maria Stenzel/NGIC; 260 (LO CTR), Bill Hatcher/NGIC; 260 (UP), Carsten Peter/NGIC; 260 (RT CTR), Gordon Wiltsie/NGIC; 260 (LO LE), James P. Blair/NGIC; 260 (CTR LE), Thomas J. Abercrombie/NGIC; 260 (BACK), Fabiano Rebeque/GI; 261, Rosenberg Philip/Perspectives/GI; 262, iStock/GI; 263 (LE), keyvanchan/GI; 263 (UP RT), AdemarRangel/

GI; 263 (CTR RT), Iko/SS; 263 (LO RT), Hugh Pearson/NPL/MP; 266, Yva Momatiuk and John Eastcott/MP; 267 (CTR RT), iCreative3D/SS; 267 (LE), Alex Tehrani; 267 (UP RT), Achim Baque/SS; 267 (LO RT), Stephen Nicol; 270, Nguyen Anh Tuan/SS; 271 (LO RT), Daniel Heuclin/NPL/MP; 271 (UP RT), Jon Arnold Images/DanitaDelimont.com; 271 (CTR RT), Nancy Brown/Photographer's Choice/GI; 271 (LE), John Downer/MP; 274, The Image Bank/GI; 275 (UP RT), Andrew Watson/John Warburton-Lee Photography Ltd/GI; 275, Matthew Williams-Ellis/GI; 275 (LO LE), Adam Fletcher/MP; 275 (CTR RT), David Wall Photo/GI; 278, Guillem Lopez/Cavan Images; 279 (UP RT), Roy Pedersen/SS; 279 (CTR RT), Annette Hopf/IS; 279 (UP LE), Afonso I of Portugal (litho)/The Stapleton Collection/Bridgeman Images; 279 (UP RT), Anne-Christine Poujoulat/AFP/GI; 282, Gavriel Jecan/GI; 283 (LO RT), Janie Blanchard/GI; 283 (UP RT), Rodrigo Arangua/GI; 283 (LE), Beth Zaiken; 283 (CTR RT), Neirfy/SS; 287 (CTR RT), DC_Colombia/GI; 287 (CTR LE), David Tipling/AL; 287 (UP RT), SOBERKA Richard/hemis.fr/GI; 287 (LO RT), Keren Su/GI; 293, Kelly Cheng/GI; 294, Ondrej Prosicky/SS; 298, Renate Wefers/EyeEm/GI; 301, Tim Graham/GI; 302, EyeEm/GI; 306, Nikolai Sorokin/DRMS; 309, Peter Cade/GI; 314, Steve Lovegrove/SS; 328-329, Blanscape/SS; 330 (UP), Shane Talbot/Solent News/REX/SS; 330 (LO), ZJAN/Canadian Tire Corporation/WENN/Newscom; 330 (CTR), Mario Armas/REUTERS/AL; 331, Supplied by WENN.com/Newscom; 332-333 (LO), Quaoar/SS; 333 (UP LE), Natchapon L./SS; 333 (RT), Subbotina Anna/SS; 333 (LE), Pola Damonte/SS; 333 (LO RT), Kononova Viktoriia/SS; 334 (BACKGROUND), John S Lander/LightRocket/GI; 334 (INSET UP), John S Lander/LightRocket/GI; 334 (INSET LOW), WENN Ltd/AL; 335-65 (LE), Ilona Ignatova/SS; 335 (LO RT), Brian Kinney/SS; 335 (LO CTR RT), lesapi images/SS; 335 (CTR RT), Roman Sigaev/SS; 335 (CTR), Bokic Bojan/SS; 335 (CTR LE), Songquan Deng/SS; 336 (UP LE), Pola Damonte/SS; 336 (UP RT), Rosenberg Philip/Perspectives/GI; 336 (LO LE), Blanscape/SS; 336 (LO RT), Hugh Pearson/NPL/MP

National Geographic Kids Books
gratefully acknowledges the following people for their help with the
National Geographic Kids Almanac.

Bryan Howard of the National Geographic Explorer Programs

Amazing Animals

Suzanne Braden, Director, Pandas International

Dr. Rodolfo Coria, Paleontologist, Plaza Huincul, Argentina

Dr. Sylvia Earle, National Geographic Explorer-in-Residence

Dr. Thomas R. Holtz, Jr., Senior Lecturer, Vertebrate Paleontology, Department of Geology, University of Maryland

Dr. Luke Hunter, Executive Director, Panthera

Dereck and Beverly Joubert, National Geographic Explorers-in-Residence

Nizar Ibrahim, National Geographic Explorer

"Dino" Don Lessem, President, Exhibits Rex

Kathy B. Maher, Research Editor (former), *National Geographic* magazine

Kathleen Martin, Canadian Sea Turtle Network

Barbara Nielsen, Polar Bears International

Andy Prince, Austin Zoo

Julia Thorson, Translator, Zurich, Switzerland

Dennis vanEngelsdorp, Senior Extension Associate, Pennsylvania Department of Agriculture

Wonders of Nature

Anatta, NOAA Public Affairs Officer

Dr. Robert Ballard, National Geographic Explorer-in-Residence

Douglas H. Chadwick, Wildlife Biologist and Contributor to *National Geographic* magazine

Susan K. Pell, Ph.D., Science and Public Programs Manager, United States Botanic Garden

Space and Earth
Science and Technology

Tim Appenzeller, Chief Magazine Editor, *Nature*

Dr. Rick Fienberg, Press Officer and Director of Communications, American Astronomical Society

Dr. José de Ondarza, Associate Professor, Department of Biological Sciences, State University of New York, College at Plattsburgh

Lesley B. Rogers, Managing Editor (former), *National Geographic* magazine

Dr. Enric Sala, National Geographic Explorer-in-Residence

Abigail A. Tipton, Director of Research (former), *National Geographic* magazine

Erin Vintinner, Biodiversity Specialist, Center for Biodiversity and Conservation at the American Museum of Natural History

Barbara L. Wyckoff, Research Editor (former), *National Geographic* magazine

Culture Connection

Dr. Wade Davis, National Geographic Explorer-in-Residence

Deirdre Mullervy, Managing Editor, Gallaudet University Press

Going Green

Eric J. Bohn, Math Teacher, Santa Rosa High School

Stephen David Harris, Professional Engineer, Industry Consulting

Catherine C. Milbourn, Senior Press Officer, EPA

Brad Scriber, Senior Researcher, *National Geographic* magazine

Paola Segura and Cid Simões, National Geographic Emerging Explorers

Dr. Wes Tunnell, Harte Research Institute for Gulf of Mexico Studies, Texas A&M University–Corpus Christi

Natasha Vizcarra, Science Writer and Media Liaison, National Snow and Ice Data Center

History Happens

Dr. Sylvie Beaudreau, Associate Professor, Department of History, State University of New York

Elspeth Deir, Assistant Professor, Faculty of Education, Queens University, Kingston, Ontario, Canada

Dr. Gregory Geddes, Professor, Global Studies, State University of New York–Orange, Middletown-Newburgh, New York

Dr. Fredrik Hiebert, National Geographic Visiting Fellow

Micheline Joanisse, Media Relations Officer, Natural Resources Canada

Dr. Robert D. Johnston, Associate Professor and Director of the Teaching of History Program, University of Illinois at Chicago

Dickson Mansfield, Geography Instructor (retired), Faculty of Education, Queens University, Kingston, Ontario, Canada

Tina Norris, U.S. Census Bureau

Parliamentary Information and Research Service, Library of Parliament, Ottawa, Canada

Karyn Pugliese, Acting Director, Communications, Assembly of First Nations

Geography Rocks

Dr. Kristin Bietsch, Research Associate, Population Reference Bureau

Carl Haub, Senior Demographer, Conrad Taeuber Chair of Public Information, Population Reference Bureau

Dr. Toshiko Kaneda, Senior Research Associate, Population Reference Bureau

Dr. Walt Meier, National Snow and Ice Data Center

Dr. Richard W. Reynolds, NOAA's National Climatic Data Center

United States Census Bureau, Public Help Desk

Bold indicates illustration; **bold** page spans include text and illustrations.

347